D0868517

# The Messages of Medjugorje

## The Complete Text, 1981-2014

A CHRONOLOGICAL CORPUS OF ALL THE MESSAGES OF OUR LADY OF MEDJUGORJE FROM THE BEGINNING

*With Introduction by;*
*Medjugorje-Apologia.com*

© 2014 Medjugorje-Apologia.com. All rights reserved
ISBN 978-1-304-86163-4

# TABLE OF CONTENTS

# PUBLISHER'S NOTE

Section heading "A Bief Timeline of Events" is printed with permission from Medjugorje Apologia (Medjugorje-Apologia.com), authored by David Bianchini.

Chapter one, entitled "Main Body of Messages," is taken from the text "MESSAGES AND TEACHINGS OF MARY AT MEDJUGORJE: Chronology of the Messages.The Urgency to Return to God," by René Laurentin and René LeJeune. Translated by Juan Gonzales, Jr., Ph.D. Edited and Published by THE RIEHLE FOUNDATION, P.O. BOX 7, MILFORD, OHIO 45150, Copyright © 1988.

Chapter two, entitled "Messages Following" is taken from Medjugorje Web, by Steve Shawl, www.medjugorje.org

# A Brief Timeline of Events

**June 24th-25th, 1981:** Six young children, ages10 - 16 (Marija, Mirjana, Vicka, Ivan, Jakov, and Ivanka), allegedly begin receiving visions in the small village of Medjugorje, located in Bosnia-Hercegovina (diocese of Mostar). [1]

[1] Just a few days after the apparitions began, the communist government began to persecute the children, believing that they were anti-socialist nationalists, and hostile to the Communist Party. The police took the children by force to the Mostar mental facility, to a morgue, and to various other places intended to scare the children into confessing the staging of lies to subvert the government. [1] At one point, the police even held a gun to Vicka's head, believing her to be the leader of the children and the mastermind behind the hoax. They also proceeded to harass the parents of the children as well, taking them into custody and ordering them to forbid their children from going to the church. [2]

**1981:** The local parish priest, Father Jozo Zovko does not believe the children at first, and even warns the bishop not to be so haste in his acceptance of the apparitions. [1]

[1] Father Jozo was skeptical of the apparitions at first, since the people were gathering on the hill leaving the church empty (The madonna later corrected the people, gently telling them that if they had to choose between gathering on the hill to witness an apparition, or going to the church to pray, they should choose the church). [2b] It wasn't until one morning while in prayer, he heard a voice say, *"Protect the children."* At the same moment, the children ran into the church in tears, fleeing from the communist soldiers. Fr. Jozo then hid the children in a small room in the church, and went out to speak to the soldiers. It was in this moment that he knew he had to protect the children. [3]

**1981:** *July 25th.* After interviewing the children, the local Bishop of Mostar (bishop Zanic) is initially sympathetic to the apparitions, stating in a homily that same day; *"Six simple children like these would have told all in half an hour if anybody had been manipulating them. I assure you that none of the priests has done any such thing. The accusation is insulting and must be firmly rejected. Furthermore, I am convinced the children are not lying. They are saying only what they most profoundly believe. [...] One thing is certain; something has stirred in people's hearts. Confession, prayer, reconciliation between enemies - that is a most positive step forward."*[1] [4]

**1981:** As Fr. Jozo begins to believe in the apparitions, he becomes more and more outspoken in his protection of the children against the unjust Communist persecutions. He is soon targeted as a primary suspect, arrested, and placed on a mock trial for conspiracy to overthrow the Communist constitution. False witnesses are brought in to testify against him, without the ability to make his own defense. He is then sentenced to three and a half years in prison. 5 [1]

[1] The Communist regime redoubled their efforts in suppressing the Medjugorje phenomenon. They banned the children from going to the hill of the apparition site, set up around-the-clock police guard, planted informers and false pilgrims to incite an uprising, set up blockades to prevent cars from passing, detained pilgrims for questioning, and, in an effort to control all the media, they imprison the only two journalists who supported Medjugorje. 5

**1981:** Bishop Zanic, still favorable to the apparitions, protests the atrocities committed by the Communists, stating; *"...these irresponsible calumnies and these attacks whose bad taste will in no way facilitate a calm appraisal of the events which have been taking place in Medjugorje. Such behavior violates fundamental human and civic rights."* 6 [1]

[1] Bishop Zanic was later summoned to Sarajevo by the Communist State Police and interogated over his involvement in Medjugorje. The interogators, being true to form, also threatened the bishop with imprisonment, just as they had to Fr. Jozo, if he did not stop supporting the apparitions. 6b Ap1

**1981:** With Fr. Jozo now in prison, there is no one to protect the children against the Communist guards. However, another Franciscan priest, Father Tomislav Vlasic, is soon transferred to Medjugorje, who acted as a temporary replacement to Fr. Jozo. For two years he remains the children's spiritual director, before deciding to leave Medjugorje for Italy. [1]

[1] Critics of Medjugorje seem to want to cast doubt over the apparitions by attacking the character of Fr. Vlasic, in an attempt to convince readers that he and Fr. Jozo were somehow the mastermind behind Medjugorje, manipulating the children at will. Due to the pervasive and paranoid nature of these charges, we have addressed them in more detail on our website at medjugorje-apologia.com.

**1981:** At the same time when these events are unfolding in Medjugorje, Bishop Zanic and the local Franciscans are in continual tension over the *"Herzegovinian Affair"*. Like the bishop Ule before him, bishop Zanic too begins pressuring the Franciscans to hand over more of their parishes to him. The Franciscans, after already handing over nearly half of their parishes, feel it unjust for the bishop to continue demanding more, and thus resist his efforts while at the same time petitioning Rome for assistance. Out of this conflict, the bishop targets two Franciscans priests (Fr. Ivica Vego and Fr. Ivan Prusina), and, ultimately, sees to their expulsion from the Franciscan order and the dissolution of their vows. [1]

[1] Normally this incident would have no relevance to Medjugorje, and would thus not be included in this timeline. However, the local townspeople, sympathetic to the two priests, encouraged them to approach the children to ask Our Lady for counsel. Upon inquiry, the Lady instructed them to relay the following message; *"The Gospa wants it said to the bishop that he has made a premature decision. Let him reflect again, and listen well to both parties. He must be just and patient. She says that both priests are not guilty."* This admonishment, according the bishop Zanic, is what compels him to change his opinion from favorable to negative on the apparitions (see; "But the Blessed Virgin would never admonish a bishop"). Furthermore, since the Lady said that the two priests were not guilty, their innocence was then implicated in the evaluation of the apparitions. And as we will see, 12 years later in 1993, the Holy See indeed affirmed their innocence by dropping all the charges against the two priests, indirectly siding with the Lady.

**Oct. 30, 1984:** Bishop Zanic changes his position on Medjugorje, issuing a *Positio* (public statement) to the press in writing, stating that he had a *"moral certitude that the Medjugorje events are a case of collective hallucination".* [7] According to the bishop, his change of mind was on the grounds that *"the Blessed Virgin would never admonish a bishop."* [1] As he stated; *"This support given against the authority of the Church, proves that it is not the Virgin."* And again, he states; *"That fact convinced me that it did not deal with the Madonna, and that she could not defend the two priests expelled by the Order and released from their vows. That would be to destroy the hierarchy and the Church"* [8]

[1] As the bishop notes, his position on Medjugorje hinges on the fact that the Lady admonished him over his actions against the two guilty Franciscan priests, Fr. Ivica Vego and Fr. Ivan Prusina. According to him, this was sufficient proof he needed to determine the falsity of Medjugorje. And for the remaining years of his episcopate, he routinely returns to this position when other recourse fails. However, as we shall see, the Holy See opened an investigation into this matter in 1993, and over-turned the decree by the bishop, vindicating the two priests (see 1993).

**1984:** Higher authorities in the Church urge bishop Zanic to open a formal investigation into the events before arriving at a final judgment (in accordance with the CDF's 1978 "Norms in Judging Alleged Apparitions"). Bishop Zanic obeys by forming a local commission of fourteen members, including theologians and medical professors. However, of the fourteen members, ten of them were known opponents of Medjugorje. [1] [9] Fr. Gandic, a member of this local commission, states in an interview; "They were so prejudiced--some members of the commission--that they went on an on about the Herzegoninian Case, and hadn't time to discuss the Medjugorje phenonmenon." [9b]

[1] We must be clear to our readers, that while we strive to give due reverence and respect to a shepard of the Church, we must nonetheless remain faithful to history. At the time, it had been common knowledge to everyone involved that bishop Zanic had one goal in mind; to prove Medjugorje false. This was no secret. Even bishop Zanic

himself on a number of occasions let his sentiments be known. For example, when asked about whether the Commission will approve Medjugorje, he responded; "I am the Commission". [9] And on another occasion, he stated; "Either I or Medjugorje must die". [9] Furthermore, when he formed a preliminary four-person commission to investigate the aparitions, all four theologians he selected had already announced prior that they believed the visionaries were frauds (the one member who actually met with the visionaries, changed his mind from negative to positive, after which he was dismissed from the comminion by the bishop). [9c] Despite this opposition, however, the Lady continually reminded the children to pray and fast for the bishop, and to respect him; *"Pray very much for the Bishop and for those who are responsible for the church. No less than half of their prayers and sacrifices must be devoted to this intention. Pray my dear children...he is tormented by anxiety. He has taken upon himself all the problems of the diocese...I will ask Almighty God for the grace to be able to comfort the bishop. [...] It is necessary to respect the leaders and to obey them."* [10]

**1984:** While the Commission is meeting, a number of medical doctors and professors request permission to perform various tests and experiments on the children. The children are questioned and subjected to numerous tests by doctors from all over the world. They are poked with needles, burnt with matches, and tested with various medical equipment. All the doctors, without question, agree that the children are not in any way hallucinating, hysteric, neurotic, cataleptic, or pathological. Furthermore, they also rule out the possibility of deception on the part of the children. Instead, the doctors are continually impressed by how level-headed, well-mannered, and ordinary the children seem, especially under such stressful circumstances. [11]

[1] Despite the positive findings of science, the bishop's Commissioner rejected this evidence as inadmissible, since the foreign doctors did not speak Serbo-Croatian and had to rely on interpreters. [12]

**Oct. 30, 1984:** While ten of its members had known prejudices against Medjugorje, the local commission eventually becomes deadlocked. Bishop Zanic, anxious to stop the influx of pilgrims, pre-empts the commission by circulating a new decree to all the bishops around the world on the *"Actual (Unofficial) Position of the Diocese of Mostar on the Medjugorje events"*, in which he asserts again the verdict of "collective hallucination". [12b] This decree, though unofficial, is given to the media as well, which in turn publish articles that Rome has condemned Medjugorje.

In an official memorandum of the Vatican State Secretary Office, Cardinal Casaroli charged Cardinal Franjo Kuharic to convey to bishop Zanic that he should *"suspend the airing of his own personal statements and renounce making judgments, until such time as all the elements could be conclusively gathered together, and the happenings could be clarified"* [13]

**1984:** Fr. Rene Laurentin, a known proponent of Medjugorje, writes to the bishop, asking him why he willfully ignored the results of the scientific experiments performed on the children, which proved that they were neither hallucinating nor pathological. The bishop responds;

*"The word hallucination is too flattering for what goes on in that apparition room. There are witnesses to testify that there are no ecstasies, no hallucinations, but simply parrot-like performances of a comic show. Therefore, I declare the word "hallucination" too generous a description for such wicked play-acting. It will all blow up in your face sooner or later, and then your precious encephalograms and cardiograms and all your scientific apparatus will sink without trace."* [14]

**Dec. 1984:** Cardinal Hans Urs von Balthasar, after reading bishop Zanic's unofficial decree, responds with the following;

*"My Lord, what a sorry document you have sent throughout the world! I have been deeply pained to see the episcopal office degraded in this manner. Instead of biding your time, as you were recommended to do by higher authority, you fulminate and hurl thunderbolts like Jupiter. While you denigrate renowned people who are innocent , deserving of your respect and protection, you bring out accusations that have been refuted a hundred times over."* [15]

**1986:** Bishop Zanic submits a negative decision to Cardinal Ratzinger, then prefect of the Congregation for the Doctrine of the faith. Instead of accepting the negative decision by the bishop, Cardinal Ratzinger dissolves the bishop's Commission, and convenes a new Commission of all the Yugoslavian Bishops in the region.

According to bishop Zanic, Cardinal Ratzinger told him forthright; *"No, you are going to dissolve your diocesan commission. The verdict is transferred to the Bishops Conference."* [16]

**Dec. 23, 1990:** Now out of the hands of bishop Zanic, the new Yugoslavian Commission initiates a formal investigation into the apparitions, which continue over a course of three years. Cardinal Franjo Kuharic, President of the Yugoslav Bishops' Conference, gives a general report of the progress of the Commission, stating that the bishops *"have a positive opinion of Medjugorje events."* [17]

**1991:** The Yugoslavian Bishops Conference votes to classify Medjugorje in one of three ways; 1) certain of supernatural origin, 2) not yet certain of supernatural origin, 3) certain of *no* supernatural origin. The conference rejects the 3rd classification by a vote of 19 to 1, and after much deliberation between the 1st and 2nd classification, decides that Medjugorje cannot yet be confirmed supernatural, but also expresses its favorability to the apparitions; *"The Church is not in a hurry. We, the bishops, after three years of examination by the Commission, have declared Medjugorje a place of prayer and a Marian sanctuary. This means that we are not opposed to people coming on pilgrimage to Medjugorje to venerate the Mother of God there, in conformity with the teaching and faith of the universal Church. As to the supernaturality of the apparitions,* *we have declared: Up to this moment, we cannot affirm it. We leave it for later. The Church is not in a hurry."* [18]

[1] This statement is the most concise summary of the Church's position on Medgjugorje in layman's terms, and provides us with the proper context for reading the "1991 Zadar Declaration" (the formal decision of the commission in church language). Without the proper context above, one can easily misinterpret the Zadar Declaration, and in fact many critics have fallen into this error, believing the commission held a negative position rather than one of cautiously optimistic neutrality. In reality, the Commission was largely amiable to the apparitions, but tempered its favorability due to the strong opposition of bishop Zanic (see our website medjugorje-apologia.com.

**1991:** Cardinal Ratzinger (prefect of the CDF), quotes the Yugoslavian Bishops as stating the following; *"We want to be concerned that this place, which has become a place of prayer and faith, remain and come to be even more in the most interior unity with the entire Church."* [19]

**1991:** The local bishop (now bishop Peric) voices his disagreement with the progress of the Yugoslavian Bishops Conference, stating;*"My conviction and my position is not only 'non constat de supernaturalitate', but likewise, 'constat de non supernaturalitate' of the apparitions or revelations in Medjugorje*".

Like bishop Zanic, his predecessor bishop Peric, also does not believe in the apparitions, and considers the decision of the Yugoslav Bishop's Commission and its acceptance by Rome to be an error. However, the CDF later responded to the bishop's statement with the following; "*What Bishop Peric said...declaring: "My conviction and my position is not only 'non constat de supernaturalitate', but likewise, 'constat de non supernaturalitate' of the apparitions or revelations in Medjugorje", should be considered the expression of the personal conviction of the Bishop of Mostar which he has the right to express as Ordinary of the place, but which is and remains his personal opinion.*" [20]

**1993:** Having no other choice, bishop Peric concedes to the findings of the Yugoslavian bishop's conference, stating; *"Medjugorje is officially accepted as a place of prayer and pilgrimage."* [21]

**1993**: The two Franciscan priests who were unjustly expelled from the order in 1981, finally receive vindication from Rome, after 12 years of failed appeals and delays in the lower tribunals. After the case was elevated to the Apostolic Signatura, the Tribunal responded definitively, declaring that Bishop Zanic's expulsion and laicization of the two priests was done illegally and unjustly. [1] [22]

[1] The results of this investigation are monumentous, since it was bishop Zanic himself who based his negative judgment on the supposed guilt of these two priests and the Lady's declaration of their innocence. While the findings of the Tribunal have been

made public, the Tribunal has forbidden the publishing of its 13-page report on the investigation. Thus, we cannot post the details of the report publicly. However, certain individuals who have read this report (Fr. Laurentin being one), have verified conclusively how damaging it really is [23] Ultimately, what we can say with certitude, is that the laicization of the two priests was revoked and the priests were permitted to return to their community in good standing. However, one of the priests, Ivica Vego, had since married. Thus, tragically, a priest was robbed of his priesthood through this ordeal.

**1998:** The secretary of the CDF responds in a letter of inquiry from Bishop Gilbert Aubry on the status of Medjugorje. He re-iterates the Church's position by stating it; 1) he defers all authority to the 1991 Bishop's Conference, 2) the bishop's opinion is merely his own opinion, and should not be considered the judgment of the Church, 3) private pilgrimages are permitted *"so long as they are not regarded as an authentication of events still taking place and which still call for an examination by the Church"* (complete text at medjugorje-apologia.com).

[1] We have seen some critics argue that the Church as prohibited private pilgrimages to Medjugorje, based on a faulty interpretation of the above statement; *"So long as they are not regarded as an authentication of..."* This statement means exactly what it says; that the presence of pilgrims from all over the world should not be regarded as proof of the supernaturality of the events still taking place. As we have seen, the Church expressly permits, and even encourages pilgrimages to Medjugorje (being a "place of prayer and Marian sanctuary"), while she continues her investigation of the phenomenon.

**2002**: The pope elevates Sister Emmanuel's community (the same sister who Bishop Zanic condemned and said that as she was not a nun, she had no right to call herself 'Sister') to full recognition.

**2008:** Cardinal Bertone of the CDF writes; *"Bishop Peric's statement expresses a personal opinion of his own. It is not a definitive official judgment on the part of the Church, The Church defers to the Zadar statement issued on 10th April 1991 by the bishops of the former Yugoslavia and the statement leaves the door open to further investigations of the affair. So the process of verification needs to move forward."* [24]

**2010:** The Holy See forms a new commission to investigate the apparitions of Medjugorje. [1]

[1] The stated objective of this Commission is principally of a technical matter; to disseminate and publicize the details of the 1991 Yugoslavian Bishops Conference, which as we have also seen, had a positive view of the events. Therefore, we should expect a likewise positive result from this Commission.

**2014:** The Vatican commission completes its investigation of Medjugorje and submits its findings to the Congregation for the Doctrine of the Faith. The judgment awaits final approval from pope Francis.

---


1. Mary Craig, *Spark From Heaven: The Mystery of the Madonna of Medjugorje*, Ave Maria Press 1988, p41,54,68-77. *(impartial BBC journalist)*
[See also Mirjana Stanislava Vasilj-Zuccarini *Our Lady's Call from Medjugorje,* p76, 116-124. *(local villager and eye witness)]*
2. Vasilj-Zuccarini *op. cit.,* p35,68,72.
2b. Fr. Rene Laurentin, *Messages and Teachings of Mary at Medjugorje: Chronological Corpus of the Messages*, The Riehle Foundation 1988, p314. [complete text at medjugorje-apologia.com]
3. Craig, *op. cit.* p56.
4. Craig, *op. cit.* p68.
5. Craig, *op. cit.* p76, 71, 72.
6. Craig, *op. cit.* p74.
6b. Fr. Ljudevit Rupcic, *The Truth About Medjugorje*, p. 70-75 (*Fr. Rupcic served on the Theological Commission of the Yugoslavian Bishops Conference from 1969 to 1980 and also was imprisoned by the Communists for a number of years*).
7. Antonio Gaspari (EWTN), *Medjugorje: Deception of Miracle?* ("Inside the Vatican", Nov. 1996) [link at medjugorje-apologia.com]
8.Laurentin, *op. cit.* Ap. 329-331. [complete text medjugorje-apologia.com] (note, appendix is missing in the linked source)
9. Craig, *op. cit.* p124, 129
9b. The Madonna of Medjugorje, Franciscan University of Steubenville, 1987 [see clip of interview at medjugorje-apologia.com]
9c. Randall Sullivan, *The Miracle Detective*, Grove Press 2004, p.122 (impartial journalist for Rolling Stone)
10. Laurentin, *op. cit.* p.203, Ap. 336, 340
11. Among the professors, psychiatrists, and medical doctors who have tested the children, are; Nicolas Bulat, Professor of Dogma at the University of Split, Dr. Mario Botta, Dr. Lucia Capello, Dr. Enzo Gabrici, Professor Maria Franchini, Professor Henri Joyeux, Dr. Jacques Philippot, Dr. F. Rouquerol, Professor Santini, Dr. Paolo Maestri, and Professor Margnelli. See Craig p125, 133, 134, 135,
12. *Glas Koncila*, Oct. 20th, 1985 issue.
12b. Craig, *op. cit.*, p144.
13. Vatican State Secretary Office, Cardinal Casaroli, No. 150.458, April 1st, 1985.
14. Laurentin, *Dermieres Nouvelles de Medjugorje,* op.cit. [see also; Craig p.145]
15. Kevin Delvin, *The Medjugorje Story*, RAD Background Report/72.
16. Laurentin, *The Position of Medjugorje in the Church*, July, 1997, sec. *The Local Bishop*. [link at medjugorje-apologia.com]
17. Interview on Croatian public television, Dec. 23, 1990] [link at medjugorje-apologia.com]
18. Declaration printed in Vecernji List, August 1993, Latest News 13, page 41. [see also; Glas Koncila, August, 1993]
19. *Gebetsaktion*, #22, 1992, p.4.
20. Congregation of the Doctrine of the Faith, Tarcisio Bertone (Secretary) to Bishop Gilbert Aubry of Saint-Denis de la Reunion [complete text at medjugorje-apologia.com]
21. Laurentin, *Medjugorje-13 Years Later,* The Riehle Foundation, 1994, p36.
22. Apostolic Signatura Tribunal, Case No. 17907/86CA ly.
23. Laurentin, *Medjugorje-13 Years Later*, The Riehle Foundation, 1994, p43, 42.
24. Cardinal Bertone, *The Last Secret of Fatima*, p.94


*Appendix I:*

*(fn. 6b.)* While bishop Zanic and father Jozo were both threatened with imprisonment if they did not stop supporting Medjugorje, it was only Fr. Jozo who ultimately went to prison. Just after Fr. Jozo was released from prison, he met with the bishop, who explained to him that he was forced by the Communists to change his opinion on Medjugorje from open/supportive to negaitve, saying; *"I could not have gone to prison for Medjugorje"*, and *"How could I have acted differently?"*, and *"nor did I wish to go from being bishop to assistant pastor of a village"* (referring to the pressure from his diocesan priests, who were insisting that he condemn the apparitions). [6b] Due to the serious nature of this evidence, however, and based on the testimony of one man, we

purposely ommitted it from the main body of the timeline. Although Fr. Jozo is a realiable witness with no *credible* blunders against his character, this evidence alone will not suffice in the mind of a critic, nor do we wish for our readers to imitate the methods of some critics by reducing the issue to a deragatory soundbyte by saying; "The bishop was a coward!". Our Lady has shown us the example by which we should live by; pray for our shepards, fast for them, respect them, obey them. She will take care of the rest.

# COMMON MISCONCEPTIONS

**1. The local Franciscan priests are the "mastermind" behind Medjugorje.**
The genesis of this claim dates back to the first days of the apparitions, when the Communist regime saw Medjugorje as a threat to its government, and thus initiated a media campaign to undermine the apparitions. [1a] They printed cartoons which depicted the six visionaries manipulated by evil Franciscans, or the Virgin armed with a machine gun [1] (the Communist government had full control over the media in the region, and imprisoned the only two journalists who spoke favorably about Medjugorje [2]). Suffice to say, those who continue to level these claims today, are, as Cardinal Hans Urs von Balthasar stated when he scolded the local bishop for his opposition to the apparitions; "bringing out accusations that have been refuted a hundred times over". In reality, the apparitions started with the children before the priests ever heard of Medjugorje, and were sustained by the children long after the priests were gone. The three priests who were closest to the children (Fr. Jozo, Fr. Vlasic, and Fr. Barbaric) were there acting in their office as spiritual director, guiding the children and also protecting them from harm from the Communist persecution. In the eyes of a secularist, it is easy to see how spiritual direction can appear like "manipulation".

**2. Pope John Paul II and Mother Teresa didn't support Medjugorje. Those are just fabrications.**
Those who put forth this claim have likely not reviewed the evidence on the matter, which includes not only testimonies from eyes witnesses, but also documents written in their own handwriting as well. Due to the compelling nature of this evidence, we have included it on our website page; "Position of the Church". There can be no doubt that both of these mystics (who were arguably more qualified at discerning supernaturality than anyone else living at the time) believed in and supported the apparitions at Medjugorje.

**3. The children said the apparitions would occur for "only three more days".**
The Church teaches us that even true visionaries can draw false interpretations of their own visions. Such is this situation in question. During the first days of the apparitions, the children were still very ignorant about apparitions in the Catholic Church, and so Fr. Jozo had lent them a book to read about Lourdes. They read about how the Blessed Virgin appeared to Bernadette only eighteen times, and thus assumed that all apparitions occur in the same way. 3 This faulty assumption is what prompted Mirjana to conclude that the apparitions in Medjugorje would only occur for three more days. As she stated; "That's what happened in Lourdes, so that is what will happen here". This human error does not impugn the authenticity of Medjugorje. In fact, it is a natural occurrence in most (if not all) approved apparitions, for the visionaries to interpret minor inaccuracies based on their own human understanding. This is the nature of private revelation, which is not free from error as public revelation is.

> *Congregation for the Doctrine of the Faith, 1978 norms for judging alleged apparitions:*
> "taking into account, however, the possibility that the subject may add something by their own activity—even if this is done unconsciously—of some purely human elements to an authentic supernatural revelation"

**4. The messages have continued for years with no end in sight (unlike Lourdes or Fatima).**
There have been approved apparitions that have occurred for nearly half a century, or more. For example, the apparitions in Laus France occurred for 54 years. St. Brigid of Sweden received apparitions for more than a quarter-century. And St. Hildegard received visions for nearly 70 years. 4 According to the Congregation for the Doctrine of the Faith (herein termed the CDF), the "length of apparitions" is not a factor in determining the authenticity of alleged apparitions. The Church does not set arbitrary standards for judging alleged apparitions, but instead has specific criteria that it follows (see 1978 CDF Norms for Judging Alleged Apparitions and Revelations). Jakov, one of the visionaries, has been asked this question many times. His response has always been the same; "Instead of asking 'why'; 'why have they been occurring for so long', we instead should be saying something else; we should be saying 'thank you', and giving thanks to Our Lord for allowing Our Blessed Mother to be with us for so long."

> Mirjana: "Why have the apparitions been lasting so long?"
> Our Lady: "Because so many people are taking so long to convert. There have never been so many unbelievers."
>
> "Today is the day that I was going to stop giving messages because certain people do not accept them. The parish has responded and I wish to continue to give messages to a degree, such as has never before been witnessed in the world, since the beginning of history. Try to remain in my heart. Do not remain outside of it." - April 4th, 1985

**5. The Lady said that all faiths are equal.**
There are two points to consider here: 1) A possible faulty English translation of the original Croation (translated by Juan Gonazales, Jr, Ph.D.), which took a narrower interpretation. 2) Context. We have included a passage below which helps illustrate the proper context of the alleged statement. Upon reading the complete text, it becomes evident that the Lady did not say all faiths are equal. She was rather correcting a mistaken notion of the children that everyone who is not Catholic is damned. This hard-lined view was found not only among Feeneyites and some traditionalists, but also in isolated pockets of the world where Catholicism was the dominant religion (Medjugorje). We might also point out to the reader that Mother Teresa has made similar statements. It was not her objective to convert others, but to love. It is in loving that the greatest number of conversions occur.

> "Tell this priest, tell everyone, that it is you who are divided on earth. The Muslims and the Orthodox, for the same reason as Catholics, are equal before my Son and me. You are all my children. Certainly, all religions are not equal, but all men are equal before God, as St. Paul says. It does not suffice to belong to the Catholic Church to be saved, but it is necessary to respect the commandments of God in following one's conscience. Those who are not Catholics, are no less creatures made in the image of God, and destined to rejoin someday, the House of the Father. Salvation is available to everyone, without exception. Only those who refuse God deliberately, are condemned. To him, who has been given little, little will be asked for. To whomever has been given much (to Catholics) , very much will be required. It is God alone, in His infinite justice, Who determines the degree of responsibility and pronounces judgment."
>
> "All religions are similar before God. God rules over them just like a sovereign over his kingdom. In the world, all religions are not the same because people have not complied with the commandments of God. They reject and disparage them."

**6. The messages detract from the Catholic Faith**

Those who would make this claim have likely not read the messages in their entirety. It should suffice to include a short list of exerts from the messages, to illustrate their fidelity to the Catholic faith (see below).

> "Let Holy Mass be your life. Understand that the Church is God's palace, the place in which I gather you and want to show you the way to God. Come and pray! Neither look at others, nor slander them. Rather let your life be a testimony on the way of holiness. Churches deserve respect and are set apart as holy because God, who became man, dwells in them day and night."
>
> "Pray for priests. My Son gave them to you as a gift."
>
> "I urge you to ask everyone to pray the rosary. With the rosary you will overcome all the troubles which Satan is trying to inflict on the Catholic Church. Let all priests pray the rosary. Give time to the rosary."
>
> The Blessed Virgin kisses an image of the Pope and says: "It is your father, the spiritual father of all."
>
> "It is intentional that all apparitions are under the auspices of the Catholic Church."
>
> "Dear children! In the great love of God, I come to you today to lead you on the way of humility and meekness. The first station on that way, my children, is confession. Reject your pride and kneel down before my Son."
>
> "The West has made civilization progress, but without God, as if they were their own creators. ...Monthly Confession will be a remedy for the Church in the West. One must convey this message to the West. [...] Whole sections of the Church could be cured, if the believers would go to confession once a month. "
>
> "Do not go to confession through habit, to remain the same after it. No, it is not good. Confession should give an impulse to your faith. It should stimulate you and bring you closer to Jesus. If confession does not mean anything for you, really, you will be converted with great difficulty."
>
> "My children, I wish that the holy mass be for you the gift of the day. Attend it, wish for it to begin. Jesus gives Himself to you during the mass. Thus, look forward to that moment when you are cleansed. Pray very much so that the Holy Spirit will renew your parish. If people attend mass with lukewarmness, they will return to their homes cold, and with an empty heart."
>
> "I would like to guide you spiritually, but I would not know how to help you, if you are not open. It suffices for you to think, for example, where you were with your thoughts yesterday during mass. When you go to mass, your trip from home to church should be a time of preparation for mass. You should also receive Holy Communion with an open and pure heart; purity of heart and openness. Do not leave the church without an appropriate act of thanksgiving. I can help you only if you are accessible to my suggestions; I can not help you if you are not open."

**7. She said her birthday is August 5th. But the Church celebrates it on Sept. 8th.**

It may appear like Our Lady is correcting the Church, when in actuality She is not. We have to remember that the Church calendar is a liturgical calendar, not an indication of a historic date. The calendar is not set in stone. It can be revised, altered, feasts shifted, saints added, others dropped, etc.

When asked the same question, Colin B. Donovan (EWTN) responded; "That is a liturgical celebration by the Church, not an assertion of an historical date. The association of Mary with August 5th historically is the apparition of Our Lady of the Snows, a day on which, as promised by a vision, snow fell in Rome to mark the place where the Pope was to build a "temple" to the Blessed Virgin. That "temple" is the Pontifical Basilica of St. Mary Majors (the highest ranked Marian church in the world), the dedication of which is celebrated each August 5th. Could that be the actual day of Mary's birth? Who knows? One could even argue that snow better signifies her Immaculate Conception than her birth."

**8. But the Blessed Virgin would never admonish a bishop.**
In 1981, bishop Zanic had two local Franciscans priests (Ivica Vego and Ivan Prusina) expelled and laicized from the order for reasons concerning the "Hercegovinian Affair". The two priests, believing they were innocent, did not know what to do. Encouraged by a few locals, they asked the children to inquire to the Blessed Virgin about the situation. The Virgin told the children to respond in this way;

> "The Gospa wants it said to the bishop that he has made a premature decision. Let him reflect again, and listen well to both parties. He must be just and patient. She says that both priests are not guilty."

This point is critical, because this is the reason that caused the the bishop to change his mind about Medjugorje. As he states; "This support given against the authority of the Church, proves that it is not the Virgin." And again, he states; "That fact convinced me that it did not deal with the Madonna, and that she could not defend the two priest expelled by the Order and released from their vows. That would be to destroy the hierarchy and the Church" So we see clearly, the bishop had set this issue as the pillar of his negative opinion of Medjugorje. And yet, in 1993, the Holy See initiated an investigation into this matter and found that the priests were innocent of the actions taken against them by the bishop; that their laicization had been done illegally and unjustly, and thus reinstated the priests back to good standing. 5 (see also medjugorje-apologia.com, timeline; 1993) So we see that the Virgin was indeed correct. Yet despite knowing they were completely innocent, the Virgin still emphasized to the children the importance of obedience and reconciliation (see text below).

It is also interesting to note, that some of our Orthodox brethren make a similar argument against the apparitions at Guadalupe, where Our Lady asked to have a shrine built in her honor. Their words are almost identical; "The Virgin Mary would never ask to have a shrine built to her. If She was truly the Virgin, She would instead ask to have a shrine built to Her Son." Here we see how this arbitrary standard is used to criticize an approved Catholic apparition. The premise in both these cases is clearly faulty; appealing to Mary as she was on earth 2,000 years ago, not the now glorified Mary Who is now Queen of Heaven and Mother of the Church. As our mother, She is only concerned about the good of souls. And so every action and word from Her, must be seen in this light. When She was asked about the two Franciscan priests, She responded in truth, against an injustice. And undoubtedly, it was for the good of the souls of these two hot-headed priests, who would have otherwise become embittered against the bishop, and have harbored this resentment for the rest of their lives.

> After the locals involved the children in the affair, they composed questions to present to Our Lady:
>
> CHILDREN: "The bishop is protesting because you said that Father Ivica Vego and Father Ivan Prusina are not guilty. He has the feeling that you are not the Blessed Virgin

because you do not respect the decision of the leaders. Do you want us to explain your point of view?"

OUR LADY'S RESPONSE: "It is necessary to respect the leaders and to obey them, but they also make mistakes. They must do penance for their mistakes and rectify their errors. The bishop and those who influence him in this regard, do harm to the faith. I do not find fault with Father Vego and Father Prusina."

Q: "What do you recommend to our bishop, and to other bishops in order to resolve this problem? How can they resolve it? What must they do to arrive at an understanding and reconciliation?"

A: "It is necessary to pray very much. They must pray. Let them know that without my help, they can do nothing, because I am your Mother. Let them ask for my help, because I want to save all of them. They can be saved only by making peace among them, and by renouncing all forms of jealousy. That is the only way to find a solution."

Q: "What do you recommend to Fathers Ivica Vego and Ivan Prusina so that they may be able to approach the bishop and establish a dialogue with him?"

A: "Let them pray for him, and let every misunderstanding be forgotten as if nothing existed. Let them love the bishop and let them pray very much for him. It is in this manner that the problems will be able to be resolved."

Q: What do you ask of the bishop so that he can acknowledge you, and that the question of Herzegovina be resolved?"

A: "I addressed the bishop many messages, but he has not accepted them. Then I sent you to him, but he still did not receive the Queen of Peace because he is tormented by anxiety. He has taken upon himself all the problems of the diocese instead of confiding them to my Son for a solution. Pray, my dear children, so that he will accept me. From my side, I will ask Almighty God for the grace to be able to comfort the bishop."

**9. But one of the laicized priests, Ivica Vego, married a nun.**
It is true that after being expelled from the Franciscans and released of his vows (including the vow of chastity), Fr. Vego was forced to return to the secular life. During this time, a nun took pity on him, and they eventually married within the Church. This unfortunate consequence of expelling an innocent priest resulted just as Our Lady predicted in 1981 (see transcript below). As She says, if they stop being priests, "things could get even worse". This does not excuse Fr. Vego from marrying a nun however, though he was free to marry. We must remind the reader, however, this priest had only a peripheral involvement in the apparitions, over the course of just a few months. It is thus irrational to assert that the behavior of this priest later in his life can be used to condemn Medjugorje.

OUR LADY, 1981: "if they stop being priests, things could get even worse."
QUESTION: "The bishop is not in the habit of saying: 'Our Lady protects rebel Franciscans and does not listen to the Church. Can Our Lady tell us what she wishes to accomplish by such actions? Could she explain to the bishop that she is on his side and on the side of the Church?

ANSWER: "I want to guard the Church and all those who are responsible. I want to protect all priests, the good and the bad, because Jesus said; 'It is not those who are in good health who are in need of a physician.' But that does not mean that I do not protect the bad priests. Understand that well. They could not be good without my protection! Understand well: I want to protect and put on the right path all priests, because it is necessary that they do my will."

**10. But Fr. Vlasic was also laicized, and he was the children's spiritual director!**
First, we might point out that Fr. Vlasic was only temporarily stationed in Medjugorje as a replacement to Fr. Jozo (Fr. Jozo was the original priest and spiritual director in Medjugorje, who was imprisoned by the communist police for defending the children). Fr. Vlasic had only been the children's spiritual director for two years after he began plans to found a new Franciscan community in Italy in 1984. Thus, for the past 27 years, Fr. Vlasic has remained in Italy, no longer involved in the children's lives. Critics, however, nonetheless attempt link Fr. Vlasic to Medjugorje, as if they are one in the same ("guilt by proxy" is not grounded in canon law, nor right reason). Furthermore, we should also point out that the laicization of Fr. Vlasic in 2008 was due to the express request of Fr. Vlasic himself, not as a punishment against his own wishes.

Intent on getting the approval of the Blessed Virgin, Fr. Vlasic evidently pressured Marija to give a positive approval to form a new community. 5b However, the Virgin did not give explicit approval. Nevertheless, Fr. Vlasic requested to be transferred to Italy to pursue his intentions of founding the aforementioned community. His request was granted in 1986.

Fr. Vlasic: "Should we found here a community just like that of Saint Francis of Assisi?"
Our Lady: "God has chosen Saint Francis as His elected one. It would be good to imitate his life. In the meantime, we must realize what God orders us to do."

**11. The children and Franciscans were disobedient to the bishop.**
When the bishop ordered the apparitions to cease taking place in the parish church, they complied by moving to a small private room. 6 When the bishop ordered the children to make no further public appearances in the parish, the children stopped publicly speaking about the messages in church, and instead wrote the apparitions on paper. 6 When the bishop ordered the new statue of Our Lady of Medjugorje to be taken down from the altar, they complied by moving it to the small apparitions room. When the bishop banned the three Franciscan priests (Fr. Jozo, Fr. Vlasic, Fr. Rupcic) from celebrating Mass or preaching in the parish, they complied. When the bishop banned all mention of the apparitions in homilies, it was not necessary to comply since the priests never mentioned the apparitions in homilies to begin with. When the bishop ordered the Franciscans to hand over all written material including the diary, they could not comply entirely because the supposed "diary" never existed. When the bishop forbade the children from stepping foot into the church, Fr. Vlasic refused, since the church was the only safe place for the children against the communist police. In short, the children obeyed exceedingly well to the bishop's demands. And Fr. Vlasic, while he did not obey in this one instance, he is also not the children (critics often seem to want to tether the Franciscans to the children, as if they are one in the same). Though they all felt the bishop's actions were unjust, they nonetheless meekly accepted them as necessary trials, just as the Mother of God said;

The Virgin instructs how to respond to the bishop's orders;

"Beginning today, the Lord wants to try the parish in a special way, in order to strengthen it in faith... You the members of this parish have a large and heavy cross to bear. But do not be afraid to carry it. My Son is here to help you." - (On the same day the demands from the bishop were announced, April 11, 1985)

"Carry out well your responsibilities and what the Church asks of you to do."

"It is necessary to respect the leaders and to obey them, but they also make mistakes. They must do penance for their mistakes and rectify their errors."

"Obey, and do what the priests and your parents tell you. Go often to holy Mass and receive Communion. Be very attentive..."

**12. But the local bishop condemned Medjugorje. Therefore, we should be obedient.**
Normally, this would be true, since the local bishop is typically the first authority in judging alleged apparitions within his jurisdiction. However, Medjugorje is unique in that Rome has intervened on a number of occasions, opposing the bishops negative opinion that Medjugorje should be condemned. For a complete analysis on the Church's position on Medjugorje, please see medjugorje-apologia.com, "What is the Position of the Church?".

**13. But even the 1991 Yugoslavian Bishop's Conference was against Medjugorje.**
Those who make this claim have likely not studied the history on this Commission. The Yugoslavian bishop's conference was more favorable towards Medjugorje than not. The evidence on this account is clear and unambiguous, to the degree that it is unclear how critics could claim otherwise. Due to the importance of this Commission, we have devoted an entire section on it on medjugorje-apologia.com, "What is the Position of the Church?".

**14. The children went to the hill to smoke cigarettes!**
While it is true that, out of the six children, two of them had went to the hill was to smoke cigarettes, we must also remember that the use of tobacco was commonplace during that time, especially in that region of Bosnia, where tobacco farms were the only source of income for families. And so, the children were exposed to it at a young age. However, it is also important to note, ever since the apparitions first started, the children never smoked again in their lives. Thus, we see from this incident another good fruit (which is what the Church is more concerned about when investigating apparitions). Furthermore, the Church does not require the visionaries to be saints or to have never made any mistakes (the visionaries have always said they were just ordinary children, no better than anyone else). In fact, there have been approved apparitions in which some of the children started off as trouble-makers. In Kibeho, for example, Marie-Claire was known to be a bully to the other children, nominally Catholic, and often teased and chided the idea of apparitions. Yet once Our Lady began appearing to her, she grew out of her childish ways. Although the children of Medjugorje have always been well-mannered, respectful, and level-headed, they nonetheless had to mature in their faith under the instruction of the Lady.

Mirjana: "Why are you appearing to us? We are not better than others."
Our Lady smiles: "I do not necessarily choose the best ones."

Mirjana: "She said Herself that we were ordinary and average, and that She needed us that way."

**15. The children told lies!**

In all the years of exemplary conduct, one of the children (Ivan), in the midst of a difficult time in his young life, did tell a lie to the commissioner (which the Madonna scolded him for afterwards. As the Virgin gently corrected; "Only prayer will undo Ivan's silly mistake."), it was nonetheless an out-of-character fault which he did not repeat. It was during his time in the seminary (1985), studying to become a priest, but disillusioned at the prospect (The seminary was not what he had expected. But who can blame him? Seminaries during the 1980's were not entirely the most orthodox or faithful). He was asked by the commissioner what he had written down on a piece of paper that was sealed in the archives. Ivan responded that he had written nothing; that he left the paper blank. When they opened the envelope, they found written on the paper a description of a sign. After the incident, Fr. Slavko Barbaric reprimanded Ivan for his behavior, and began to investigate the matter. However, the Madonna again gently corrected; "It wasn't Ivan's fault. I've scolded him enough now. Let him alone."

We must also remember that the Church does not require visionaries to be immaculate, or even saints. If it did, then it would never have approved the apparitions in La Salette or Kibeho for example. What matters to the Church is evidence of spiritual growth and good fruit as a result from the apparitions. During the first few years of the apparitions, the children were still young and overwhelmed by what was happening. They needed time to mature in their faith, under the guidance of the Virgin. As they said themselves; "we were just ordinary children, no different from everyone else."

The Virgin Instructs the Children as a Mother;

> "Listen attentively at holy Mass. Be well mannered. Do not chatter during holy Mass."
>
> "Be together, and do not argue, do not be disorderly. My angels, I will make you attentive. I will guide you on a sure way."
>
> "Obey your grandmother and help her because she is old."
>
> "Dear children, do not permit Satan to become the master of your heart, because in that case, you will become the image of Satan, and not mine. I invite you to pray, in order to become witnesses of my presence. Without you, the Lord cannot realize what He wishes. The Lord has given each one a free will, and you can dispose of it."
>
> "Dear children, if you knew how much I love you, your heart would weep over it. If there is someone who asks you for something, give it to him. I also present myself to many hearts, and they do not open up. Pray so that the world may welcome my love.

**16. But Marija even admitted to lying!**

This claim refers to the situation involving the departure of Fr. Vlasic from Medjugorje, who transferred to Italy in 1986 to found a new community of Franciscans (see also #10; "But Fr. Vlasic was also laicized, and he was the children's spiritual director!"). In 1984, Fr. Vlasic had petitioned the Virgin (through Marija) on whether he should establish the new community. In response, the Lady stated that it was good to imitate the life of St. Francis, and that one must open to the will of God [1]. Fr. Vlasic had convinced himself that this response was an approval by the Virgin, and thus pressured Marija to give a written statement to the fact. Marija refused to comply with his request at first, not understanding how the Virgin's response could be construed as an approval. But Fr. Vlasic continued to pressure Marija, insisting that she had an obligation to the whole world to write the declaration.Torn between obedience to the priest (who at the time was her spiritual director), and fidelity to the visions, Marija chose obedience. Thus, she wrote the statement demanded by Fr. Vlasic. A few years later, she retracted the statement publicly stating; "My first declaration...does not correspond to the truth." [2]

We might offer three points of consideration regarding this situation; 1) This is the one instance where a critic can appropriately use the word "manipulation" on the part of a Franciscan priest toward the children. Although Fr. Vlasic started off well, helping to protect the children from the Communist persecutions, he allowed his increasingly myiopic preoccupation with his plans to overshadow his otherwise good judgemenet. 2) Some may still fault Marija for acquiescing to the pressure of Fr. Vlasic. And, if Vlasic was not a priest, we would agree. However, since Fr. Vlasic was not only a priest, but also the child's spiritual director, the degree of her culpability was further diminished, if not entirely removed. 3) Interestingly enough, this situation provides a subtle example of Marija's docility to the Church, through her willingness to place obedience to her spiritual director over her private revelation (The Virgin had taught them of the importance of obedience, and the deep reverence due to priests). Later, after Fr. Vlasic has transferred to Italy and began his plans, she publicly set the record straight for the welfare of the souls involved.

> [1] *Fr. Vlasic:* "Should we found here a community just like that of Saint Francis of Assisi?"
> *Our Lady*: "God has chosen Saint Francis as His elected one. It would be good to imitate his life. In the meantime, we must realize what God orders us to do."
>
> [2] "My first declaration, as published in Croatian and Italian, does not correspond to the truth. I personally had no desire to give any sort of written declaration. Father Tomislav V. kept suggesting to me, stressing over and over again, that I as a seer should write the declaration which the world was waiting for. [...] After seven years of daily apparitions, after having the most intimate experiences of the gentleness and wisdom of the Madonna's advice and the Madonna's answers to my personal questions, I can affirm that the idea of the heavenly plan and the numerous messages given in Medjugorje cannot be construed as supporting the undertaking and program initiated in Italy by Father Tomislav Vlasic and Agnes Heupel." 5b

**17. The children lost their vocation!**

This claim is based on one of the messages the Virgin once gave to the children; "I would like for all of you to become priests and religious, but only if you desire it. You are free. It is up to you to choose." We might first point out that the Lady encouraged the children in this direction, but left them free to choose. Even though they did make an honest attempt at following the Virgin's counsel, they all eventually married. As a result of this, critics attempt to cast doubt on Medjugorje by pointing to the failure of the children. However, just as we cannot blame the Virgin for the shortcomings of the children, neither can we necessarily blame the children for the shortcomings of seminary and religious institutions of the 1980's. We have to remember the state of these institutions during this time was one of radical upheaval, following the wake of the cultural revolution of the 1960's. It was not uncommon for seminaries to feel more like country clubs--with bars, swimming pools, and smoking lounges--rather than a sanctuary of prayer and recollection. Often times, the most faithful catholics who prayed their rosaries were the ones most ridiculed and persecuted by their peers. Suffice to say, it should be no surprise that the children became discouraged at the prospect of a priestly or religious vocation, though they tried.

We might also point out that there have been approved apparitions in which the visionaries tried to become a priest or religious, but failed. For example, the visionary of La Salette, Maximino, entered seminary but had difficulties with the studies, not unlike Ivan. He eventually left seminary just like Ivan did.

> "During the time I spent in the 'Little Seminary' in Dubrovnik, I suffered very much, truly, very much, because of my relations with my colleagues and professors." - Ivan

**18. But the Lady endorsed a book that was condemned by the Vatican!**
There are some Medjugorje followers who seem to want to deny any connection between Medjugorje and "The Poem of the Man-God" (by Maria Valtorta), likely due to the fact that it was once included on the Catholic Church's Index of Forbidden Books. To anyone who has not studied the history of this book, it may seem justified to harbor such reserve and caution with regard to it. After all, what more compelling sound-byte is there (in an age where sound-bytes govern our culture and media, rather than thorough scholarship) than; "It was on the Index of Forbidden Books. Stay away."? It would not be an exaggeration to say that this "one-liner"--this single sentence alone--has discouraged thousands, if not millions of people, from reading this book. And yet, any serious scholar of Maria Valtorta will agree that it is only a half-truth; one which does not reflect the Church's true position with regard to this book.

It cannot be denied that the visionaries of Medjugorje have explicitly stated, on numerous occasions, that Our Lady not only permits the reading of this work, but also encourages people to read it if they want to know Jesus (see evidence below). And yet despite this, some Medjugorje followers continue to refuse to acknowledge the evidence. Well-intentioned though they may be, they nonetheless do a disservice to the apparitions and to Our Lady for their persistent denial of this truth (It should be no surprise that the greatest lies are those mixed with a little truth). Was the Poem listed on the Index of Forbidden books? Yes. But what we fail to hear, is that it was only the first edition that was placed on the Index, and for reasons of a legal stipulation (Canon 1385), which required all private revelations to have an Imprimatur prior to publishing. What critics also fail to mention, is that in 1966, Pope Paul VI not only suppressed Canon 1385, but also abolished the Index of Forbidden Books altogether. What is also glossed over, is the fact that the Holy Office later gave the publishers permission to freely distribute the second edition of the book. Nor do we hear about the fact that Pope Pius XII explicitely gave permission for the book to be published and read. It is also never mentioned that Saint Faustina's diary was also included on the aforementioned Index, as was Alexander Dumas' "Three Musketeers" and " Count of Monte Cristo", or Galileo's writings on celestial bodies. Nor was it mentioned that the same Cardinal that was responsible for all this, was also the one who banned Padre Pio for excercising his priestly faculties.

All this and much more could be said in defense of this book. But rather than provide a lengthy rebuttal to the many misconceptions surrounding this work (and why the faithful may, in fact, read it in good conscience), it should suffice to refer our readers to a webpage which has already done the work for us; www.maria-valtorta.net. For those who would like to investigate further, we believe that this website provides a good starting point. Here is also a website with links to additional websites of study; www.mariavaltortawebring.com. And finally, we will also provide a link to the publisher's website, which provides 1,000 free pages of the book online, for those who would like to review the work directly; valtorta.org.

> *Vicka*: "They are true. Yes, yes, true. Authentic, yes. You can read these, they are true." (listen to audio recording at medjugorje-apologia.com)
>
> Marija: "You can read it." (EWTN Interview, March 4, 1992, Archbishop Hannan Focus program)
>
> Vicka: "Yes. The Poem of the Man-God by Maria Valtorta, ten volumes. Our Lady says The Poem of the Man-God is the truth. Our Lady said if a person wants to know Jesus he should read Poem of the Man-God by Maria Valtorta. That book is the truth." (Interview with Attorney Jan Connell of the Pittsburgh Center for Peace on January 27, 1988, image1, image2)
>
> *Marija*: "Our Lady says The Poem of the Man-God is the truth." [cf. R. Laurentin, Dernieres Nouvelles de Medjugorje No 15, OEIL, 1996, p. 19]

see also; www.mariavaltortawebring.com/Pages/014_1988.htm

**19. The visionaries live in big houses and drive expensive cars!**
The visionaries do not live lavishly, contrary to what some may believe. They live very simple lives dedicated to prayer, to serving the pilgrims, and spreading the message of Medjugorje. They have always firmly rejected donations. Their houses and cars are not atypical for the region--in fact they are quite average. Furthermore, their houses are used primarily to accommodate pilgrims, not for the visionaries themselves. The Lady of Medjugorje was clear about the abuse of money and the temptation for earthly riches;

(relating to the exploitation of some pilgrims.)

> "Right now, many are greatly seeking money, not only in the parish, but in the whole world. Woe to those who seek to take everything from those who come, and blessed are those from whom they take everything."

**20. The Lady told the children they are already saved. This is Protestant theology.**
A biblical scholar will remind us that to properly understand Scripture, one must also understand the context from which the passages come from, as well as other factors that may alter its meaning, such as translation errors. Otherwise, there will be no limit to the number of false interpretations people can make. In much the same way, the exegesis of private revelations must proceed in kind. Regarding the Lady's statement to the children, it is important to understand that She was teaching the children how to pray better, since in the beginning, they were still self-interested in their prayers. She was teaching the children not to become so absorbed in self; to rather direct their prayers outwards, and in this way, they will also obtain grace for themselves. Padre Pio once said that if you want to receive the most graces, then dedicate your life to praying for others. The more one prays for the salvation of souls, the more our own hearts will be converted. St. Therese of Lisiuex also said that she never made more progress in the spiritual life, than the day she began devoting all her prayers for others. This is a foundational part of the message of Medjugorje. Our Lady continually reminds of our obligation to pray for poor sinners, who are casting themselves into hell more today than ever before in the history of the world. It is in this context that we must read the passage in question;

> "Do not be afraid for yourselves, you are already saved. Pray rather for those who are in sin and who do not believe."
>
> While crying: "There are so many men who live in sin. Here there are likewise among you some people who have offended my heart. Pray and fast for them."
>
> "Pray, pray! How many persons have followed other beliefs or sects and have abandoned Jesus Christ. They create their own gods; they adore idols. How that hurts me! If they could be converted. Like the unbelievers, they are many. That will change only if you help me with your prayers."

**21. Fruits are not really a factor in determining authenticity. False apparitions sometimes have good fruits.**
According to the Catholic Church, fruits are one of the most important factors in judging alleged apparitions. 7 Furthermore, while it it is true that a small number of conversions have occurred at

the sites of condemned apparitions (the Holy Spirit can work even in the midst of falsehood), these numbers are marginal--a handful at most--compared to Medjugorje which is seeing conversions every year by the thousands. The number of conversions occurring in Medjugorje is so great, that it exceeds that of many approved apparitions. In fact, according to EWTN correspondent Antonio Gaspari, "More confessions are heard in Medjugorje than in any other parish of the entire world; more than 150 confessors work without interruption there every day. In the year 1990 (before the outbreak of civil war), 1,900,000 people took Communion (more than at Fatima); 30,000 priests and over 100 bishops have visited the site. Many conversions are reported, even among those who come out of curiosity, or simply to accompany friends or relatives." 8

A hoax does not produce a massive number of conversions, surpassing that of even approved apparitions. Nor does a hoax bring about peace and reconciliation between peoples, or produce numerous miracles and healings. A hoax is by nature a barren tree; it cannot produce good fruit. This is why Church norms place such a strong emphasis on fruits when judging alleged apparitions, because it eliminates every possibility, even that of diabolic origin ("a house divided against itself cannot stand"). In fact, to believe Medjugorje is a hoax or diabolical in origin, requires a greater leap of faith than to believe in the apparitions are authentic.

**22. The messages are simple and boring.**
We believe that those who have the eyes to see, will see in the messages exactly what they need to hear. On the surface, the words of the messages may seem simple and repetitive. But Our Lady did not come to communicate lofty theolgical treatises. She came to communitcate love. And it is precisely in simplicity and humility that love is best communicated. In our human nature, we have a tendency to complicate things. Our Lady is trying to get us back to the basics again; to teach us how to love, and how to rescue souls in the simplest and easiest way possible. She has effectively given us a formula for converting souls and producing saints, to a degree never before seen in the history. We believe this has been Her mission in Medjugorje, which She never ceases to repeat. However, in order to understand this, one must read the messages in their entirety. It does not suffice to read a few paragraphs. To really grasp the message of Medjugorje, one must start from the beginning, June 24th, 1981, and read, message by message, on a daily basis, so that they will be absorbed and transformative. For this, we recommend reading the complete body of messages contained in this book.

**23. Why is Medjugorje so important? Why not just believe in approved apparitions such as Fatima and Lourdes?**
Every time Our Lady has appeared throughout history, it has been to help guide man back to God from the errors of that particular period in history. This is a basic teaching of the Church on private revelations. Even the Catechism of the Catholic Church reminds us of this purpose of private revelation; "It is not their role to improve or complete Christ's definitive Revelation, but to help live more fully by it in a certain period of history." (CCC, 67)

It is thus, that Medjugorje is more relevant to us today than any other private revelation in the history of Christianity. Medjugorje is THE message of our time. And so, we would do well to listen to what Our Mother has to say to us who are living today.

Furthermore, there is a particular sense of urgency in the messages, more so than in past apparitions (yet it is also balanced with great hope as well, which separates Medjugorje from condemned apparitions that typically only focus on the negative)

> "Dear children! You are not aware of the importance of the messages which God is sending you through me. He is giving you great graces and you do not realize it. Pray to

the Holy Spirit for enlightenment. If only you knew how many graces God is giving you, you would pray without ceasing."

"These apparitions are the last for humanity." [...] "I have come to call the world to conversion for the last time. Later, I will not appear any more on this earth. [...] "These apparitions are the last in the world."

"One day he [Satan] appeared before the throne of God and asked permission to submit the Church to a period of trial. God gave him permission to try the Church for one century. This century is under the power of the Devil, but when the secrets confided to you come to pass, his power will be destroyed. Even now he is beginning to lose his power and has become aggressive. He is destroying marriages, creating division among priests and is responsible for obsessions and murder You must protect yourselves against these things through fasting and prayer, especially community prayer. Carry blessed objects with you. Put them in your house, and restore the use of holy water."

"A great battle is about to take place. A battle between my Son and Satan. Human souls are at stake. "

"I have prayed; the punishment has been softened. Repeated prayers and fasting reduce punishments from God, but it is not possible to avoid entirely the chastisement. Go on the streets of the city, count those who glorify God and those who offend Him. God can no longer endure that."

"My angel, pray for unbelievers. People will tear their hair, brother will plead with brother, he will curse his past life, lived without God. They will repent, but it will be too late. Now is the time for conversion. I have been exhorting you for the past four years. Pray for them."

"Hurry to be converted. Do not wait for the great sign. For the unbelievers, it will then be too late to be converted. For you who have the faith, this time constitutes a great opportunity for you to be converted, and to deepen your faith. Fast on bread and water before every feast, and prepare yourselves through prayer."

"Dear children! I continually need your prayers. You wonder what all these prayers are for. Look around, dear children, and you will see how much ground sin has gained in this world. Because of that, pray that Jesus conquers."

"The hour has come when the demon is authorized to act with all his force and power The present hour, is the hour of Satan."

"How many people come to church, to the house of God, with respect, a strong faith, and love of God? Very few! Here you have a time of grace and conversion. It is necessary to use it well."

"Be converted! It will be too late when the sign comes. Beforehand, several warnings will be given to the world. Have people hurry to be converted. I need your prayers and your penance. (CP. 131). My heart is burning with love for you. It suffices for you to be converted. To ask questions is unimportant. Be converted. Hurry to proclaim it. Tell everyone that it is my wish, and that I do not cease repeating it. Be converted, be converted. It is not difficult for me to suffer for you. I beg you, be converted. I will pray to my Son to spare you the punishment. Be converted without delay. You do not know the plans of God; you will not be able to know them. You will not know what God will send, not what He will do. I ask you only to be converted. That is what I wish. Be converted! Be ready for everything, but, be converted. That is all I wish to say to you. Renounce everything. All that is part of conversion. Goodbye, and may peace be with you. "

"The sign will come, you must not worry about it. The only thing that I would want to tell you is to be converted. Make that known to all my children as quickly as possible. No pain, no suffering is too great to me in order to save you. I will pray to my Son not to punish the world; but I beseech you, be converted.You cannot imagine what is going to happen nor what the Eternal Father will send to earth. That is why you must be converted! Renounce everything. Do penance. Express my acknowledgement to all my children who have prayed and fasted. I carry all this to my Divine Son in order to obtain an alleviation of His justice against the sins of mankind. (C. 145 - 146). I thank the people who have prayed and fasted. Persevere and help me to convert the world."

"Where are the prayers which you addressed to me? My clothes were sparkling. Behold them soaked with tears. Oh, if you would know how the world today is plunged into sin. It seems to you that the world sins no longer, because here, you live in a peaceful world where there is no confusion or perversity.If you know how lukewarm they are in their faith, how many do not listen to Jesus. Oh, if you knew how much I suffer, you would sin no more. Oh, how I need your prayers. Pray!"

Jelena: "Why are you so beautiful?"
I am beautiful because I love. If you want to be beautiful, love. There is no one in the world who does not desire beauty.

As a final note, we include on our website (medjugorje-apologia.com) a documentary created by a young woman from Russia who visited Medjugorje. For those who have not yet braved the pilgrimage, we believe this homemade video will help to capture a small glimpse into the Medjugorje experience, which communicates in subtly, in peace, and in silence. Although there exists many documentaries about Medjugorje, what we like about this documentary is that it is not flamboyant or excessively talkative. Rather, it conveys the simple day-to-day sights and sounds of a typical pilgrimage to Medjugorje, and the open hearts of those involved.

---

FOOTNOTES:
1a. Randall Sullivan, The Miracle Detective, Grove Press 2004, p.116 (impartial journalist for Rolling Stone)
1,2. Mary Craig, Spark From Heaven: The Mystery of the Madonna of Medjugorje, Ave Maria Press 1988, p58,61. See also p41, 46, 54-56. (impartial BBC journalist). See also; Mirjana Stanislava Vasilj-Zuccarini, Our Lady's Call from Medjugorje, p71 (local villager and eye witness).
3. Craig, op. cit. p 58.
4. Dr. Mark Miravalle & Wayne Weible, Are the Medjugorje Apparitions Authentic?, New Hope Press 2008, p.19. [link]
5. Apostolic Signatura Tribunal, Case No. 17907/86CA ly.
[see also; Laurentin, Medjugorje-13 Years Later, The Riehle Foundation, 1994, p43, 42.]
5b. Marija Pavlovic, written statement, Nov. 7, 1988. [link]
6. Craig, op. cit. p 154,155.
7. Congregation for the Doctrine of the Faith, Norms for Judging Alleged Apparitions and Revelations, 1978. [link]
8. Antonio Gaspari (EWTN), Medjugorje: Deception of Miracle? ("Inside the Vatican", Nov. 1996) [link]

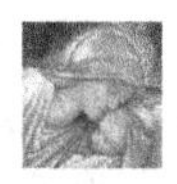

# CHAPTER I.

## MAIN BODY OF MESSAGES *(1981-1987)*

**WEDNESDAY, JUNE 24TH 1981** A silent and distant apparition of the white silhouette on the hill of Crnica; the first time in the afternoon, the second time, towards 6:00 p.m.

**THURSDAY, JUNE 25TH 1981**
The date of the first apparition for the group of six seers, who see the Gospa nearby on the hill: *Praised be Jesus!* (DV.1). ***Ivanka:***"Where is my mother?" (Her mother had died two months previously.) *She is happy. She is with me.* (A variation on this wording *is) She is your angel in heaven.* (Lj.15). ***The seers:*** "Will you return tomorrow?" The apparition acquiesces with a nod of the head. ***Mirjana:***"No one will believe us. They will say that we are crazy. Give us a sign!" The apparition responds only with a smile. Mirjana believed she had received a sign. Her watch had changed time during the apparition. (Bu 24; D4; K21). *Goodbye, my angels.* (BU.24). *Go in the peace of God.* (DV.1).

**FRIDAY, JUNE 26TH 1981**
In the presence of a crowd of 2,000 to 3,000 people, drawn there by the luminary signs coming from the hill of the apparitions, Vicka sprinkles the apparition with holy water and says: "If you are the Gospa, stay with us, if not, go away." The apparition only smiles. ***Ivanka:***"Why have you come here? What do you desire? *I have come because there are many true believers here. I wish to be with you to convert and to reconcile the whole world.* (According to others: To *convert all of you.)* (K.26). ***Ivanka:***"Did my mother say anything?" *Obey your grandmother and help her because she is old.* (K.26; Lj.16; BU.28). ***Mirjana:*** *"How is* my grandfather?" (He had recently died.) *He is well.* (K.26). ***The seers*** on a request from the crowd: "Give us a sign which will prove your presence." *Blessed are those who have not seen and who believe.* (L.2,24). ***Mirjana:***"Who are you?" *I am the Most Blessed Virgin Mary.* (L.1, 37). "Why are you appearing to us? We are not better than others." *I do not necessarily choose the best.* "Will you come back?" *Yes, to the same place as yesterday.* (L.2, 25). On returning to the village after the apparition, Maria sees the Virgin again, in tears, near a cross with rainbow colors: *Peace, Peace, Peace! Be reconciled! Only Peace.* (D.7). *Make your peace with God and among yourselves. For that, it is necessary to believe, to pray, to fast, and to go to confession.* (F.2, 126; D.5).

**SATURDAY, JUNE 27TH 1981**
*Praised be Jesus!* ***Jakov:***"What do you expect of our Franciscans?" *Have them persevere in the faith and protect the faith of others.* (DV.1). ***Jakov*** and ***Mirjana:***"Leave us a sign because the people treat us as liars." *My angels, do not be afraid of injustice. It has always existed.* (L.2,33). ***The seers:*** "How must we pray?" *Continue to recite seven Our Father's and*

*seven Hail Mary's and Glory Be's, but also add the Creed.* (Bl.12). *Goodbye, my angels. Go in the peace of God.* And to ***Ivan,*** alone, aside: *Be in peace and take courage.* ("And what a beautiful smile when she left me," noted Ivan.) (L.2,33).

**SUNDAY, JUNE 28TH 1981**
***The seers:*** "What do you wish?" *That people believe and persevere in the faith.* ***Vicka:***"What do you expect from the priests?" *That they remain strong in the faith and that they help you.* "Why don't you appear to everyone in church?" *Blessed are they who believe without having seen.* "Will you come back?" *Yes, to the same place.* "Do you prefer prayer or singing?" *Both, pray and sing.* ***Vicka:***"What do you wish from the crowd which has gathered here?" This question remained without any response except for a glance of love, with a smile, said the seers. Here the Virgin disappeared. The visionaries prayed so that she might return because she had not said, *Goodbye, my angels.* During their song, "You Are All Beautiful," she reappears. *Vicka:* "Dear Gospa, what do you expect of this people?" She repeated the question three times and finally was given this answer: *That those who do not see believe as those who see.* ***Vicka:***"Will you leave us a sign so that people believe that we are not liars nor comedians?" No other response, only a smile. *Go in the peace of God,* she said, as she disappeared. (The responses for the 28th of June were taken om the tape recorder of Grgo Kozina.) (L.2,37-38).

**MONDAY, JUNE 29TH 1981**
***The seers:*** "Dear Gospa, are you happy to see so many people here today?" *More than happy* ("She smiles," writes Vicka). "How long will you stay with us?" *As long as you will want me to, my angels.* "What do you expect of the people who have come in spite of the brambles and the heat?" *There is only one God, one faith. Let the people believe firmly and do not fear anything.* "What do you expect of us?" *That you have a solid faith and that you maintain confidence.* "Will we know how to endure persecutions which will come to us because of you?" *You will be able to, my angels. Do not fear. You will be able to endure everything. You must believe and have confidence in me.* Here Vicka writes a question from Dr. Darinka Glamuzina: "May I touch Our Lady?" She gives this response: *There have always been doubting Thomases, but she can approach.* Vicka shows her where to stretch out her hand. Darinka tries to touch her. The Gospa disappears, then reappears in her light. (L2,33). The parents of a three-year-old child, Daniel Setka, who had suffered from septicemia since the fourth day of his birth, asked the seers to intercede for the handicapped child. "Dear Gospa, is little Daniel going to speak some day? Cure him so that they all will believe us. These people love you very much, dear Gospa. Perform a miracle ... It is watching... it ... Dear Gospa, say something." They repeated this petition and conveyed the response: *Have them believe strongly in his cure. Go in the peace of God.* (L.2, 42-43).

# THE HIDDEN PHASE
## (JUN 30, 1981 TO DEC 31, 1981)

During this period, the Gospa appeared where the seers (who were being tracked down), discreetly awaited her, away from the patrols of the police.

**TUESDAY, JUNE 30TH 1981**
Apparition at Cerno. (L.2,40-41). ***Mirjana:*** 'Are you angry that we were not on the hill?" *That doesn't matter.* "Would you be angry if we would not return any longer to the hill, but we would wait in the church?" *Always at the same time. Go in the peace of God.* (L.2,50). On that day, Mirjana thought that she understood that the Gospa would return for three more days, until FRIDAY. But it was only her interpretation.

**WEDNESDAY, JULY 1ST 1981**
Apparition in the van (L.2,56: no words were reported).

**THURSDAY, JULY 2ND 1981**
*Jakov:* "Dear Gospa, leave us a sign." The Virgin seemed to acquiesce with a nod: *Goodbye, my dear angels.* (L.2,60). The apparitions from the 3rd to the 20th of July, 1981, have left few traces, almost uniquely the diary of Vicka (July 21-29, Aug. 22-Sept. 6, Oct. 10-Dec. 24), and the parish Chronicle (which begins Aug. 10, 1981).

**FRIDAY, JULY 3RD 1981**
Apparition at the rectory. No message was preserved.

**SATURDAY, JULY 4TH 1981**
The seers believe the apparitions had ended, but the Gospa appeared to each one of them separately, where he or she was. No message was preserved.

**TUESDAY, JULY 21ST 1981** (27th apparition, according to Vicka's diary).
Just like every day, we spoke with the Gospa. At 6:30 when she arrived, she greeted us: *Praised be Jesus!* Then we asked her if she would give us a sign. She said yes. Then we asked her how longer still would she come to visit us. The Blessed Virgin responded: *My sweet angels, even if I were to leave the sign, many people will not believe. Many people will only come here and bow down. But people must be converted and do penance.* Then we questioned her on the subject of the sick. For some, the Gospa said that they would be cured only if their faith was strong; and for others, no. Then she prepared to depart. Upon leaving, she said to us: *Go in the peace of God.* (DV.1,2).

**WEDNESDAY, JULY 22ND 1981:** (28th apparition, 6:30, according to Vicka's diary). (DV.1,2).
On arriving she said: *Praise be Jesus Christ.* All of us questioned her on the subject of some sick people who had been recommended to us. Then we prayed with the Blessed Virgin. She only said the Our Father and Glory Be, and during the time that we said the Hail Mary, she was silent. The Gospa told us that: *A good many people have been converted and among them some had not gone to Confession in 45 years, and now, they are going to Confession.* Then she said: *Go in the peace of God.* She began to depart and, while she was departing, a cross appeared in the sky.

**THURSDAY, JULY 23RD 1981** (29th apparition, according to Vicka's diary.) (DV.1,2).
Vicka only mentions the greeting from Our Lady: *Praised be Jesus Christ.*

**FRIDAY, JULY 24TH 1981** (3Oth apparition, 6:30, according to Vicka's diary). (DV.1,2).
Today, also, we went to the place of the apparitions about 6:20, and while praying and singing, we waited for the Blessed Virgin. At exactly 6:30 we saw the light which slowly approached. Then we saw the Blessed Virgin and heard her customary greeting. To our questions, relative to the majority of the sick, the Gospa answered quickly: *Without faith, nothing is possible. All those who will believe firmly will be cured.*

**SATURDAY, JULY 25TH 1981** (31st apparition, according to Vicka's diary). (DV.1,2).
After the usual questions on the subject of the ill, the Gospa responded: *God, help us all!*

**MONDAY, JULY 27TH 1981** (33rd apparition, at 6:30, according to Vicka's diary). (DV.1,3).
Only four of us came because they put pressure on Ivica, Ivanka and Mirjana to go to Sarajevo. At 6:30 exactly, the Gospa appeared. Vicka asked her about certain sick people, took some objects which had been given to her by some people, and approached Our Lady so that she could bless them. The Gospa made the Sign of the Cross and said: *In the name of the Father, and of the Son, and of the Holy Spirit.* Then we questioned her on the subject of the sign, and the Gospa answered: *Await, it will not be for long. If I will leave you a sign, I will still appear to you.* Vicka

asked if we would be able to see her again one more time this evening on the hill. The Gospa agreed and said: *I will come at 11:15 p. m. Go in the peace of God.* Saying this, she began to disappear and we saw in the heavens the heart and the cross. Mary said: *My angels, I send you my Son, Jesus, Who was tortured .for His faith, and yet He endured everything. You also, my angels, will endure everything.* Jesus had long hair, brown eyes, and a beard. We only saw His head. (We transpose this phrase which came before the word of Mary.) She said that we prayed and sang beautifully: *It is beautiful to listen to you. Continue in this manner.* In conclusion she said: *Don't be afraid for Jozo.* (The pastor who had been threatened by the police).

**WEDNESDAY, JULY 29TH 1981** (35th apparition, 6:30, according to Vicka's diary). (DV.1,3). Today we waited for the Blessed Virgin in Vicka's room. At exactly 6:30, the Gospa came and greeted us. *Praised be Jesus!* Jakov was the first to question her on the subject of a person who was ill. The Blessed Virgin said: *She will be cured. She must believe firmly.* Vicka asked why she had not come yesterday. The Blessed Mother said something, smiled, but no one heard it. Then Maria and Jakov asked her about certain sick people. We then took some articles and all four approached the Gospa so that she would bless them. When we were doing this, our hands became very cold. Jakov asked if we could embrace her. The Blessed Virgin said that we should approach and embrace her. Then we asked her to leave us the sign. She said: *Yes.* Then: *Go in the* peace of God. And she began to disappear. On the ceiling the Cross and the Heart were visible. The cross, the heart and the sun are mentioned by Vicka in her diary, in later apparitions. (Aug. 22, 27, 30 and 31, Sept. I and Nov. 22, 1981, as well as on Feb. 6 and Mar. 12, 1982). In church we saw the Blessed Virgin a second time toward eight o'clock in the choir loft. While we were praying, the Blessed Virgin prayed with us. (DV.1, 3).

**THURSDAY, JULY 30TH 1981**
We did not go to the hill. (DV.1, 4). (Vicka's diary contains no more observations until August 22nd.)

**JULY 1981**
*Carry out well your responsibilities and what the Church asks you to do.* (BL.307).

**SUNDAY, AUGUST 2ND 1981**
Maria sees the Virgin in her room: *All of you together go to the meadow at Gumno. A great battle is about to take place. A battle between my Son and Satan. Human souls are at stake.* The seers, accompanied by some 40 people, went to the praire of Gumno, 200 meters from Vicka's house. *Everyone here may touch me.* (D). After many people had touched her, a black stain appeared on the dress of the Virgin. Maria cried. Marinko, invited the people who were present to go to Confession.
**THE BEGINNING OF AUGUST 1981**
"What do you wish that we do later?" *I would like for you to become priests and religious, but only if you, yourselves, would want it. It is up to you to decide.* (L.2, 83).

**THURSDAY, AUGUST 6TH 1981** (FEAST OF THE TRANSFIGURATION)
*I am the Queen of Peace.* (L.1, 75).

**FRIDAY, AUGUST 7TH 1981**
On Mt. Krizevac, at two o'clock in the morning: *That one do penance for sins.* (L.2, 76).

**SATURDAY, AUGUST 8TH 1981**
*Do penance! Strengthen your faith through prayer and the sacraments.* (D.).

**MONDAY, AUGUST 17TH 1981**

*Do not be afraid. I wish that you would be filled with joy and that the joy could be seen on your faces. I will protect Father Jozo.* (The latter was the pastor of the parish at Medjugorje who was imprisoned). (BL.338).

**SATURDAY, AUGUST 22ND 1981**
*Father Jozo has nothing to fear. All that will pass.* (DV.1, 3).

**SUNDAY, AUGUST 23RD 1981**
*Praised be Jesus! I have been with Ivica until now.*(This diminutive refers sometimes to Ivan, sometimes to Ivanka. Here, the context does not permit one to be more specific). *Pray, my angels, for this people. My children, I give you strength. I will give you some of it always. "When you need me, call me.* (DV.1, 4).

**MONDAY, AUGUST 24TH 1981**
In her diary, for the date of August 25th, Vicka writes: "Yesterday, MONDAY the 24th at 10:45, Mirjana and I were at Ivan's house. We heard an uproar and we went out running. Outside, everybody was looking at the cross on Krizevac. At the spot of the cross, Mirjana, Jakov, Ivan and I saw the Blessed Virgin, and the people saw something like her statue which began then to disappear, and the cross appeared again. Over the entire sky one saw, written in letters of gold, MIR: "PEACE." Vicka's diary then reports the apparition on August 25th. (DV. 1, 4). A little after the Virgin prayed for peace, a large inscription appeared on top of Krizevac. The word "Peace" (MIR in Croatian). The inscription was seen by the pastor and many persons of the village. There is written testimony by those who saw the inscription. The seers affirmed that the Blessed Virgin Mary promised that there would still be many other signs as forerunners at Medjugorje, and in other parts of the world, before the great sign. (K58, which observes the event one evening in July 1981).

**TUESDAY, AUGUST 25TH 1981**
Some persons who were present said ... to request of the Blessed Virgin the permission to touch her. The Gospa said: *It is not necessary to touch me. Many are those who do not feel anything when they touch me.* (DV.1, 4). She also said that, among those present, there was a spy (no other clarification was given on this point). *On the matter of the sign, you do not have to become impatient for the day will come.* (DV.1, 4).

**WEDNESDAY, AUGUST 26TH 1981**
Today, for the first time, we waited for the Blessed Virgin at the home of Zdenka Ivankovic. There were five of us, because Ivanka had not yet returned. The Blessed Virgin appeared and said: *Praised be Jesus.* She said that tomorrow the people did not have to come, and thus we would be by ourselves. Then also: *Do not give advice to anyone. I know what you feel and that will pass, also.* (DV.1,4).

**THURSDAY, AUGUST 27TH 1981**
Maria and I came to Jakov's house today about six o'clock. We helped Jakov's mother to prepare supper. At six o'clock the Blessed Virgin came toward us. I was outside when the Blessed Virgin Mary came. She said that they should not have to make one suffer so. We asked her with respect to the sign, and she said: *Very soon, I promise you.* We commended certain sick people to the Holy Virgin. She stayed with us for 15 minutes. Then we left for the home of Marinko Ivankovic in order to wait for the Blessed Virgin there. She came at 6:30. She told Ivan (Dragicevic): *Be strong and courageous.* She left, and the cross, the heart and the sun appeared. (DV. 1, 5).

**FRIDAY, AUGUST 28TH 1981**
At the hour of the apparitions, the seers wait in the room of Father Jozo, who is in prison. The Virgin does not appear. It is the second time that this has happened. They go to church and pray. She appears to them: *I was with Father Jozo. That is why I did not come. Do not trouble*

*yourselves if I do not come. It suffices then to pray.* (DV.1, 5). Today, Ivan entered the seminary of Visoko: *You are very tired. Rest, so that you can find strength. Go in the peace of God. Goodbye.* (Adieu: Ivan's Journal).

**SATURDAY, AUGUST 29TH 1981**
***Jakov:*** "Are you also appearing to Ivan in the seminary?" *Yes, just like to you.* "How is Ivan Ivankovic, son of Pero, and cousin of Vicka, one of the four men at Bijakovici who bear this name. He had been arrested by the police August 12th, on the hill of the apparitions, and imprisoned.) *He is well. He is enduring everything. All that will pass. Father Jozo sends you greetings.* (DV.1). "What is the news from our village?" *My angels, you are doing your penance well.* "Will you help us in our studies?" *God's help manifests itself everywhere. Go in the peace of God with the blessing of Jesus and mine. Goodbye.* (Ivan's Journal: C76). ***Ivanka:*** "Will you leave us a sign soon?" *Again, a little patience.* (DV.1).

**SUNDAY, AUGUST 30TH 1981**
At 6:20, we began to pray at the home of Marinko Ivankovic. The Virgin arrived and said: *Praised be Jesus!* ***Vicka*** asked the Virgin: "People say that since they locked up Father Jozo in his cell, the doors unlocked by themselves. Is that true?" *It is true, but no one believes it.* ***Ivanka:*** "How is Mirjana? What are her feelings?" *Mirjana is sad because she is all alone. I will show her to you.* Suddenly, we saw Mirjana's face. She was crying. "Dear Gospa, there are some young people who betray our faith." *Yes, there are many.* She mentions some names. ***Vicka***asks the Virgin concerning a woman who wanted to leave her husband because he was making her suffer. *Let her remain close to him and accept her suffering. Jesus, Himself, also suffered.* On the matter of a sick young boy: *He is suffering from a very grave illness. Let his parents firmly believe, do penance, then the little boy will be cured.* ***Jakov***asks her about the sign: *Again, a little patience.* (DV.1, 6). *Ivan,* who had been several days without an apparition: "How will I do in this seminary?" *Be without fear. I am close to you everywhere and at all times.* (L.2, 84). ***Ivan's diary:*** 'Are the people pious in our village?" *Your village has become the most fervent parish in Hercegovina. A large number of people distinguish themselves through their piety and their faith.* (c.77).
**END OF AUGUST 1981:**
"Which is the best fasting?" *A fasting on bread and water I am the Queen of Peace.* (L.1, 98 and 187; MM6).

**TUESDAY, SEPTEMBER 1ST 1981** "Will there be a Mass on Mt. Krizevac?" *Yes, my angels.* ***Jakov:***'Are the police setting up a trap around the church'?" *There's nothing at all. Have the people pray and remain in church as long as possible. Go in the peace of God.* The cross, the heart, and the sun appeared. (DV.1, 6). ***Ivan's diary:*** "I prayed with her so that Jesus might help me in my vocation. Then we recited the rosary. The Gospa smiled with kindness." *Do not be afraid. I am close to you and I watch over you.* (c.77).

**WEDNESDAY, SEPTEMBER 2ND 1981** Concerning the young man who hanged himself: ***Vicka:*** "Why did he do that?" *Satan took hold of him. This young man should not have done that. The Devil tries to reign over the people. He takes everything into his hands, but the force of God is more powerful, and God will conquer.* (DV.1, 6). ***Ivan's diary:*** "How will things go for Anton, Dario, Miljenko, my friends in the seminary, and for me?" *You are, and you will always be my children. You have followed the path of Jesus. No one will stop you from propagating the faith in Jesus. One must believe strongly.* (C.78).

**THURSDAY, SEPTEMBER 3RD 1981**
***Jakov:*** "When will the sign which was announced come?" *Again, a little patience.* (DV.1, 6).

**FRIDAY, SEPTEMBER 4TH 1981**
***Ivanka***and ***Maria:*** "We will not be at home except on

SATURDAYs and SUNDAYs. The other days we will be far away in school. What must we do?" *It is enough for you to pray. Come here SATURDAYs and SUNDAYs. I will appear to all of you.* (DV.1, 6). To Ivan in the seminary: *The sign will be given at the end of the apparitions.* ***Ivan:***"When will that be?" *You are impatient, my angel. Go in the peace of God.* (L.2, 84).

**SATURDAY, SEPTEMBER 5TH 1981**
***Ivan's diary:*** "I was praying in the chapel. The Gospa came when I was reciting the Our Father." *Praise be Jesus and Mary.* (The Virgin was using a salutation of pious people in Croatia, probably with the desire to revive it.) *Go in the peace of God, my angel. May the blessing of God accompany you. Amen. Goodbye.* (C.79).

**SUNDAY, SEPTEMBER 6TH 1981**
***Ivan's diary:*** "I was praying in the chapel. Suddenly there was a great light." *Pray especially on SUNDAY, so that the great sign, the gift of God may come. Pray with fervor and a constancy so that God may have mercy on His great children. Go in peace, my angel. May the blessing of God accompany you. Amen. Goodbye.* (C.79).

**MONDAY, SEPTEMBER 7TH 1981**
***Ivan's diary:*** *Be converted all of you who are still there. The sign will come when you will be converted.* (C.79).

**TUESDAY, SEPTEMBER 8TH 1981** (FEAST OF THE NATIVITY OF THE VIRGIN)
***Ivan's diary:*** *I ask you only to pray with fervor. Prayer must become a part of your daily life, to permit the true faith to take roots.* (C.79). Jakov wishes the Blessed Virgin a happy birthday. She answers: *It is for me a beautiful day. With respect to you, persevere in the faith and in prayer.* (CP.7). *Do not be afraid. Remain in joy. It is my desire. Let joy appear on your faces. I will continue to protect Father Jozo.* (CP.8).

**THURSDAY, SEPTEMBER 10TH 1981**
***Ivan's diary:*** "We prayed a lot. Prayers filled with joy and love, prayers of the heart." Then she says: *Go in the peace of God, my angel. Amen. Goodbye.* (C.80).

**SUNDAY, SEPTEMBER 13TH 1981**
***Ivan's diary:*** "The students in the seminary prayed the rosary after they had gone to Confession." The Virgin came near the image of Jesus and said: *There is your Father, my angel. Go in the peace of God, my angels.* (C.80). Christ is our Brother, but in a sense, our Father: Formula used by some of the most renown mystics. In an apparition to Gemma Galgani, Jesus said, *I am your Father. Your Mother, here she is.* And He pointed out to her the Blessed Virgin. (J.F. Villepelée, "Vie de G. Galgani.").

**MONDAY, SEPTEMBER 14TH 1981**
To Vicka: *Stay here so that Jakov will not be alone. Persevere (both of you) with patience. You will be rewarded.* She also told her that she had scolded Mirjana and Ivanka for a behavior which was not detailed. (CP.10).

**TUESDAY, SEPTEMBER 15TH 1981**
*If this people is not converted very soon, bad things will happen to them.* (CP.10).

**WEDNESDAY, SEPTEMBER 16TH 1981**
*The militia will not stay here a long time. I will leave the sign. Be patient still. Don't pray for yourselves. You have been rewarded. Pray for others.* (CP.11).

**THURSDAY, SEPTEMBER 17TH 1981**

Concerning a sick person: *He will die very soon.* Then the Blessed Virgin encouraged the children: *Persevere and you will be rewarded.* (CP.11)

**SUNDAY, SEPTEMBER 20TH 1981**
To Vicka and Jakov: *Do not relax in your prayers. I ask both of you to fast for a week on bread and water. (Bl. 190).*

**WEDNESDAY, SEPTEMBER 30TH 1981**
*Don't ask useless questions dictated by curiosity. The most important thing is to pray, my angels.* (CP.12)

**THURSDAY, OCTOBER 1ST 1981**
Written questions asked of the seers: "Are all religions good?" *All religions are similar before God. God rules over them just like a sovereign over his kingdom. In the world, all religions are not the same because people have not complied with the commandments of God. They reject and disparage them.* (On this ambiguous response see annex 2.) "Are all churches the same?" *In some, one prays to God more. In others, less. That depends on the priests who motivate others to pray. That also depends on the power which they have.* "Why are there so many apparitions which repeat themselves so many times? Why does the Blessed Virgin appear to children who do not follow the way of God?" *I appear to you often and in every place. To others, I appear from time to time and briefly. They do not follow yet, completely the way of God. They are not aware of the gift which He has made them. That, no one deserves. With time, they also will come to follow the right way.* (CP.14).

**TUESDAY, OCTOBER 6TH 1981**
*The evening Mass must definitely be kept. The Mass of the sick must be celebrated on a specific day at a time which is most convenient. Father Tomislav must begin with the prayer group. It is very necessary. Have Father Tomislav pray with fervor.*(CP.16).

**WEDNESDAY, OCTOBER 7TH 1981**
***The seers:*** "*Is* there, outside of Jesus, other intermediaries between God and man, and what is their role?" *There is only one mediator between God and man, and it is Jesus Christ.* On the request from Father Tomislav: "Should we found here a community just like that of Saint Francis of Assisi?" *God has chosen Saint Francis as His elected one. It would be good to imitate his life. In the meantime, we must realize what God orders us to do.* (CP.16).

**THURSDAY, OCTOBER 8TH 1981**
**Maria** humbly reports that the Gospa had scolded her for having stayed (during Mass) with her school mates of religious instruction, who asked her about the apparitions: *You would have done better to attend Mass rather than to satisfy human curiosity.* (CP.17).

**SATURDAY, OCTOBER 10TH 1981**
*It is up to you to pray and to persevere. I have made promises to you; also be without anxiety.* (DV.2). *Faith will not know how to be alive without prayer.* (B1.137). *Pray more.* (CP.17).

**SUNDAY, OCTOBER 11TH 1981**
The Virgin answers, as usual, questions on the subject of people who are sick or who have disappeared: *Tomo Lovic* (an old man) *is dead.* (CP.17).

**MONDAY, OCTOBER 12TH 1981**
"Where are the Kingdom of God and of paradise?" *In Heaven.* "Are you the Mother of God?" *I am the Mother of God and the Queen of Peace.* "Did you go to Heaven before or after death?" *I went to Heaven before death.* "When will you leave us the sign?" *I will not yet leave the sign. I shall*

*continue to appear. Father Jozo sends you greetings. He is experiencing difficulties, but he will resist, because he knows why he is suffering.* (CP. 18: DV.2, 10).

**SATURDAY, OCTOBER 17TH 1981**
Questioned on the subject of the visible sign, Our Lady responds: *It is mine to realize the promise. With respect to the faithful, have them pray and believe firmly.*

**MONDAY, OCTOBER 19TH 1981**
*Pray for Fr. Jozo and fast tomorrow on bread and water. Then you will fast for a whole week on bread and water. Pray, my angels. Now I will show you Fr. Jozo.* (CP 20). The seers have a vision of Fr. Jozo in prison. He tells them not to be afraid for him, that everything was well. With respect to Marinko who protected the visionaries: *There are a few similar faithful. He is made a sufficient number of sacrifices for Jozo. He underwent many torments and sufferings. Continue, and do not let anyone take the faith away from you.*

**TUESDAY, OCTOBER 20TH 1981**
***Vicka:*** "Dear Gospa, have mercy on Fr. Jozo tomorrow during the trial. Paralyze someone; strike someone on the head. I know it is a sin to speak so, but what can we do?" The Gospa smiles at my words, then she sings: *"Jesus Christ, in Your Name.* When we finished the song, (with the Gospa) she tells us:" *Go in the peace of God.* Then she leaves. (DV.2, 13; CP. 20).

**WEDNESDAY, OCTOBER 21ST 1981**
With respect to Fr. Jozo who is awaiting sentence from the court: ***Vicka:*** "Dear Gospa, I know that you do not have the spirit of vengeance, but try nevertheless to bring certain people to reason, so that they might judge impartially." *Jozo looks well and he greets you warmly. Do not fear for Jozo. He is a saint, I have already told you.* (CP. 21). "Will Jozo be condemned?" *Sentence will not be pronounced this evening. Do not be afraid, he will not be condemned to a severe punishment. Pray only, because Jozo asks from you prayer and perseverance. Do not be afraid because I am with you.* (DV. 2, 14).

**THURSDAY, OCTOBER 22ND 1981**
*Jozo has been sentenced. Let us go to church to pray.* "We were sad because of Jozo." *You should rejoice!* (DV. 2, 14; CP 21). "Is the whiteness of the cross a supernatural phenomenon?" *Yes, I confirm it.* (DV. 2, 15; CP. 21). After many people saw the cross on Mt. Krizevac transform itself into a light, then into a silhouette of the Virgin: *All of these signs are designed to strengthen your faith until I leave you the visible and permanent sign.* (F2, 155).

**SUNDAY, OCTOBER 25TH 1981**
Three girls from Citluk, returning home after Mass, suddenly see a great light from which fifteen silhouettes, dressed in Franciscan frock, are apparent. They go down on their knees, pray and cry. The Blessed Virgin was questioned on this subject: *It was a supernatural phenomenon. I was among the saints.* (CP. 23).

**MONDAY, OCTOBER 26TH 1981**
The Blessed Virgin appeared smiling: *Praise be Jesus. You are not to ask me any more questions on the subject of the sign. Do not be afraid, it will surely appear. I carry out my promises. As far as you are concerned, pray, persevere in prayer.* (DV. 2, 16: CP. 23-24).

**WEDNESDAY, OCTOBER 28TH 1981**
"Were you there at Krizevac yesterday for half an hour?" *Yes, didn't you see me?* (DV. 1, 17; CP. 251). Several hundred people saw, at the site of the first apparition, a fire which burned without burning up anything. In the evening, the Virgin tells the seers: *The fire seen by the faithful was of a supernatural character. It is one of the signs; a forerunner of the great sign.* (CP. 25).

**THURSDAY, OCTOBER 29TH 1981**
*You, my angels, be on your guard. There is enough mendacious news which people are spreading. Of course, I will show you my mercy. Be a little patient. Pray!* (DV. 2, 17).

**FRIDAY, OCTOBER 30TH 1981**
*Praise be Jesus!* ***Jakov*** and ***Vicka:*** "What was there in the sealed envelope which they showed us at city hall?" (Someone had told them that he would believe in the apparitions, if they would read what was in the sealed envelope.) *Do not respond anything. It is a bad trick which they are playing on you. They have already given so much false news. Do not believe them. Continue to pray and to suffer! I will make the power of love appear.* (CP 25-26; DV. 2, 18). "Should one celebrate Christmas Mass in the evening or at Midnight?" *Have them celebrate it at midnight.* (CP. 25). To the seers: *Pray! Go in the peace of God!* (DV2, 17). To Ivanka: *Pray more. The others are praying and suffering more than you.* To the seers: *Tell the young people not to allow themselves to be distracted from the true way. Let them remain faithful to their religion.* (CP 26).

**SATURDAY, OCTOBER 31ST 1981-Two versions:**
***1. Vicka's diary:*** (D. 1, 17). Mirjana arrives from Sarajevo, where she is studying at a professional school, and where she has had daily apparitions. ***Vicka*** reports: "The Gospa advises as an attentive mother would. She tells Mirjana twice that she must distrust, which persons to avoid, how to conduct herself with those who reproach her and insult God." "She also tells her to break a relationship with a girl who wanted to get her into drugs ( ... ), and; not to quarrel with anyone, to answer a point when it is useful, or to remain silent and go on her way when that is better. She tells her also that Father Jozo will not spend more than four years in prison. She was happy because all five of us were together. On the question of Danny Ljolje, the Gospa said:" *There is a lot of deception and erroneous information.* "Then she shows us a part of paradise; indescribable beauty; many people, particularly children. We were afraid. The Blessed Virgin tells us not to be afraid." *All those who are faithful to God will have that.* (DV. 2, 17).
***2. Parish Chronicle:*** T. Vlasic summarizes the advice given to Mirjana in this manner: "The Blessed Virgin advises her, as an attentive and good mother. She also shows her what she should pay attention to, which persons to avoid, how to handle those who provoke and offend God. The Blessed Virgin advised her to sever all types of relationships with a young girl who intended to get her into drugs. Then she put her on guard against other dangers. She told her not to argue with people and to answer calmly, and when she sees that serves no purpose, to keep quiet and continue on her way." "Often she would motivate her to prayer and to perseverance." "She also tells her that Father Jozo would not have more than four years in prison. The Blessed Mother shows a great joy, because the five seers were together again. To a question which was brought up again concerning Danny Ljolje, the Blessed Virgin said:" *There is enough trickery and false information.* "She asks the children to separate from such persons. And then the Gospa shows the children a part of paradise, indescribable beauty, many people, especially children. The seers were surprised and shocked. The Gospa told them not to fear:" *It will be like this for all those who are faithful to God.* "Ivanka saw her mother in paradise as well as another person who was of her acquaintance." (CP. 26-27).
**OCTOBER 1981**
Regarding the conflict between the Franciscans and the Bishop of Mostar in Hercegovina: *It is going to find a solution. We must have patience and pray.* In response to a question posed by the seers: "What will become of Poland?" *There will be great conflicts but in the end, the just will take over.* With respect to Russia: *It is the people where God will be most glorified. The West has made civilization progress, but without God, as if they were their own creators.* (K. 60).

**SUNDAY, NOVEMBER 1ST 1981**
*Be persevering! Pray! Many people are beginning to convert.* (CP. 27; DV. 2,18).
**THE BEGINNING OF NOVEMBER 1981**
The Virgin appears with a picture of John Paul II in her hand. She embraces the picture: *He is our father, and the father of all. It is necessary to pray for him.*

**MONDAY, NOVEMBER 2ND 1981**
"Why did you show us paradise the day before yesterday?" *I did it so that you could see the happiness which awaits those who love God.* Jesus appears to them crowned with thorns and with injuries all over His body. The children are afraid. *Do not be afraid. It is my Son. See how He has been martyred. In spite of all, He was joyful and He endured all with patience.* Jesus tells them: *Look at me. How I have been injured and martyred. In spite of all, I have gained the victory. You also, my angels, be persevering in your faith and pray so that you may overcome.* (CP. 28, DV. 2,18).

**TUESDAY, NOVEMBER 3RD 1981**
"The Virgin begins the song, 'Come, Come to Us Lord' and we continued it with her." *I am often at Krizevac, at the foot of the cross, to pray there. Now I pray to my Son to forgive the world its sins. The world has begun to convert.* She smiles, then leaves. (CP. 28, DV.2, 18).

**FRIDAY, NOVEMBER 6TH 1981**
"After twenty minutes, the Gospa disappears and before us Hell appears. Later she tells us:" *Do not be afraid! I have shown you Hell so that you may know the state of those who are there.* (DV. 2, 19).

**SUNDAY, NOVEMBER 8TH 1981**
The Blessed Virgin kisses an image of the Pope and says: *It is your father, the spiritual father of all.* (L2, 90). The seers have a vision of Fr. Jozo in prison. The Blessed Virgin tells them: *Have you seen how our Fr. Jozo struggles for God?* (dv. 2, 20).

**MONDAY, NOVEMBER 9TH 1981**
"Jakov and I were alone in the room. We were speaking of the militia which passed by. The Virgin arrived:" *Do not be afraid of the militia. Do not provoke anybody. Be polite with everybody.* (DV. 2, 20).

**TUESDAY, NOVEMBER 10TH 1981**
*Do not give in. Keep your faith. I will accompany you at every step.* (DV. 2, 20).

**FRIDAY, NOVEMBER 13TH 1981**
*Praise be Jesus!* ***The seers:*** "Always Jesus and Mary." "Then the Blessed Virgin shows us beautiful landscapes. The Baby Jesus was walking there. We were not able to recognize Him. She said:" *It is Jesus. On my arrival and when I depart always sing the song, 'Come, Come to us 0 Lord.'* "Then she blessed us." (DV. 2, 21: CP. 29).

**SUNDAY, NOVEMBER 15TH 1981**
"We were in Fr. Jozo's room. The Gospa did not come. She appeared to us in the church after the prayers of 7 Our Father's, Hail Mary's, and Glory Be's. We asked her why she had not appeared. She answered that she had not appeared because someone had installed something there." *The world is on the point of receiving great favors from me and from my Son. May the world keep a strong confidence.* (CP. 29; DV. 2,22).

**MONDAY, NOVEMBER 16TH 1981**
*The Devil is trying to conquer us. Do not permit him. Keep the faith, fast and pray. I will be with you at every step.* (CP. 31). **To Jakov and Vicka:** *Persevere with confidence in prayer and in faith.* (DV. 2, 22).

**SUNDAY, NOVEMBER 22ND 1981**
"We asked the Blessed Virgin what the cross, the heart and the sun, seen during the apparition, meant:" *These are the signs of salvation: The cross is a sign of mercy, just like the heart. The sun*

*is the source of light, which enlightens us.* (DV. 12,24; cf. 29XI; DV. 12, 19; CP. 33). A shining silhouette takes the place of the cross again on Krizevac. The seers ask the Virgin if it was she. *Why do you ask me my angels? Have you not seen me?* (L21, 92). *The world must find salvation while there is time. Let it pray with fervor. May it have the spirit of faith.* (CP. 33).

**MONDAY, NOVEMBER 23RD 1981**
"The Gospa was all dressed in gold. Around her veil, on her dress, everything shined and sparkled. It was indescribable. She was very, very beautiful." *The people le have begun to convert. Keep a solid faith. I need your prayers.*

**THURSDAY, NOVEMBER 26TH 1981**
"This evening, the Blessed Virgin was smiling. We prayed and sang with her. We asked her questions about the sick." *Have a strong faith, pray and fast and they will be cured. Be confident and rest in joy. Go in the peace of God. Be patient and pray for the cure. Goodbye, my dear angels.* (CP. 34; DV. 2, 25).

**SATURDAY, NOVEMBER 28TH 1981**
"We were five, Ivan was absent. Profound harmony reigned over us. The Virgin came at the moment when we began to say the Our Father. We conversed with her. Then she blessed the objects. She looked at us with sweetness and said , " *Ah, it is so beautiful to see all of you together! Go in the peace of God, my angels. Goodbye.* (DV. 2, 26).

**SUNDAY, NOVEMBER 29TH 1981**
*It is necessary for the world to be saved while there is still time; for it to pray strongly and to have the spirit of faith.* (CP. 34).
**NOVEMBER 1981:**
*The Devil tries to impose his power on you. But you must remain strong and persevere in your faith. You must pray and fast. I will be always close to you.* ***Vicka:*** "This warning concerns everybody." (C 100).

**WEDNESDAY, DECEMBER 2ND 1981**
***Maria, Vicka*** and ***Jakov:*** "We asked the Blessed Virgin on the matter of a young man who had suddenly lost his memory and stopped learning. She said," *It is necessary to hospitalize him.* "We still questioned her. She did not respond to some of the questions." *It is not necessary to ask questions on every subject.* "She greeted us then, as usual." (CP. 35; DV. 2, 28).

**THURSDAY, DECEMBER 3RD 1981**
*Pray, and persevere through prayer.* (CP. 35; DV. 2,29).

**SUNDAY, DECEMBER 6TH 1981**
*Be strong and persevering. My dear angels, go in the peace of God.* (DV. 2,30).

**MONDAY, DECEMBER 7TH 1981**
*The people are converting. It is true, but not yet all.* She spoke while looking at the crowd which was present at the different sites of the apparitions. (C53). Apparition at Jakov's home: "The blessed Virgin prayed all the time with us. She then said: " *Pray and persist in prayers.* (DV. 2, 30 and CP. 36). On the walls there was written in letters of gold "MIR LJUDIMA" (Peace to the people). (CP. 36).

**TUESDAY, DECEMBER 8TH 1981** (Feast of the Immaculate Conception).
Responding to a question from the seers with respect to their future: *I would like for all of you to become priests and religious, but only if you desire it. You are free. It is up to you to choose.* (L1, 136). *If you are experiencing difficulties or if you need something, come to me.* (K.72). *If you do not have the strength to fast on bread and water, you can give up a number of things. It would be*

*a good thing to give up television, because after seeing some programs, you are distracted and unable to pray. You can give up alcohol, cigarettes and other pleasures. You yourselves know what you have to do.* (T. 55). On this day of the Feast of the Immaculate Conception, the Gospa was serious; she knelt down with arms extended while praying: *My beloved Son, I beseech you to be willing to forgive the world its great sin through which it offends you.* (C 53).

**WEDNESDAY, DECEMBER 9TH 1981**
"While we were saying our prayers, the Blessed Virgin intervened: " *Oh, My Son Jesus, forgive these sins, there are so many of them!* "Then we were all silent." *Continue to pray, because that is the salvation of this people.* (CP. 37; DV.2, 31).

**FRIDAY, DECEMBER 11TH 1981**
***Vicka:*** "I recommend to the Gospa my parents who are in Germany." *I promise to protect them. Everything will go well.* (DV. 2, 32; CP 37).

**SATURDAY, DECEMBER 12TH 1981**
As vacation approached, which permitted the seers to be back, the Blessed Virgin was happy: *Very soon you will all be united. You will be able to have a good time together.* (CP. 38, DV. 2,32).

**WEDNESDAY, DECEMBER 16TH 1981**
*Kneel down, my children, and pray. Persevere in prayer.* (CP. 38). **Jakov** and ***Vicka:*** "Every word of the Blessed Virgin invited us to be joyful." (CP. 39).

**FRIDAY, DECEMBER 18TH 1981**
"The Blessed Virgin did not respond to our questions. She sang: 'Jesus Christ, in Your Narne.' After the first verse, she said: " *Come on, sing more joyfully. Why are you so pensive?* "After the prayer, she began, 'Queen of the Holy Rosary' and she departed." (CP. 39).

**SATURDAY, DECEMBER 19TH 1981**
It is the date of the first ambiguous oracle on the Bishop. Complete text, which is questionable and disputed, has been referred to Annex 1.

**MONDAY, DECEMBER 21ST 1981**
*Be on your guard, my children. Prepare yourselves for difficult days. All kinds of people will come here.* (CP. 40).

**THURSDAY, DECEMBER 24TH 1981**
*Celebrate the days which are coming. Rejoice with my Soil. Love your neighbor. May harmony reign among you.* (CP. 41).

**FRIDAY, DECEMBER 25TH 1981**
*Love one another, my children. You are brothers and sisters. Don't argue among yourselves.* Then she blesses them and leaves. (CP. 41). After having had a vision of Jesus: *Give glory to God, glorify Him and sing, my angels.* (Bl. 53).

**WEDNESDAY, DECEMBER 30TH 1981**
In response to some questions concerning the sick, she began prayer with the "Our Father," then the song "The Queen of the Holy Rosary," and she departed. (CP. 42).

**THURSDAY, DECEMBER 31ST 1981**
Ivan: "How can one put priests, who do not believe in the apparitions, on the right track?" *It is necessary to tell them that, from the very beginning, I have been conveying the message of God to the world. It is a great pity not to believe in it. Faith is a vital element, but one cannot compel a*

*person to believe. Faith is the foundation from which everything flows.* "Is it really you who appears at the foot of the cross?" *Yes, it is true. Almost every day I am at the foot of the cross. My Son carried the cross. He has suffered on the cross, and by it, He saved the world. Every day I pray to my Son to forgive the sins of the world.* (CP 42; cf. L2, 126).

# The Apparitions in the Chapel Opposite the Sacristy (Jan-Feb 1982 To Apr 11, 1985)

The apparitions, since July 1981, often taking place in the church, where they occurred spontaneously toward the end of the rosary, are transferred to the room serving as a storeroom. It is opposite the sacristy and provided privacy from the curiosity of the pilgrims and every provocation on part of the police. This room was cleaned and decorated. Subsequently, it has since been called "chapel of the apparitions." Before the end of February this transfer was definitive, except for rare occasions (apparitions in the sacristy, when the chapel was found overrun or certain days for medical exams).

**MONDAY, JANUARY 11TH 1982**
*I invite you very specially to participate at mass. Wait for me at church, that is the agreeable place.* (CP. 43).

**THURSDAY, JANUARY 14TH 1982**
After the prayers, the songs and the questions, The Gospa reprimanded two seers because of their behavior, and recommended to them not to behave in this manner again. In case of observation, the other seers did not understand what the Gospa told those she reprimanded, and observed only her expression and guessed what it was all about. Those whom she reprimanded say that at that moment, she was gentle and attentive in respect for them. (CP. 44).

**MONDAY, JANUARY 18TH 1982**
On the matter of a sick person with heart problems: *There is little hope for her. I will pray for her.* After her departure, the children see the cross, the heart and the sun, signs which they perceive from time to time. (CP. 46).

**WEDNESDAY, JANUARY 20TH 1982**
Must the children from Izbicno meet us tomorrow? They say that you told them of this meeting. *It is not necessary for you to meet them.* They want to transfer Fr. Tomislav from here. What must he do? *If it is in God's design, that he depart, as has been the case with Fr. Jozo, have him abandon himself to the will of God. He must think very much, and you must pray for him.* (CP. 47).

**THURSDAY, JANUARY 21ST 1982**
***The seers:*** Why don't you leave a concrete sign, so that the priests are convinced and that they be converted, in order to be able to convert the others? *The sign will appear at the desired time.* Why are there apparitions in different places in Hercegovina? *My children, don't you see that the faith begins to extinguish itself, and that it is necessary to awaken the faith among men?* What must we do so that peace may reign among the priests? *Fast and pray!* (CP. 46).

**FRIDAY, JANUARY 22ND 1982**
Is the apparition at Izbicno coming from God or from the devil? *It is coming from God.* (CP. 47).

**TUESDAY, FEBRUARY 2ND 1982**
When must one celebrate the feast of The Queen of Peace? The Blessed Virgin smiled as she answered: *I would prefer that it take place June 25th. The faithful have come for the first time on that day, on the hill.* (CP. 48).

**MONDAY, FEBRUARY 8TH 1982**
Jakov and I were in the sacristy. When we began to pray the "Our Father," the Gospa arrived. It was five minutes after six. We questioned her on the matter of a person who was sick, emotionally: *He must pray. I will- help him within the limitation of my power.* To the Slovenes who were praying while she was with us: *Persevere in prayer.* Then she blessed some articles, (DV3, 3).

**TUESDAY, FEBRUARY 9TH 1982**
At the fourth "Our Father," the Blessed Virgin- arrived. We always ask questions with respect to the sick: *Pray for all the sick. Believe firmly. I will come to help, according to that which is in my power I will ask my Son, Jesus, to help them. The most important thing, in the meantime, is a strong faith. Numerous sick persons think that it is sufficient to come here in order to be quickly healed. Some of them do not even believe in God, and even less, in the apparitions, and then they ask for help from the Gospa!* (Dv3,3).

**WEDNESDAY, FEBRUARY 10TH 1982**
Jakov and I were alone. Just as every evening, we prayed, conversed with the Blessed Virgin, and asked many questions. To them she responded: *Pray, Pray! It is necessary to believe firmly, to go to confession regularly, and likewise receive Holy Communion. It is the only salvation.* Her preferred prayer is the "Creed." When we recite it, the Blessed Virgin does not cease to smile. I think that no one has seen her happier than during this prayer. (DV3, 4).

**THURSDAY, FEBRUARY 11TH 1982**
Just like every evening, except on
FRIDAYs,
SATURDAYs, and
SUNDAYs, Jakov and I are alone. The Blessed Virgin begins first or all to pray the "Our Father," then the "Glory Be." We recommend the sick and then present her questions: *Pray my angels, persevere! Do not let the enemy take possession of you in anything. Be courageous. Go in the peace of God, my angels. Goodbye.* (DV3,4).

**FRIDAY, FEBRUARY 12TH 1982**
*Be more calm, more poised. Do not take sides with other children. Be agreeable, well mannered, pious!* When the Gospa prays, she joins her hands. When she speaks she opens them and raises them toward Heaven, her palms turned upwards. (DV3,5).

**SATURDAY, FEBRUARY 13TH 1982**
To the seminarians who were present: *Through prayer, one obtains everything.* (C.52).

**SUNDAY, FEBRUARY 14TH 1982**
We are four seers today. When we are in a group, I feel a little happier and joyful in the presence of the Holy Virgin. Likewise, the other four: *Be together like brothers and sisters. Do not argue. Satan exists! He seeks only to destroy. With regards to you, pray, and persevere in prayer. No one will be able to do anything against you.* (DV3, 6).

**TUESDAY, FEBRUARY 16TH 1982**

The Blessed Virgin began "Jesus in Your Name." Since she has appeared to us she hasn't been sad. Whatever she says, her countenance is smiling and filled with serenity. Her joy attracts us. She wants us to be joyful, we also, wanting nothing to deceive us, any intrigue, or inventive story. *Satan only says what he wants. He interferes in everything. You, my angels, be ready to endure everything. Here, many things will take place. Do not allow yourselves to be surprised by him.* (DV3, 7).

**FRIDAY, FEBRUARY 19TH 1982**
We asked if we could pray the "Hail Mary." She said yes. And while we prayed, she looked at us with a smile, but without praying with us. Truly, her beauty is indescribable. Since I have seen the Blessed Virgin, I have been filled with joy. Whatever her words may be, what she has told me, I have always done it. I have obeyed. She makes attentive remarks, as a mother. *Listen attentively at holy Mass. Be well mannered. Do not chatter during holy Mass.* (DV3, 8).

**SUNDAY, FEBRUARY 21ST 1982**
*Be together, and do not argue, do not be disorderly. My angels, I will make you attentive. I will guide you on a sure way.* (DV3, 9).

**TUESDAY, FEBRUARY 23RD 1982**
When we asked the Gospa, she did not answer, but began immediately to pray. When we asked her if such a person were alive, she says: *Do not ask me any more questions! I know what there is in each sick person, or what there is in my power to help him. I will pray to my Son to put out His mercy on each one.* (DV3, 10).

**THURSDAY, FEBRUARY 25TH 1982**
*Be persevering and courageous. Do not fear anything. Pray, and do not pay attention to others.* We asked for news about Fr. Jozo: *Do not fear for him.* (DV3, 12).

**SUNDAY, FEBRUARY 28TH 1982**
*Thank Tomislav very much, for he is guiding you very well.* Then she smiles, and begins to say the "Glory Be." *Go in the peace of God, my angels!* (DV3, 15).
**END OF FEBRUARY AND BEGINNING OF MARCH, 1982.**
Messages received by Jelena:Dear *children, if you would know how much I love you, your heart would weep over it. If there is someone there who asks you for something, give it to him. I also present myself to many hearts, and they do not open up. Pray so that the world may welcome my love. Dear children, I would like for the whole world to be my child, but it does not want it. I wish to give everything for it. For that, Pray!* (L2, 131).

**MONDAY, MARCH 1ST 1982**
*All of you be happy, and may my blessing accompany you at each step.* She blessed many articles; she touched them with her hands. (DV3, 16). Since the Yugoslavian authorities demanded that they put an end to the prayer meetings for the young people, the Blessed Virgin was questioned and responded: *It is better to temporarily suspend prayer meetings and those of meditation because of the authorities. Take them up later, when it will be possible. (CP. 49).*

**TUESDAY, MARCH 2ND 1982**
A woman, who had come from Osijek, brought two large pictures of the Pope. The Blessed Virgin came at six o'clock with her smile. I believed she was smiling at us; but it was because of the pictures on the table. She said: *He is your father, my angels.* Then she began the "Our Father." On leaving she said: *Open the door well, follow the Mass well! Go in the peace of God, my angels! If you suffer for a just cause, blessings will be still more abundant for you.* (DV3,17).

**THURSDAY, MARCH 4TH 1982**

I asked questions with respect to a woman who had no children. She is not of our faith. The Blessed Virgin said: *Let her believe firmly. God, who comes to help everyone, will likewise help her. Be patient, my angels, do not be afraid of anything. I am at your side and guard you. If you have any problems, whatever it be, call me. I will come immediately and help you in advising you on best resolving the difficulty.* (DV3, 19). *Go in peace, my angels. Goodbye.*

**FRIDAY, MARCH 5TH 1982**
I questioned the Blessed Virgin on the matter of an Italian, who was very sick, and about another man who acquired cancer. She responded: *Tell them to pray and to put themselves in the hands of God. I too, will call on the mercy of my Son. I will do everything in my power to help them. But it will be necessary to believe completely. Without a strong faith, nothing is possible. Goodbye my angels.* (DV3, 19).

**SUNDAY, MARCH 7TH 1982**
The Blessed Virgin said that she has been with Ivan (at the Seminary at Visoko): *He prays well; he is obedient. He follows my instructions.* (DV3, 20).

**MONDAY, MARCH 8TH 1982**
Concerning a boy named Bora, (age 16), from Metkovic, who disappeared for a week: *He left because of many troubles. He himself, created some of the problems.* (DV3, 21).

**TUESDAY, MARCH 9TH 1982**
On the matter of a young man from Hadromilje, named Mladen, who disappeared from his home: *He has serious problems. It is necessary to pray for him very much, my angels. The people are beginning to be converted. Prayer has been taken up again, in the homes, where people had no longer prayed.* (DV3, 21).
**THE BEGINNING OF APRIL 1982:**
***Mirjana:***Do you wish the establishment of a special feast in your honor? *I wish a feast for the Queen of Peace, on the 25th of June, anniversary of the first apparition.* (L2, 127).
**HOLY WEEK: APRIL 4TH - APRIL 10TH 1982**
Jelena sees Mary holding Jesus by the hand, and in the palm of Jesus ' hand, the inscription "Glory." Asked about the meaning, the Blessed Virgin responded: *These are the names of all those who have been inscribed in the heart of Jesus.* (L2, 132).
**EASTER**
**SUNDAY, APRIL 11TH 1982**
Is it necessary to establish prayer groups, formed by Priests, Sisters and laity in the parish? *It is necessary, but not only here. Communities of prayer are necessary in all parishes.* (CP.54). (It does not mean just "Charismatic Groups," as the polemists, adversaries of this movement, have indicated.

**WEDNESDAY, APRIL 21ST 1982**
Father Vlasic questioned the seers. They say that the Blessed Virgin continues to appear to them everyday. The messages can be summarized thusly: *Be patient! Everything is developing according to God's plan. His promises will be realized. May one continue to pray, to do penance, and to be converted.* (CP 55).

**THURSDAY, APRIL 22ND 1982**
Are the luminous signs at the cross on Krizevac natural, or do they come from God? What does the letter "S" and the letter "T," which appear on the cross mean? *They are signs of God, and not of natural phenomena. "S" and "T" are signs of salvation.* (Bl.55; CP.55).

**SATURDAY, APRIL 24TH 1982**

What must one do in order to have more cures? *Pray! Pray and believe firmly. Say the prayers which have already been requested. (Seven "Our Father's, " "Hail Mary's, "Glory Be's " and the "Creed.) Do more penance.* (CP.55).

**SUNDAY, MAY 2ND 1982**
*I have come to call the world to conversion for the last time. Later, I will not appear any more on this earth.* (L2,128).

**THURSDAY, MAY 6TH 1982**
May we write on a piece of paper, the date of the great sign, describe it, seal it, and put it in the archives? (as requested by the commission).
*No! I have entrusted that only to you. You will unveil it when I will tell you. Many persons will not believe you, I know, and you will suffer very much for it. But you will endure everything, and you will finally be the happiest.* (CP.56).

**THURSDAY, MAY 13TH 1982**
After the attempt on the life of John Paul II: *His enemies have wanted to kill him, but I protected him.* (Bu. 151).
**SPRING, 1982**
Question asked at the request of the pastor at Izbicno, alleged place of other apparitions: Why are there so many signs in Hercegovina? *It is God who gives them. My children, have you not observed that faith began to extinguish itself? There are many who do not come to church except through habit. It is necessary to awaken the faith. It is a gift from God.* People are surprised that you are appearing in so many places: *If it is necessary, I will appear in each home.* (C.92-93). With respect to the little seers from Izbicno : (Izbicno, 60 kilometers from Medjugorje. In 1982-83, 18 persons mostly females, said they had apparitions. The seers from Medjugorje were said to have received kind words for those from Izbicno, but the Blessed Virgin reminded them strongly, that they must not have any contact with these persons, nor invite them to Medjugorje.) *Did I not tell you not to come together with those children? I am your mother, you must obey me.* (C93). For Jakov, who was crying to see Vicka ill: *The cross is necessary because of the sins of the world.* (L2, 128).

**WEDNESDAY, JUNE 23RD 1982** (Possibly a few days preceding)
Just before the anniversary of June 24th, Vicka answered some questions asked by Fr. Tomislav Vlasic, who reported them in the parish Chronicle, on June Keith, regarding responses of Our Lady:
*The most important thing is that you, the seers, remain united. Let peace be among you. Pay very close attention to that. Obey, and do what the priests and your parents tell you. Go often to holy Mass and receive Communion. Be very attentive these days. Some dishonest people will come to you, in numbers, in order to tempt you. Be careful of your statements. These days, I am expecting of you, a very special discipline. Do not move around anywhere, or often, and do not separate from one another.* (Some of the seers understood that these words were directed specifically to them, and they began to cry).
*A number of those who have been very enthusiastic will cool* off. *But you, persist, and be proud of each of my words. Have the people pray very much. Have them pray more for salvation, and only for salvation, because it is in prayer And let the people be converted so long as it is possible. There are many sins, vexations, curse words, lies and other bad things. Let them be converted, go to confession and receive Holy Communion.*
*Let them not print books on the apparitions before the anniversary has passed, because that could have some undesirable consequences.* (Repression by the authorities?).
*You have asked me to keep in this parish good and faithful priests who will continue the work. Do not be afraid of anything. This grace will be given to you. From priests, I do not demand anything other than prayer, with perseverance, and preaching. May they be patient and wait for the promises of God.*

With respect to the two Franciscans who had been suspended, see the Annex 1.
With respect to a question from a theologian:
Does the Holy Spirit have two natures? *He has only one; the Divine nature.*
*The seers:* They have said that these would be the last apparitions on earth? Is it true?
*These apparitions are the last in the world.*
"As far as I have understood," observes Tomislav Vlasic, "her answer is not only given in Medjugorje, but also in other parts of the world."

**THURSDAY, JUNE 24TH 1982 OR**
**FRIDAY, JUNE 25TH 1982**
Before the evening Mass, during the apparition, the Virgin told the priests, through the intermediary of the seers: *Thank the people in my name for the prayers, the sacrifices and the penance. Have them persevere in prayer, fasting and conversion, and have them wait with patience the realization of my promise. Everything is unfolding according to God's plan.*(C 98; CP 60 and 64).

**MONDAY, JULY 12TH 1982**
Will there be a third world war? *The third world war will not take place.* (CP 68).

**WEDNESDAY, JULY 21ST 1982**
To the response conveyed by Father T. Vlasic on Purgatory: *There are many souls in Purgatory. There are also persons who have been consecrated to God: some priests, some religious. Pray for their intentions, at least seven Our Father's, Hail Mary's and Glory Be's and the Creed. I recommend it to you. There is a large number of souls who have been in Purgatory for a long time because no one prays for them.* A response to a question on fasting: *The best fast is on bread and water. Through fasting and prayer, one can stop wars, one can suspend the laws of nature. Charity cannot replace fasting. Those who are not able to fast can sometime replace it with prayer, charity and a confession; but everyone, except the sick, must fast.* (CP 69).

**SATURDAY, JULY 24TH 1982**
Answer to some questions which were asked: *We go to Heaven in full conscience: that which we have now. At the moment of death, we are conscious of the separation of the body and the soul. It is false to teach people that we are re-born many times and that we pass to different bodies. One is born only once. The body, drawn from the earth, decomposes after death. It never comes back to life again. Man receives a transfigured body. Whoever has done very much evil during his life can go straight to Heaven if he confesses, is sorry for what he has done, and received Communion at the end of his life.* (CP 70).

**SUNDAY, JULY 25TH 1982**
A response to questions asked regarding Hell: *Today many persons go to Hell. God permits his children to suffer in Hell due to the fact that they have committed grave unpardonable sins. Those who are in Hell, no longer have a chance to know a better lot.* (CP 71). Response to questions regarding cures: *For the cure of the sick, it is important to say the following prayers: the Creed, seven Our Father's, Hail Mary's and Glory Be's, and to fast on bread and water. It is good to impose one's hands on the sick and to pray. It is good to anoint the sick with holy oil. All priests do not have the gift of healing. In order to revive this gift, the priest must pray with perseverance and believe firmly.* (CP 71).

**FRIDAY, AUGUST 6TH 1982** (Feast of the Transfiguration)
A response to questions which were asked concerning Confession: *One must invite people to go to Confession each month, especially the first*
*SATURDAY. Here I have not spoken about it yet. I have invited people to frequent Confession. I will give you yet some concrete messages for our time. Be patient because the time has not yet come. Do what I have told you. They are numerous who do not observe it. Monthly Confession*

*will be a remedy for the Church in the West. One must convey this message to the West.* (CP 72). That night the Gospa gave a sign to a group of young people who prayed with Ivan Dragicevic: two luminary signs descended on Krizevac and the church. This phenomenon was observed by Father Tomislav Vlasic near the church. Ivan commented on this phenomenon to all those who were there and added, "The Blessed Virgin told me that she would appear to you now in Heaven." (CP 72).

**TUESDAY, AUGUST 10TH 1982**
No special message, but the visionaries only said-the Blessed Virgin told us that now we can give some information in writing to people according to the plan which we had already worked out. (CP 73).

**WEDNESDAY, AUGUST 11TH 1982**
No special message. The Blessed Virgin only scolded the seers for their lack of seriousness during the evening Mass.

**SUNDAY, AUGUST 15TH 1982**
The vision lasted about seven minutes. The Gospa entrusted a new secret to Vicka and Ivanka-only to them. The others saw that it was about a secret, but they did not understand anything. (CP 74).

**MONDAY, AUGUST 16TH 1982**
No special message. The Gospa only corrected "the very resonant and very rapid prayer of the seers and the people in church." ***Mirjana***says that, at the time of the apparition, she sees heavenly persons: Jesus, Mary, angels, in three-dimensions, and earthly persons in two-dimension, at the same time she sees Father Jozo, or Ivan Ivankovic imprisoned because of their faith. (CP 74).

**WEDNESDAY, AUGUST 18TH 1982**
Mirjana reports to Fr. Tomislav Vlasic what the Gospa has told her concerning the sick: *Have them believe and pray; I cannot help him who does not pray and does not sacrifice. The sick, just like those who are in good health, must pray and fast for the sick. The more you believe firmly, the more you pray and fast for the same intention, the greater is the grace and the mercy of God.* (CP 76). Asked with respect to a plan of marriage between a Catholic and an Orthodox: *In my eyes and in the sight of God, everything is equal. But for you, it is not the same thing because you are divided. If it is possible, it is better if she were not to marry this man because she will suffer and her children also. She will be able to live and follow only with difficulty, the way of her faith.* (CP77). (On this ambiguous message, see Annex 2.)

**SUNDAY, AUGUST 29TH 1982**
With reference to the critiques according to which the apparitions have divided the priests in Hercegovina: *I have not desired your division. On the contrary, I desire that you be united. Do not ignore the fact that I am the Queen of Peace. If you desire a practical advise: I am the Mother who has come from the people; I cannot do anything without the help of God. I, too, must pray like you. It is because of that, that I can only say to you: Pray, fast, do penance and help the weak. I am sorry if my preceding answer was not agreeable to you. Perhaps you do not want to understand it.* (CP 79).

**TUESDAY, AUGUST 31ST 1982**
*I do not dispose all graces. I receive from God what I obtain through prayer. God has placed His complete trust in me. I protect particularly, those who have been consecrated to me. The great sign has been granted. It will appear independently of the conversion of the people.* (CP 79).
**THE END OF AUGUST 1982**

Ivan is on the hill of Bijakovici with his friends. The Virgin appears to him. *Now, I am going to give you a sign in order to strengthen your faith.* They see two rays of light, one on the church, the other on the cross at Krizevac. (L2, 129).

**SATURDAY, SEPTEMBER 4TH 1982**
*Jesus prefers that you address yourselves directly to Him rather than through an intermediary. In the meantime, if you wish to give yourselves completely to God and if you wish that I be your protector, then confide to me all your intentions, your fasts, and your sacrifices so that I can dispose of them according to the will of God.* (CP 80).

**SUNDAY, SEPTEMBER 26TH 1982**
For a religious who had come from Rome: *Have her strengthen the faith of those who have been entrusted to her.* For Father Faricy and Forrest: *They are on the good path, have them persist.* For the Pope: *Have him consider himself the father of all mankind, and not only of Christians. Have him spread untiringly and with courage the message of peace and love among all mankind.* (CP 82).

**FRIDAY, OCTOBER 1ST 1982**
*I am happy because you have begun to prepare the monthly feast of the sacrament of Reconciliation. That will be good for the whole world. Persevere in prayer. It is the true way which leads you toward my Son.* (CP. 83).

**THURSDAY, NOVEMBER 4TH 1982**
Questioned with respect to a vision of Andja, from Mostar, who had seen one evening during prayer, 13 persons coming from the East; another evening six persons: *It is about a true vision. They were some souls of her close family from Purgatory. It is necessary to pray for them.* (CP 85).

**SATURDAY, NOVEMBER 6TH 1982**
Frightened by the eighth secret, Mirjana prayed to the Blessed Virgin to preserve humanity from this calamity:
*I have prayed; the punishment has been softened. Repeated prayers and fasting reduce punishments from God, but it is not possible to avoid entirely the chastisement. Go on the streets of the city, count those who glorify God and those who offend Him. God can no longer endure that.* (CP 86).

**MONDAY, NOVEMBER 8TH 1982**
Father Tomislav has the seers ask the Virgin if it is necessary to write to the Bishop and to priests so that they can call the faithful to intensify their prayers, or if it is better to wait for other events: *It is better to wait than to precipitate that.* (CP 86).

**MONDAY, NOVEMBER 15TH 1982**
**Jakov:** "Must Vicka take the prescribed medicines, or must she have herself admitted to a hospital in Zagreb?" *It is necessary to send Vicka to Zagreb.* Vicka refused to question the Blessed Mother on this subject. She said that she wanted to accept what God would send her. (CP 87).

**SATURDAY, DECEMBER 18TH 1982**
With respect to the article of the Bishop of Mostar in the journal, "Vijesnik," on the events of Medjugorje, Fr. Tomislav Vlasic had the seers ask: Must we respond to the Bishop in writing? *Yes, respond!* (CP. 91).

**MONDAY, DECEMBER 20TH 1982**

With respect to the same article (Dec. 18, 1982), the visionaries ask: Is it necessary to give the faithful of Mostar objective information concerning the case in Hercegovina? *No!*(CP 95). Is it better for the seers to pray with you, and for the pilgrims to ask their questions to the priests instead? *Yes, it is better that the children pray with me, and that the pilgrims ask the priests and look for solutions with them. In the meanwhile I will continue to answer the questions which they ask me.* (CP. 95).

**THURSDAY, DECEMBER 23RD 1982**
To Mirjana: *On Christmas I will appear to you for the last time.* (F. 11,74).

**SATURDAY, DECEMBER 25TH 1982**
To Mirjana after she had received the tenth secret:
*Now you will have to turn to God in the faith like any other person. I will appear to you on the day of your birthday and when you will experience difficulties in life.* (F2, 149-150). *Mirjana, I have chosen you, I have confided in you everything that is essential. I have also shown you many terrible things. You must now bear it all with courage. Think of Me, and think of the tears I must shed for that. You must remain courageous. You have quickly grasped the messages. You must also understand now that I have to go away. Be courageous.* (G. 1, 22).

**MONDAY, DECEMBER 27TH 1982**
Today the statue of the Queen of Peace was finished. It was sculptured by Vipotnik, a sculptor from Slovenia, and painted by Luka Stojaknac and Florijan Mickovic, who wanted to maintain anonymity. This statue has been a source of grace for Luka, who is Orthodox; he put his marriage in order. ***The Seers:*** "May we put the statue in church?" *Yes, you may!* (CP. 96). It is this statue which had been venerated for a long time in the nave. it was removed from there on orders from the bishop on March 25th, 1985. It then found itself consigned to the small chapel of the apparitions.

**WEDNESDAY, DECEMBER 29TH 1982**
***Jelena:***"May I know the ten secrets?" *I did not appear to you as to the other six because my plan is different. To them I entrusted messages and secrets. Forgive me if I cannot tell you the secrets which I have entrusted to them; it concerns a grace which is for them, but not for you. I appeared to you for the purpose of helping you to progress in spiritual life and through your intermediary I want to lead people to holiness.* (Bo. 37).

**FRIDAY, DECEMBER 31ST 1982**
On Vicka's request, the Blessed Virgin gives this message for the new year: *Pray as much as possible and fast!* In the evening, to the seers: *You must persevere in prayer and fasting.* (C. 140). *I wish that the new year will be spent in prayer and penance. Persevere in prayer and in sacrifice, and I will protect you and will hear your prayers.* (CP. 98).
***1983***

**SATURDAY, JANUARY 1ST 1983** (The Feast of Holy Mary, Mother of God.)
***Ivanka:*** "Are you still appearing to Mirjana?" *After Christmas, I am no longer appearing to her for the present.* (CP. 99).
**BEGINNING OF 1983**
***Jelena***asks the Blessed Virgin on the authenticity of the apparitions of the six seers, and on the sign *which has* been promised: *Pardon me, but you cannot know it; it is a special gift for them. You will have to believe it like all the others. In the meantime, everything that they say corresponds to truth.* (Bo.38).

**WEDNESDAY, JANUARY 5TH 1983**
Tomislav receives, from the four seers present (Ivan, Jakov, Maria and Vicka), the following information: Maria has received 7 secrets, Vicka 8, Jakov, Ivanka and Ivan 9, and Mirjana 10. We

do not know how long the apparitions will last, nor why she no longer appears to Mirjana after Christmas. The Gospa invites us constantly to prayer, to fasting, to conversion. She confirms her promises. Ivan thinks that the apparitions have ceased for Mirjana because she did not pray enough outside of the apparitions. The Gospa probably did it so that Mirjana would learn to pray in the faith, he volunteers. (According to other interpretations, the end of the apparitions would be, on the contrary, a sign of achievement and maturity.) Questioned with respect to the time of the sign: "Which month? Which year?" **Ivan** says: "It is forecast." (CP. 103-104).

**FRIDAY, JANUARY 7TH 1983**

Mary begins to tell her life to the visionaries. They are invited to write down her testimony. They will not be able to make it public until they have received her authorization. (CP. 105). This transmission will last:
for Jakov until April, for Ivanka, until May 22nd, for Maria, until July 17th.
Maria, who was still attending the school for hairdressers in Mostar, received only an abridged account, the days when she was in Medjugorje. For Vicka, it lasted until April 10th, 1985: a long account which filled three notebooks. Up to this day, the seers have not received authorization to reveal these contents.

**MONDAY, JANUARY 10TH 1983**

Confidences from Mirjana to Father Tomislav Vlasic: "During the 18 months that I saw the Gospa, a great intimacy was established between us. I felt her maternal love. I could ask her all kinds of questions. Thus I asked her why God was so merciless in sending sinners to Hell for eternity?" *Men who go to Hell no longer want to receive any benefit from God. They do not repent nor do they cease to swear and to blaspheme. They make up their mind to live in Hell and do not at all contemplate leaving it.* (CAROL). (Man's refusal is an irreversible choice.) Questioned on the subject of Purgatory, the Blessed Virgin says: *There is there, different levels of which the lowest are close to Hell and the highest gradually draw near to Heaven. It is not on all souls day, but at Christmas, that the greatest number of souls leave Purgatory. There are in Purgatory, souls who pray ardently to God, but for whom no relative or friend prays for them on earth. God makes them benefit from the prayers of other people. It happens that God permits them to manifest themselves in different ways, close to their relatives on earth, in order to remind men of the existence of Purgatory, and to solicit their prayers close to God who is just, but good. The majority go to Purgatory. Many go to Hell. A small number go directly to Heaven.* (C. 103).

**WEDNESDAY, JANUARY 12TH 1983**

Regarding an American television team: "Will they be able to finish without difficulties? *There will be some difficulties, but it will be for the glory of God.* (CP. 108).

**TUESDAY, MARCH 1ST 1983**

To Jelena:*Transcribe all the lessons which I give you for the spiritual* life; *later you will deliver them to the authorities of the Church.* (T. 64).

**APRIL 4TH 1983** (Easter
MONDAY)

A message addressed by Jelena to Tomislav, who had written on Good
FRIDAY, April 1st, a letter of protest on the subject of the problems suffered in the parish. "I was expecting the corrections from a Canonist and no one knew anything except the Pastor" he observes in detail.
MONDAY, Jelena appeared without knowing anything, and tells me: "Do not have recourse to anyone. When you have a problem, you must remain smiling and praying. When God begins a work, no one will stop it." Father Vlasic judges this fundamental message as per (VB. 4, p. 100), "the Madonna does not stop telling us": *Pray, fast, and allow Got to act.* Jelena transmits the message from the Blessed Virgin: *Do not pity anyone. If the police cause you some anxiety, continue on your way joyful and calm. Pray for them. "en God begins His work, no one can stop it.* (CP.127-bis). Father Vlasic notes in the "Parish Chronicle" the internal locutions which have

been received by Jelena after December 15, 1982. The Madonna's message: *Hurry to be converted. Do not wait for the great sign. For the unbelievers, it will then be too late to be converted. For you who have the faith, this time constitutes a great opportunity for you to be converted, and to deepen your faith. Fast on bread and water before every feast, and prepare yourselves through prayer.*
*Fast once a week on bread and water in honor of the Holy Spirit outside of FRIDAY.*
*Have the largest possible number of persons pray and fast during the novena of the Holy Spirit, so that it may spread over the church. Fast and pray for the Bishop.* (CP. 127 bis).

**WEDNESDAY, APRIL 20TH 1983**
To Jelena, the Blessed Virgin, in tears: *I give all the graces to those who commit grave sins, but they do not convert. Pray! Pray for them! Do not wait for FRIDAY. Pray now. Today your prayers and your penance are necessary to me.* (CP. 130).

**THURSDAY, APRIL 21ST 1983**
*You* (the visionaries), *must behave well; be pious and set a good example for the faithful.* Jakov admits that the Blessed Virgin has made remarks to him several times, concerning his conduct. She has taught him how to participate at Mass, to pray, and to behave around others. (CP. 130).

**SUNDAY, APRIL 24TH 1983**
Message for an Italian doctor who is present: *I bless him just as those who work with him at the hospital in Milan, for everything they are doing. Have them continue, and pray. I bless the sick of this hospital, just like the sick for whom you have prayed this evening, and those for whom you will pray.* (Bo. 11).

**MONDAY, APRIL 25TH 1983**
Message received by Jelena, these last days: *Be converted! It will be too late when the sign comes. Beforehand, several warnings will be given to the world. Have people hurry to be converted. I need your prayers and your penance.* (CP. 131). *My heart is burning with love for you. It suffices for you to be converted. To ask questions is unimportant. Be converted. Hurry to proclaim it. Tell everyone that it is my wish, and that I do not cease repeating it. Be converted, be converted. It is not difficult for me to suffer for you. I beg you, be converted. I will pray to my Son to spare you the punishment. Be converted without delay. You do not know the plans of God; you will not be able to know them. You will not know what God will send, not what He will do. I ask you only to be converted. That is what I wish. Be converted! Be ready for everything, but, be converted. That is all I wish to say to you. Renounce everything. All that is part of conversion. Goodbye, and may peace be with you.* (CP. 132).

**FRIDAY, APRIL 29TH 1983**
Marijana, (aged 11) sees the Blessed Virgin at the same time as Jelena, but she does not hear her words. ***Jelena:***"Why doesn't Marijana hear?" *I do not want to separate you.* (CP. 133). (Does the Gospa wish to mean that these two adolescents compliment each other?)

**THURSDAY, MAY 5TH 1983**
With respect to a sick person from Vienna: The doctor has diagnosed schizophrenic. Some priests think it is a question of diabolical possession. *It is a diabolic possession. One can succeed only through prayer.* (CP 135).

**WEDNESDAY, MAY 25TH 1983**
To Jelena:*Assemble about twenty young people who are ready to follow Jesus, without reservation. Bring them together within a months notice. I will initiate them into the spiritual life. They can likewise be more than twenty. Even some adults and children can participate, all those who will accept the rule. I will ask these people to do penance for certain intentions. They will fast*

*and pray for the Bishop. They will give up what they cherish the most, drink, coffee, pleasures, television. It is necessary to have persons who wish to consecrate themselves more specifically to prayer, and to fast. I will give them the rules to follow.* (see June 16, 1983) *The persons who will follow these rules, will be consecrated whatever their state in life may be.* (CP 136).

**SATURDAY, MAY 28TH 1983**
To Jelena:*It is very beautiful to remain*
*THURSDAYs, for the adoration of my Son in the Blessed Sacrament of the altar. It is likewise beautiful to venerate the cross each*
*FRIDAY. I wish that every*
*SATURDAY, which is the day that the Church had dedicated to me, you will consecrate to me at least a quarter of an hour. Meditate during this time, on my life, my messages, and pray.* (CP. 141).

**WEDNESDAY, JUNE 1ST 1983**
*Dear Children: I hoped that the world would begin to be converted on its own. Do now, everything you can, so that the world can be converted.* (CP. 137).

**THURSDAY, JUNE 2ND 1983**
*Read what has been written about Jesus. Meditate on it, and convey it to others.* (CP. 137).

**FRIDAY, JUNE 3RD 1983**
Father Vlasic has begun to form a prayer group requested by the Virgin on May 25th. (Jakov, Vicka, Ivanka). "What do you expect of Fr. Tomislav? Has he begun well?" *Yes, it is good. Have him continue.* "What should one do so that people will not drive from here, the priests who work with faith and love?" *Pray and fast for this intention. I will tell you when the moment comes, what you must do.* "Father Tomislav wants to call the parish to prayer and fasting, so that the church recognizes that the events here are supernatural. It is a good way?" *Yes, it is a good way. Have the parish pray for this gift. Have them pray also for the gift of the Holy Spirit so that all those who come here will feel the presence of God.* (CP. 138).

**FRIDAY, JUNE 10TH 1983**
Jelena, Marijana and Anita, (age 11), are arguing. The first two make peace, but Anita refuses. The other two enter the church. Anita follows them, and suddenly extends to them, her hand. An indescribable joy penetrates their hearts. *I had been waiting for quite a while for your success. Continue in this manner,* says the Gospa. (CP. 142-143).

**SUNDAY, JUNE 12TH 1983**
**Ivan:** May the priests begin new work around the church or must they request authorization from the authorities? *Do not begin the work until receiving permission from the authorities. Otherwise, someone will inform the latter and the works would be forbidden. Go, and kindly request the authorization. It will be given to you.* (CP. 145).

**TUESDAY, JUNE 14TH 1983**
**Ivan:** What do you wish that the priests preach during the ten anniversary days of the first apparitions? *Have them do what they think is best. It would be good to remind the faithful of the events which have been revealed here in relation to my coming. Have them remind them the reasons for my coming here.* (CP.145).

**THURSDAY, JUNE 16TH 1983**
On May 25, 1983, the Blessed Virgin has repeated her desire that a prayer group, totally abandoned to Jesus, be formed. On June 16th she dictated to Jelena the rules for this group: *Renounce all passions and inordinate desires. Avoid television, particularly evil programs, excessive sports, the unreasonable enjoyment of food and drink, alcohol, tobacco, etc.*

*Abandon yourselves to God without any restrictions.*
*Definitely eliminate all anguish. Whoever abandons himself to God does not have room in his heart for anguish. Difficulties will persist, but they will serve for spiritual growth and will render glory to God.*
*Love your enemies. Banish from your heart, hatred, bitterness, preconceived judgments. Pray for your enemies and call the Divine blessing over them.*
*Fast twice a week on bread and water. Reunite the group at least once a week.*
*Devote at least three hours to prayer daily, of which at least, half an hour in the morning and half an hour in the evening. Holy Mass and the prayer of the Rosary are included in this time of prayer. Set aside moments of prayer in the course of the day, and each time that circumstances permit it, receive Holy Communion. Pray with great meditation. Do not look at your watch all the time, but allow yourself to be led by the grace of God. Do not concern yourself too much with the things of this world, but entrust all that in prayer to Our Heavenly Father. If one is very preoccupied, he will not be able to pray well because internal serenity is lacking. God will contribute to lead to a successful end, the things of here below, if one strives to do his utmost in working on his own. Those who attend school or go to work must pray half an hour in the morning and in the evening, and, if possible, participate in the Eucharist. It is necessary to extend the spirit of prayer to daily work (that is to say, to accompany work with prayer.)*
*Be prudent because the Devil tempts all those who have made a resolution to consecrate themselves to God, most particularly, those people. He will suggest to them that they are praying very much, they are fasting too much, that they must be like other young people and go in search of pleasures. Have them not listen to him, nor obey him. It is to the voice of the Blessed Virgin that they should pay attention. When they will be strengthened in their faith, the Devil will no longer be able to seduce them.*
*Pray very much for the Bishop and for those who*
*are responsible for the church. No less than half of their prayers and sacrifices must be devoted to this intention.*
To Jelena:*I have come to tell the world that God is truth; He exists. True happiness and the fullness of life are in Him. I have come here as Queen of Peace to tell the world that peace is necessary for the salvation of the world. In God, one finds true joy from which true peace if derived.* (L1, 100).
**SPRING 1983**
*Hasten your conversion. Do not await the sign, which has been announced, for those who do not believe. It will be too late. You who believe, be converted and deepen your faith.* (L1, 99). To Jelena, concerning Anita, to whom the Blessed Virgin appeared after Good
FRIDAY, and who only seldom gets together with Jelena and Marijana, because of her many obligations: *If she cannot come because of her responsibilities, have her pray for a quarter of an hour at least, and I will appear to her and bless her.*

**WEDNESDAY, JUNE 22ND 1983**
To Jelena:*Love your enemies and bless them!* (L1. 100).

**FRIDAY, JUNE 24TH 1983**
*The sign will come, you must not worry about it. The only thing that I would want to tell you is to be converted. Make that known to all my children as quickly as possible. No pain, no suffering is too great to me in order to save you. I will pray to my Son not to punish the world; but I beseech you, be converted. You cannot imagine what is going to happen nor what the Eternal Father will send to earth. That is why you must be converted! Renounce everything. Do penance. Express my acknowledgement to all my children who have prayed and fasted. I carry all this to my Divine Son in order to obtain an alleviation of His justice against the sins of mankind.* (C. 145 - 146). *I thank the people who have prayed and fasted. Persevere and help me to convert the world.* (CP. 151).

**SUNDAY, JUNE 26TH 1983**

*Love your enemies. Pray for them and bless them.* (MM. 24).

**TUESDAY, JUNE 28TH 1983**
To Jelena:*Pray for three hours a day. You pray very little. Pray at least a half hour in the morning and in the evening.* (L2. 133).

**FRIDAY, JULY 1ST 1983** (toward 11 o'clock at night on Krizevac)
*I thank all those who have responded to my call. I bless all of you. I bless each of you. In these days, I ask you to pray for my intentions. Go in the peace of God.* (Bl. 81).
**THE BEGINNING OF JULY 1983**
Concerning the tensions which involved the diocese: *Fast two days a week for the intentions of the Bishop, who bears a heavy responsibility. If there is a need to, I will ask for a third day. Pray each day for the Bishop.* (L2. 134).

**SATURDAY, JULY 2ND 1983**
To Jelena:*Devote five minutes to the Sacred Heart. Each family is an image of it.* (L1. 100).

**MONDAY, JULY 4TH 1983**
To Jelena:*You have begun to pray three hours a day, but you look at your watch, preoccupied with your work. Be concerned with only the essential. Let yourself be guided by the Holy Spirit in depth, then your work will go well. Do not hurry. Let yourself be guided and you will see that everything will be accomplished well.* (L1. 100).

**TUESDAY, JULY 26TH 1983**
To Jelena:*Be on your guard. This period is dangerous for you. The Devil is trying to lead you astray from your way. Those who give themselves to God will be the object of attacks.* (L. 2. 134). To Maria: *Dear children, today I would like to invite you to constant prayer and penance. Particularly, have the young people of this parish become more active in their prayer.* (F2, 113).

**TUESDAY, AUGUST 2ND 1983**
To Jelena:*Consecrate yourself to the Immaculate Heart. Abandon yourselves completely. I will protect you. I will pray to the Holy Spirit. Pray to Him also.* (L2, 134).

**SATURDAY, AUGUST 6TH 1983**
On orders form the Bishop, Father Pervan, the parish priest put an end to the custom which calls for the seers beginning the prayers of the Rosary and the seven Our Father's, Hail Mary's and Glory Be's. Jakov questioned the Blessed Virgin on this subject: *If it is so, then do not go against it so as not to provoke any quarrels. If it is possible, talk about it tomorrow among yourselves. All of you come to an agreement beforehand.* (CP. 165).

**FRIDAY, AUGUST 12TH 1983**
This was an exceptionally long apparition (38 minutes). The Blessed Virgin gives the seers instructions to guide their lives which only concerned them: *Pray more for your spiritual life. Do your utmost in this sense. Pray for your Bishop.* (CP. 158).

**MONDAY, AUGUST 15TH 1983**
To Jelena:*See how I am happy here! There are many who have come to honor me. In the meanwhile, do not forget that in other places there are still more persons who hurt me and offend me.* (CP 160). *Do not be in anxiety. May peace unite your hearts. Every disorder comes from Satan.* To the young people who are returning to school: *Be careful not to diminish the spirit of prayer.* (L1. 101). *Satan is enraged against those who fast and those who are converted.* (U. 101).

**TUESDAY, AUGUST 23RD 1983**

With respect to Father Emilien Tardif, the Canadian priest of the charismatic renewal: *Have him announce my messages to the whole world. Let Jesus, only Jesus, be at the center of his efforts.* (Bl. 368; CP. 162).

**THURSDAY, AUGUST 25TH 1983**

Father Tardif, Father Raucourt and Dr. Phillippe Madre have been arrested and expelled by the Yugoslavian authorities: *Do not worry for them. Everything is in God's plan.* (CP. 163).

**MONDAY, AUGUST 29TH 1983**

For the intention of a group of young people before their departure on their pilgrimage to Brijeg: *I wish that you pray throughout your trip, and at you glorify God. There, you will be able to meet other young people. Convey the messages which I have given you. Do not hesitate to speak to them about it.* (CP. 159). *Some begin to pray and to fast just as they have been told, but they get tired very quickly, and thus loose the graces which they have acquired.* (CP. 159).

**MONDAY, SEPTEMBER 5TH 1983**

The mother of Jakov (12 years old) dies. The Blessed Virgin consoles him and reveals to him: *Your mother is with me in Heaven.* (CP. 163).

**MONDAY, SEPTEMBER 12TH 1983**

*Pray. When I give you this message, do not be content to just listen to it. Increase your prayer and see how it makes you happy. All graces are at your disposal. All you have to do is to gain them. In order to do that, I tell you again-Pray!* (BN 5, 7).

**FRIDAY, SEPTEMBER 16TH 1983**

*Pray, pray, pray! Do not be discouraged. Be in peace because God gives you the grace to defeat Satan.* (Bl. 288).

*In my messages, I recommend to everyone, and to the Holy Father in particular to spread the message which I have received from my Son here at Medjugorje. I wish to entrust to the Pope, the word with which I came here: 'MIR, (peace),' which he must spread everywhere. And here is a message which is especially for him: That he bring together the Christian people, through his words and his preaching; that he spread particularly among the young people, the messages which he has received from the Father in his prayers, when God inspires him.* (CP. 169).

**MONDAY, SEPTEMBER 26TH 1983**

*My Son suffers very much because the world is not converting. May the world be converted and make peace.* (CP.171).

**THURSDAY, SEPTEMBER 29TH 1983**

To Jelena:*I desire for a great peace and a great love to grow in you Consequently, Pray!* For three priests from Liverpool: *Preach my messages. Speak about the events at Medjugorje. Continue to increase your prayers.* (Bl. 368).

**SATURDAY, OCTOBER 15TH 1983**

To Jakov: *My Son suffers very much because men do not want to be reconciled. They have not listened to me. Be converted, be reconciled.* (CP, not paged).

**THURSDAY, OCTOBER 20TH 1983**

To Jelena, for the prayer group: *I ask you for a commitment of four years. It is not yet the time to choose your vocation. The important thing is first of all, to enter into prayer. Later, you will make the right choice.* For the parish: *Have all the families consecrate themselves to the Sacred Heart each day. I am very happy when the entire family meets to pray each morning, for half an hour.* (L1. 101).

**FRIDAY, OCTOBER 21ST 1983**

*The important thing is to pray to the Holy Spirit, so that He may descend on you. When one has Him, one has everything. People make a mistake when they turn only to the saints to request something.* (L1. 101).

**MONDAY, OCTOBER 24TH 1983**

To Jelena, for the prayer group: *If you pray, a source of life will flow from your hearts. If you pray with strength, if you pray with faith, you will receive graces from this source, and your group will be strengthened.* (Ba. 45).

**TUESDAY, OCTOBER 25TH 1983**

To Jelena:*Pray! Pray! Prayer will give you everything. It is with prayer that you can obtain everything.* (Ba. 45).

**WEDNESDAY, OCTOBER 26TH 1983**

To Jelena:*I pour out my blessing over you, and my heart wishes to be with you.* (Ba. 45).

**THURSDAY, OCTOBER 27TH 1983**

To Jelena:*Pray, pray, pray. You do not learn anything from chatter, but only from prayer. If someone asks you about me, and about what I say, answer: 'That doesn't explain anything. It is in praying that we will understand better'* (Ba. 45).

**FRIDAY, OCTOBER 28TH 1983**

To Jelena:*I see that you are tired. I wish to support you in your effort, to take you in my arms so that you may be close to me. All those who wish to ask me questions, I will answer: 'There is only one response, prayer, a strong faith, an intense prayer, and fasting.'* (Ba. 46).

**SATURDAY, OCTOBER 29TH 1983**

To Jelena:*I give you my heart; receive it! I would not want to distress you, nor to stop talking to you, but I cannot stay always with you. You have to get used to it. In the meantime, I wish to be constantly with you, from the bottom of my heart. It is necessary to pray very much, not to say: 'If today we have not prayed, it is nothing serious.' You must strive to pray. Prayer is the only road which leads to peace. If you pray and fast, you will obtain everything that you ask for.* (Ba. 46).

**SUNDAY, OCTOBER 30TH 1983**

To Jelena:*Why do you not put your trust in me? I know that you have been praying for a long time, but really, surrender yourself Abandon your concerns to Jesus. Listen to what He says in the Gospel: And who among you, through his anxiety, is able to add a single cubit, to the length of his life.' (Mt.* 6:27). *Pray also, in the evening when you have finished your day. Sit down in your room, and say to Jesus: 'Thank you.' If in the evening you fall asleep in peace, and in prayer, in the morning you will walk up thinking of Jesus. You will then be able to pray for peace, but if you fall asleep in dis traction, the day after will be misty, and you will forget even to pray that day.* (Ba. 46).

**MONDAY, OCTOBER 31ST 1983**

To Jelena:*I know that you prayed today, and that you did all your work while praying. Still, I have a particular intention for which I am asking you to say each day, seven Our Father's, seven Hail Mary's, and the Creed.* (Ba. 47).

**FRIDAY, NOVEMBER 4TH 1983**

To Jelena:*I wish that you tell them, that tomorrow is a day of fasting, in order to sanctify yourselves in the Holy Spirit. And pray! Let this message be conveyed to the group.* (Ba. 47).

**SATURDAY, NOVEMBER 5TH 1983**

*Jelena:*"Our Lady looked at us tenderly and said:" *I know my children, that you have worked and prayed today. But, I beseech you, be generous, persevere, continue to pray.* (Ba 47).

**SUNDAY, NOVEMBER 6TH 1983**
To Jelena:*Where are the prayers which you addressed to me? My clothes were sparkling. Behold them soaked with tears. Oh, if you would know how the world today is plunged into sin. It seems to you that the world sins no longer, because here, you live in a peaceful world where there is no confusion or perversity. If you know how lukewarm they are in their faith, how many do not listen to Jesus. Oh, if you knew how much I suffer, you would sin no more. Oh, how I need your prayers. Pray!* (Ba. 47).

**MONDAY, NOVEMBER 7TH 1983**
To Jelena:*Do not go to confession through habit, to remain the same after it. No, it is not good. Confession should give an impulse to your faith. It should stimulate you and bring you closer to Jesus. If confession does not mean anything for you, really, you will be converted with great difficulty.* (Ba. 47).

**TUESDAY, NOVEMBER 8TH 1983**
To Jelena:*Pray and fast! All that you can do for me is to pray and fast.* (Ba. 48).

**WEDNESDAY, NOVEMBER 9TH 1983**
To Jelena:*Pray! I have such a great need for your prayers. Give me your hearts.* (Ba. 48).

**THURSDAY, NOVEMBER 10TH 1983**
To Jelena:*I ask you to pray. That is all that I expect of you. Do not forget to pray to the Lord, morning and evening. Pray, Pray.* (Ba. 48).

**FRIDAY, NOVEMBER 11TH 1983**
To Jelena:*Pray! You can do everything, yes, you can do it through prayer. Place an image of the hearts of Jesus and Mary in your homes.*

**SATURDAY, NOVEMBER 12TH 1983**
To Jelena:*Give me your hearts, open them to me.* "How do we do that?" *You must redouble your efforts. Day after day, increase your fervor.* (Ba. 48).

**SUNDAY, NOVEMBER 13TH 1983**
To Jelena:*Pray, and do it with fervor. include the whole world in your prayer. Pray, because prayer makes one live.* In response to a question, the Gospa only says: *Pray and you will understand that, some day* (Ba. 49).

**MONDAY, NOVEMBER 14TH 1983**
To Jelena:*Pray, because prayer is life. Through it and in it, you live in prayer.* (Ba. 49).

**TUESDAY, NOVEMBER 15TH 1983**
To Jelena:*Pray and fast!* For the intention of the group: *I have often reproached you. Pray with me. Begin right now.* (Ba. 49).

**WEDNESDAY, NOVEMBER 16TH 1983**
To Jelena:*Pray and fast. Have all the members of your group come on TUESDAY as often as possible. Speak to them about fasting. Fast three days a week for the Bishop. If that cannot be done by everyone the same day, have each one do it whenever he is able.* (Ba. 49).

**THURSDAY, NOVEMBER 17TH 1983**

To Jelena:*Pray! If I always ask you to pray, do not think that your prayers are not good. But I invite you to prolong your personal prayer, to pray more intensely for the others.* (Ba. 49).

**FRIDAY, NOVEMBER 18TH 1983**
To Jelena:*At Medjugorje, many have begun well, but they have turned toward material goods, and they forget the only good.* (Ba. 49).

**SATURDAY, NOVEMBER 19TH 1983**
To Jelena:*My children, pray only!* (Ba. 50).

**SUNDAY, NOVEMBER 20TH 1983**
To Jelena:*My children, do not believe everything that people tell you. One must not, because of that, weaken in his faith.* (Ba. 50).

**MONDAY, NOVEMBER 21ST 1983**
To Jelena:
*TUESDAY, that is tomorrow, the whole group will find peace in prayer. All its members will be invigorated in prayer, as it is the wish of Jesus. He entrusts something to each one, and wishes something from each one. It is necessary to make them come back to their promises, which were made at the beginning, and to pray.* (Ba. 50).

**TUESDAY, NOVEMBER 22ND 1983**
To Jelena:*Pray, pray, pray... Pray, my children. Pray, because only prayer can save you.* (Ba. 50).

**WEDNESDAY, NOVEMBER 23RD 1983**
To Jelena:*Oh my sweet children, pray! I ask you only to pray. You yourselves can see that only prayer can save.* (Ba. 50).

**THURSDAY, NOVEMBER 24TH 1983**
To Jelena:*Pray and fast!* (Ba. 50).

**FRIDAY, NOVEMBER 25TH 1983**
***Jelena:***"The Blessed virgin stayed just a little time. She only said:" *Pray and fast.* (Ba 51).
**ADVENT 1983**
*Begin by calling on the Holy Spirit each day The most important thing is to pray to the Holy Spirit. When the Holy Spirit descends on earth, then everything becomes clear and everything is transformed.* (Bl. 125).

**SATURDAY, NOVEMBER 26TH 1983**
She only said: *Prayer and fasting.* (Ba. 51).

**SUNDAY, NOVEMBER 27TH 1983**
To Jelena:*My children, pray and keep your soul pure. I wish to be constantly with you.* (Ba. 51).

**MONDAY, NOVEMBER 28TH 1983**
To Jelena:*Pray, pray! Have the parish pray each day to the hearts of Jesus and Mary during the Novena of the Immaculate Conception.* (Ba. 51). This same day, some prayers were dictated or inspired by her. (Ba. 65).
**CONSECRATION TO THE HEART OF JESUS**
O Jesus, we know that You are sweet *(Mt.* 11:29). That you have given Your heart for us. It was crowned with thorns by our sins. We know that today You still pray for us so that we will not be lost. Jesus, remember us if we fall into sin. Through Your most Sacred Heart, make us all love one another. Cause hatred to disappear among men. Show us Your love. All of us love You. And

we desire that you protect us with Your Heart of the Good Shepherd. Enter into each heart, Jesus! Knock on the door of our hearts. Be patient and tenacious with us. We are still locked up in ourselves, because we have not understood Your will. Knock continuously, Oh Jesus. Make our hearts open up to you, at least in reminding us of the passion which you suffered for us. Amen

**CONSECRATION TO THE IMMACULATE HEART OF MARY**

O Immaculate Heart of Mary, overflowing with goodness, Show us your love for us. May the flame of your heart, Oh Mary, Descend upon all peoples. We love you immensely. Impress in our hearts a true love. May our hearts yearn for you. Oh Mary, sweet and humble of heart, Remember us when we sin. You know that all mankind are sinners. Through your most sacred and maternal heart, Cure us from every spiritual illness. Make us capable of looking at the beauty of your maternal heart, And that, thus, we may be converted to the flame of your heart. Amen

**TUESDAY, NOVEMBER 29TH 1983**

To Jelena:*Pray!* For the intention of the group: *I am your mother full of goodness, and Jesus is your great friend. Do not fear anything in His presence. Give Him your heart, from the bottom of your heart. Tell Him your sufferings, thus you will be invigorated in prayer, with a free heart, in a peace without fear.* (Ba. 51).

**WEDNESDAY, NOVEMBER 30TH 1983**

To Maria, for a priest: *You must warn the Bishop very soon, and the Pope, with respect to the urgent and the great importance of the message for all humanity.* This message, which was given in September was: *I have already said many times that the peace of the world is in a state of crisis. Become brothers among you, increase prayer and fasting in order to be saved.* (T. Vlasic, Apr. 22, 1984, VB. 1, 13). To Jelena:*Pray, pray, pray!* (Ba. 51).

**NOVEMBER 1983**

Before the novena to the Immaculate Conception, the Blessed Virgin tells Jelena:*Before Mass it is necessary to pray to the Holy Spirit.* "We followed this message during the novena, praying before Mass and asking the faithful to respond, '0 come Holy Spirit.' After Communion, we sang the hymn to the Holy Spirit, then we stopped doing it." In January, 1983, Jelena says that the Blessed Virgin requested that these prayers be resumed. "We should not have stopped it. The prayers to the Holy Spirit should always accompany the Mass." (Ba. 51).

**THURSDAY, DECEMBER 1ST 1983**

*Thanks to all of you who have come here, so numerous during this year, in spite of snow, ice and bad weather, to pray to Jesus. Continue, hold on in your suffering. You know well that when a friend asks you for something, you give it to him. It is thus with Jesus. When you pray without ceasing, and you come in spite of your fatigue, He will give you all that you ask from Him. For that, pray.* (Ba. 51).

**FRIDAY, DECEMBER 2ND 1983**

To Jelena:*Thank you, thanks to everyone!* That evening, it was particularly cold: *You are very good to come to mass without looking for an excuse. Show me that you have a generous heart.* (Ba. 52).

**SUNDAY, DECEMBER 4TH 1983**

To Jelena:*Pray, pray, pray only. Prayer should be for you, not only a habit, but also a source of goodness. You should live by prayer.* (Ba. 52).

**TUESDAY, DECEMBER 6TH 1983**

To Jelena:*Pray, pray! If you pray, I will keep you and I will be with you.* (Ba. 52).

**WEDNESDAY, DECEMBER 7TH 1983**

The vigil of the Immaculate Conception, To Jelena:*Tomorrow will really be a blessed day for you, if every moment is consecrated to my Immaculate Heart. Abandon yourselves to me. Strive to make your joy grow; to live in the faith, to change your hearts.* (Ba. 52).

**THURSDAY, DECEMBER 8TH 1983**
To Jelena:*Thank you my children for having come so often. Thank you. Continue your efforts and be persevering and tenacious. Pray without ceasing.* (Ba. 52).

**SUNDAY, DECEMBER 11TH 1983**
To Jelena:*Pray and fast! I wish that prayer be renewed in your heart every day Pray more, yes, more each day.* (Ba. 52).

**MONDAY, DECEMBER 12TH 1983**
To Jelena:*Pray, pray, thus I will protect you. Pray and abandon your hearts to me, because I wish to be with you.* (Ba. 52).

**TUESDAY, DECEMBER 13TH 1983**
To Jelena:*Pray and fast! I do not wish to say anything else to you.* (Ba. 52).

**WEDNESDAY, DECEMBER 14TH 1983**
*Pray and fast! I am asking you for prayer.* (Ba. *52).*

**THURSDAY, DECEMBER 15TH 1983**
*Fast on THURSDAY and FRIDAY for the Bishop.* To Jelena on the subject of catastrophic predictions: *That comes from false prophets. They say: 'Such a day, on such a date, there will be a catastrophe.' I have always said that evil will come if the world does not convert itself. Call the world to conversion. Everything depends on your conversion.* (Ba. 53).

**FRIDAY, DECEMBER 16TH 1983**
Pray and fast only! (Ba. 53).

**SATURDAY, DECEMBER 17TH 1983**
To Jelena:*Pray and fast!* (Ba. 53).

**SUNDAY, DECEMBER 18TH 1983**
To Jelena:*In this novena for Christmas, pray as much as you can. I ask you.* (Ba. 53).

**MONDAY, DECEMBER 19TH 1983**
To Jelena:*Pray!* (Ba. 53).

**TUESDAY, DECEMBER 20TH 1983**
To Jelena:*Pray!* For the intention of the group: *Fast on*
*WEDNESDAY,*
*THURSDAY, and*
*FRIDAY.* (Ba 53).

**WEDNESDAY, DECEMBER 21ST 1983**
To Jelena:*My children, I say to you again, pray and fast.* (Ba. 54).

**THURSDAY, DECEMBER 22ND 1983**
To Jelena:*Pray! What is most important for your body is prayer.* (Ba. 54).

**FRIDAY, DECEMBER 23RD 1983**
To Jelena:*Pray, pray, especially tomorrow. I desire your prayers.* (Ba. 54).

**SATURDAY, DECEMBER 24TH 1983**
To Jelena:*Pray, pray my children. I wish that this night be spent in prayer.* (Ba. 54).

**SUNDAY, DECEMBER 25TH 1983**
To Jelena:*My children, pray! I cannot tell you anything else than pray. Know that in your life, there is nothing more important than prayer.* (Ba. 54).

**MONDAY, DECEMBER 26TH 1983**
To Jelena:*My children, pray, pray more. It is not necessary to Say: 'Our Lady only repeats, pray.' I cannot tell you anything else than to pray. You would need to live this Christmas in prayer. You have rejoiced very much this Christmas, but your hearts have not attained and lived what you have desired. No one withdrew to his room to thank Jesus.* (Ba. 54). To a question from Father Laurentin, Ivan conveys this answer from the Virgin: *Our Lady prays for that. May he who undertakes it, do it in prayer. It is there that he will find his inspiration.* (Bl. 367).

**TUESDAY, DECEMBER 27TH 1983**
To Jelena:*My children, pray, pray, pray. Remember that the most important thing in our lives is prayer.* (Ba. 54).

**WEDNESDAY, DECEMBER 28TH 1983**
*My children, understand that the most important thing in our lives is prayer.* (Ba 54).

**THURSDAY, DECEMBER 29TH 1983**
To Jelena:*I wish that one love, one peace, flourish in you. Pray then.* (Ba 55).

**FRIDAY, DECEMBER 30TH 1983**
To Jelena:*My children, pray and fast. I wish to strengthen you, but prayer alone is your strength.* (Ba. 55).

**DECEMBER 1983**
*There are many Christians who are no longer faithful, because they do not pray anymore. Have them began again to recite each day, at least, seven Our Father's, seven Hail Mary's, seven Glory Be's, and the Creed, once.* (Bl. 137). *Above all, abstain from television programs. They represent a great peril for your families. After you have seen them, you cannot pray any more. Give up likewise, alcohol, cigarettes, and pleasure of this kind.* (Bl. 214; a variant of the message of Dec. 8, 1981). *The fasting which you are doing in eating fish, instead of meat, is not fasting but abstinence. The true fast consists in giving up all our sins, but one must also renounce himself and make the body participate in it.* (Bl. 191). *Monthly confession will be a remedy for the Church in the west. Whole sections of the Church could be cured, if the believers would go to confession once a month.* (Bl. 224).

**SATURDAY, DECEMBER 31ST 1983**
To Jelena:*For you, I only wish that this new year will really be a holy one. On this day, go then, to confession, and purify yourself in this new year.* (Ba. 55). She asks the group to continue to pray for the Bishop. (Ba *55)*

**1984**

**SUNDAY, JANUARY 1ST 1984**
*My children, pray! I say again, pray, because prayer is indispensable to life.* (Ba. 55).
**THE BEGINNING OF 1984**

For the intention of the pilgrims: *When you are in the room of the apparitions or at the church, you should not preoccupy yourself with taking pictures. You should rather use the time to pray to Jesus, especially in those moments of particular grace during the apparitions.* (T.58).

**MONDAY, JANUARY 2ND 1984**
*Why have you stopped saying the prayer to the Holy Spirit. I have asked you to pray always and at all times so that the Holy Spirit may descend over all of you. Begin again to pray for that.* "We had stopped saying the prayer to the Holy Spirit thinking that it was said only until Christmas." (Ba.55).

**TUESDAY, JANUARY 3RD 1984**
*My children, pray; I say it again, pray! Know that in your life the most important thing is prayer.* (J).

**WEDNESDAY, JANUARY 4TH 1984** *Before all, pray! That, I do not cease to ask you for.* (J).

**SUNDAY, JANUARY 8TH 1984** (Feast of the Epiphany)
*My children, pray! I say it again, pray! I will say it to you again. Do not think that Jesus is going to manifest Himself again in the manger; friends, He is born again in your hearts.* (DN 1, 30).

**SUNDAY, JANUARY 15TH 1984** *I know that I speak to you very often about prayer, but know that there are many people in the world who do not pray; who do not even know what to say, in prayer.* (J).

**TUESDAY, JANUARY 17TH 1984**
*Pray and fast! I wish that in your hearts prayer and fasting flourish.* (J).

**WEDNESDAY, JANUARY 18TH 1984**
*I wish to engrave in every heart the sign of love. If you love all mankind, then there is peace in you. If you are at peace with all men, it is the kingdom of love.* (DN 1, 30). To Jelena:*Pray and fast!* For the intention of the group: *Have everyone get up early, some to go to school, others to go to work, still others to help the poor like themselves, also those who need help.* (J).

**THURSDAY, JANUARY 19TH 1984**
*Pray and fast, because without prayer you cannot do anything.* (Ba55).

**SATURDAY, JANUARY 21ST 1984**
*Pray and fast. Do not give up on meditation. At home meditate at least half an hour.* (Ba55).

**SUNDAY, JANUARY 22ND 1984**
*Pray and fast. I permit all those who mortify themselves, to do it at the most three times a week. May they not prolong it.* (Ba56).

**MONDAY, JANUARY 23RD 1984**
*Pray and fast. You have not understood well, what it means to pray: If you can understand that, I desire it very much.* (Ba56).

**TUESDAY, JANUARY 24TH 1984**
*Pray very much. I desire to permeate you with prayer.* (Ba56)

**WEDNESDAY, JANUARY 25TH 1984**
*Pray and fast. You need enthusiasm in your prayer. May you pray in meditation for a long time and fervently* (Ba56).

**THURSDAY, JANUARY 26TH 1984**
*Thank you for adoring my Son in the Sacred Host. That touches me very much. With respect to you, pray! I desire to see you happy.* (Ba56).

**FRIDAY, JANUARY 27TH 1984**
*Pray and fast. I wish that you deepen and continue your life in prayer. Every morning say the prayer of consecration to the Heart of Mary. Do it in the family. Recite each morning the Angelus, five Our Father's, Hail Mary's, and Glory Be's in honor of the holy Passion and a sixth one for our Holy Father, the Pope. Then say the Creed and the prayer to the Holy Spirit. And, if it is possible, it would be well to pray a rosary.* (Ba56).

**SATURDAY, JANUARY 28TH 1984**
*I wish that all of you pray, and that my heart extend to the whole world. I wish to be with you.* (Ba57).

**SUNDAY, JANUARY 29TH 1984** *Pray and fast! I wish for you to purify your hearts. Purify them and open them to me.* (Ba57).

**MONDAY, JANUARY 30TH 1984**
*Pray! I desire to purify your hearts. Pray It is indispensable, because God gives you the greatest graces when you pray.* (Ba57).

**TUESDAY, JANUARY 31ST 1984**
To Jelena:*Pray! Do not think of anything, pray. Do not think of anything else except of those for whom you pray. Then prayer will be better and you will be faithful to it.* To the group: *Continue to help the poor, the sick, and to pray for the dead. You should not feel any fear. Let all free themselves completely and let them abandon their hearts to me so that I can be with them. Have them listen to me and discover me in the poor, and in every person.* (Ba57).

**WEDNESDAY, FEBRUARY 1ST 1984**
*It is raining at this time, and you say: 'It is not reasonable to go to church in this slush. Why is it raining so much? Why doesn 't the rain stop?' Do not ever speak like that. You have not ceased to pray so that God may send you rain which makes the earth rich. Then, do not turn against the blessing from God. Above all, thank him through prayer and fasting.* (Ba 57).

**THURSDAY, FEBRUARY 2ND 1984**
*Pray, because I need many prayers. Be reconciled, because I desire reconciliation among you and more love for each other, like brothers. I wish that prayer, peace, and love bloom in you.* (Ba57).

**FRIDAY, FEBRUARY 3RD 1984**
To Jelena:*It is up to you to pray and I will take care of the rest. You can not even imagine how powerful God is. That is why you pray. Pray because he wants to be with you and wants to cleanse you from all sin.* Our Lady gave this message on the request that we address her on the arrival of a document from the Bishop. (Jan. 13, 1984) Reference *54-84:* "The matter of the diary of Vicka Ivankovic on the apparitions," asking Mary, consequently, what we should do.

**SATURDAY, FEBRUARY 4TH 1984**
*Pray, because prayer is very necessary to you. With prayer. your body and soul will find peace. There are some young people who have consecrated themselves to me. But there are in the parish, some persons, who have not entirely given themselves. As soon as mass has ended, they are in a hurry to leave the church. That is not good. That way they will never be able to give themselves completely It is not good for them to linger about the church. One must be pious and set a good example for others, in order to awaken in them the faith. It is necessary to pray as*

*much as possible while offering your heart. They should consecrate themselves in order to become truly better.* (Ba5 8).

**SUNDAY, FEBRUARY 5TH 1984**
*Pray and fast. I desire to live in your hearts.* And especially for the prayer group: *Some of them still have a week of rest. They do not fast ... others have come here and fast on WEDNESDAY,*
*THURSDAY, and*
*FRIDAY; others help the poor and the sick; others love everybody and want to discover Jesus in each one. Some are not convinced, others are. They are mine. See how they honor me. Lead them to me so that I may bless them.* (Ba59).

**MONDAY, FEBRUARY 6TH 1984**
*Pray, pray, I ask of you.* (Ba59).

**WEDNESDAY, FEBRUARY 8TH 1984**
To Jelena:*From you, I expect only prayer. Thus, pray.* (Ba59).

**THURSDAY, FEBRUARY 9TH 1984**
*Pray, pray! How many persons have followed other beliefs or sects and have abandoned Jesus Christ. They create their own gods; they adore idols. How that hurts me! If they could be converted. Like the unbelievers, they are many. That will change only if you help me with your prayers.* (Ba59).

**FRIDAY, FEBRUARY 10TH 1984**
*Pray and fast! I desire humility from you. But you can become humble only through prayer and fasting.* (Ba59).

**SATURDAY, FEBRUARY 11TH 1984**
*Open your hearts to me, I desire to bless them fully. (Ba59).*

**SUNDAY, FEBRUARY 12TH 1984**
*Pray and fast! I ask of you. Pray for the peace and humility of your hearts.* (Ba59).

**MONDAY, FEBRUARY 13TH 1984**
To Jelena:*Fast and pray! Give me your hearts. I desire to change them completely I desire for them to be pure.* (Ba60).

**TUESDAY, FEBRUARY 14TH 1984**
*Pray and fast! I desire to purify your hearts completely. I wish to make you happy.* (Ba60).

**WEDNESDAY, FEBRUARY 15TH 1984**
In very cold weather and an icy wind: *The wind is my sign. I will come in the wind. When the wind blows, know that Jam with you. You have learned that the cross represents Christ; it is a sign of him. It is the same for the crucifix you have in your home. For me, it is not the same. When it is cold, you come to church, you want to offer everything to God. I am, then, with you. I am with you in the wind. Do not be afraid.* (Ba60).

**FRIDAY, FEBRUARY 17TH 1984**
*My children, pray! The world has been drawn into a great whirlpool. It does not know what it is doing. It does not realize in what sense it is sinking. It needs your prayers so that I can pull it out of this danger.* (Ba60).

**MONDAY, FEBRUARY 20TH 1984**

*Pray and fast! I desire to purify you and to save you. For that, help me with your prayers.* (Ba60).

**TUESDAY, FEBRUARY 21ST 1984**
*Pray and fast! I expect generosity and prayers from your hearts.* (Ba60).

**THURSDAY, FEBRUARY 23RD 1984**
*I hold all of you in my arms. You are mine. I need your prayers so that you may be mine. I desire to be all yours and for you to be all mine. I receive all your prayers. I receive them with joy.* (Ba6l).

**FRIDAY, FEBRUARY 24TH 1984**
*Pray and fast! I desire to be with you always. I desire to stay in your hearts always and for you to stay in mine.* (Ba6l).

**SATURDAY, FEBRUARY 25TH 1984**
*Know that I love all of you. Know that you are all mine. To no one do I desire to give more than to you. Come to me all of you. Stay with me. I want to be your Mother. Come, I desire all of you.* (J).

**SUNDAY, FEBRUARY 26TH 1984**
*Pray and fast! Know that I love you. I hold all of you on my knees.* (J).

**MONDAY, FEBRUARY 27TH 1984**
*Do not be tired. I desire to be with you.* (J).

**TUESDAY, FEBRUARY 28TH 1984**
*Pray and fast! Love everyone on earth, just as you love yourselves.* For the intention of the group: *Have each one decide alone. In the meantime, it would be good, that this week they fast on*
*THURSDAY. Have them read the Bible and meditate on it.* (J).

**WEDNESDAY, FEBRUARY 29TH 1984**
*Pray! It may seem strange to you that I always speak of prayer. And yet I say: pray! Why do you hesitate? In Holy Scripture, you have heard say: 'Do not worry about tomorrow, each day will have its own worries.' (Mt.* 6:34). *Then do not worry about the other days. Be content with prayer, I your Mother, will take care of the rest.* (Ba6l-62).

**THURSDAY, MARCH 1ST 1984**
Message to Marijana: *Pray and fast. When I tell you to pray, do not think that you have to pray more, but pray. Let prayer and faith awaken in your hearts.* (Ba62). To Maria, the first message of THURSDAY, addressed to the parish:
*Dear children, I have chosen particularly this parish because I wish to guide it; I watch over it with love, I would like for all of you to be mine. I thank you for having responded this evening to my call. I would like for you to be always with me and my Son. Every*
*THURSDAY I will give a special message for you.*
(NB. These messages of
THURSDAY have been widely disseminated, and have been edited by MM, and in our translation, in Medjugorje, Paris, DDB, 1987, p.26-90 L3) *Dear children, today I ask you to read the Bible in your homes, every day. Put it in a very visible place in your home, that way it will encourage all to prayer* (M53).
*THURSDAY (day of the Eucharist), may each one find his way to fast; he who smokes, may abstain from smoking; he who drinks alcohol, have him not drink. Have each one give up something which is dear to him. May these recommendations be conveyed to the parish.* (DN 1, 31). To Jelena:*Each*

*THURSDAY, read again the passage of Matthew 6, 24-34, before the most Blessed Sacrament, or if it is not possible to come to church, do it with your family.* (F2, 104).

**MONDAY, MARCH 5TH 1984**
To Jelena:*Pray and fast! Ask the Holy Spirit to renew your souls, to renew the entire world.* (DN 1 31).

**THURSDAY, MARCH 8TH 1984**
Message to the parish: *Dear children, be converted in the parish. It is my second wish. Thus all those who will come here will be able to be converted. Thank you for having responded to my call.*
**LENT 1984** (March 7 - April 22)
*Do not be afraid for yourselves, you are already saved. Pray rather for those who are in sin and who do not believe.* (T.57).

**WEDNESDAY, MARCH 14TH 1984**
*Pray and fast so that the kingdom of God may come among you. Let my Son set you aglow with His fire.* (DN 1,31).

**THURSDAY, MARCH 15TH 1984**
To Maria, for the parish: *This evening, dear children, I am particularly grateful to you for your presence. Adore continuously, the Most Blessed Sacrament. I am always present when Christians are in adoration. They then receive some particular graces.* (DN 5, 75). *Dear children, pray! All agitation comes from Satan. Your prayer should lead to peace.* (BN 18,22).

**SATURDAY, MARCH 17TH 1984**
To Jelena, during the novena in preparation for the Annunciation: *Pray and fast, so that during this novena, God will fill you with His power.* (DN 1,31).

**MONDAY, MARCH 19TH 1984**
*Dear children, sympathize with me! Pray, pray, pray!* (B.

**WEDNESDAY, MARCH 21ST 1984**
To Jelena:*Today I rejoice with all my angels. The first part of my program has been achieved.* Then, while crying: *There are so many men who live in sin. Here there are likewise among you some people who have offended my heart. Pray and fast for them.* (BN 18,22).

**THURSDAY, MARCH 22ND 1984**
Message for the parish: *Dear children, this evening I ask you in a special way during this Lenten season, to honor the wounds which my Son has received from this parish. Unite yourselves to my prayers for the intention of this parish, so that its sufferings become tolerable. Thank you for responding to my call.* (F2, 123). *Pray each day the 'Veni Creator Spiritus' (Come Holy Ghost) and the 'Angelus.' God has given each one the will to decide for himself My wish is for all to be converted, but I do not want to force anyone.* (BN 18,22). To Jelena:*Yesterday evening I said that the first wish of my plan, was realized.* (DN 1,31).

**SUNDAY, MARCH 25TH 1984** (Annunciation)
The 1,000th apparition at Medjugorje. *Rejoice with me and with my angels because a part of my plan has already been realized. Many have been converted, but many do not want to be converted. Pray.* After these words, the Blessed Virgin began to cry. (C.148).

**TUESDAY, MARCH 27TH 1984**
To Jelena:*In the group, some have given themselves up to God so that He may guide them. Let the will of God be realized in you.* (DN 1,31).

**WEDNESDAY, MARCH 28TH 1984**
*Many persons come here out of curiosity and not as pilgrims.* (BN 18,23).

**THURSDAY, MARCH 29TH 1984**
A message for the parish: *Dear children, this evening I would like to invite you to persevere in your trials. Even today the All Powerful suffers because of your sins. When sufferings occur, offer them as a sacrifice to God.* (DN *5,76).*

**FRIDAY, MARCH 30TH 1984**
*I wish that your hearts would be united to mine, like my heart is united to that of my Son.* (DN 1,32).
To Jelena:*My children, I wish that the holy mass be for you the gift of the day Attend it, wish for it to begin. Jesus gives Himself to you during the mass. Thus, look forward to that moment when you are cleansed. Pray very much so that the Holy Spirit will renew your parish. If people attend mass with lukewarmness, they will return to their homes cold, and with an empty heart.* (DN 1,31-32).

**TUESDAY, APRIL 3RD 1984**
To Jelena:*I ask for you to pray for the conversion of all men. For that, I need your prayers.* (DN 1,32).

**THURSDAY, APRIL 5TH 1984**
To Maria, for the parish: *Dear children, this evening I ask you very specially, to venerate the heart of my Son, Jesus. Make reparation for the injury inflicted on the Heart of my Son. This heart has been wounded through all kinds of sin. If you would be strong in the faith, Satan would not be able to do anything against you. Begin to walk the path of my messages. Be converted, be converted, be converted.* (BN 18,23).

**SUNDAY, APRIL 8TH 1984**
*I ask you to pray for the conversion of everyone. For that, I need your prayers.* (M 29).

**THURSDAY, APRIL 12TH 1984**
A message for the parish: *Dear children, this evening I ask you to stop your slandering and to pray for unity, because my Son and I have a special project for this parish. Prepare yourselves in a special way for Holy*
*SATURDAY.* (BN 18,24).

**SATURDAY, APRIL 14TH 1984**
To Jelena:*How can you not be happy? Jesus gives Himself to you. I wish to inundate souls. If! am sad this evening, the reason is that many have not prepared themselves for Easter. They do not permit Jesus on that day, to unite Himself to their souls.* (L 2, 138).
**HOLY WEEK APRIL 15TH-22ND 1984**
To Jelena:*Raise your hands and open your hearts. Now, at the time of the Resurrection, Jesus wishes to give you a special gift. This gift of my Son is my gift. Here it is. You will be subjected to trials and you will endure them with great ease. We will be ready to show you how to escape from them if you accept us. Do not say that the Holy Year has ended and that there is no need to pray. On the contrary, double your prayers, because the Holy Year is just another step ahead.* At this time, the risen Jesus appeared. Rays of light came forth from His wounds. He said:
*Receive my graces and tell the whole world that there is no happiness except through Me.* (M 29).
**HOLY**
**THURSDAY, APRIL 19TH 1984**
Message for the parish: *Dear children, share my compassion; pray, pray, pray!*

To Jelena:*I'm going to reveal a spiritual secret to you: if you want to be stronger than evil, make yourself a plan of personal prayer Take a certain time in the morning, read a text from Holy Scripture, anchor the Divine word in your heart, and strive to live it during the day, particularly during the moment of trials. In this way, you will be stronger than evil.* (Bl. 186). That same day, the Blessed Virgin had "dictated" to Jelena the following prayer:

**HOW TO GIVE ONESELF TO MARY MOTHER OF GOODNESS, OF LOVE AND OF MERCY**

Oh my Mother! Mother of goodness, love and mercy! I love you immensely, and I offer myself to you. Through your goodness, your love, And your mercy, save me! I wish to be yours. I love you immensely And I wish that you protect me. In my heart, oh mother of goodness, Give me your goodness, So that I go to Heaven. I ask you for your immense love That you may give me the grace That I will be able to love each one Just like you loved Jesus Christ. I ask you in grace That I be able to be merciful[1] to you. I offer myself completely to you And I wish that you will be with me at each step, Because you are full of grace. I wish never to forget your grace, And if I should lose it, I will ask, make me find it again. Amen.

1. It is an ambiguous and confusing expression on which one has commented in different ways. According to Fr. Slavko, it means: "That I know how to love your will when it differs from mine."

To T. Vlasic' question, asked by Jelena:"How could Jesus pray all night?" "With what method?" *He had a great longing for God and for the salvation of souls.* (T. Vlasic, June 1, 1984, VB 1, 39, often taken up subsequently).

*If you want to be stronger against evil, have an active conscience. For that, pray very much in the morning and read a passage from the Gospel. Plant the Divine Word in your heart and live it during the day, in this special way, in trials and in the evening, you will be very strong.* (T. Vlasic, Aug. 3, 1984).

**GOOD**
**FRIDAY, APRIL 20TH 1984**

To Jelena:*You should be filled with joy. Today, Jesus died for your salvation. He descends into Hell and opens the gates of paradise. Let joy reign in your hearts! When you pray, seek the advantage of prayer. Prayer is a conversation with God. To pray means to listen to the Lord. Prayer is for me a service, because after it all things become clear. Prayer leads to knowing happiness.*

**HOLY**
**SATURDAY, APRIL 21ST 1984**

To Jelena:*Raise your hands, yearn for Jesus because in his Resurrection, he wants to fill you with graces. Be enthusiastic about the Resurrection. All of us in Heaven are happy, but we seek the joy of your hearts. My Son's gift and mine, at this moment is this: you will be comforted in your trials, they will be easier for you because we will be close to you. If you listen to us, we will show you how to overcome them. Pray very much tomorrow. May Jesus truly rise in your families, that peace be established there, where there are wars. I wish that someone is born again in your hearts. My children, I thank you. Continue to bring about the Resurrection of Jesus in all men. The Holy Year has ended, but it represents only a step in our life. Continue to pray.* (BN 18,24).

**EASTER**
**SUNDAY, APRIL 22ND 1984**

*We all rejoice in Heaven. Rejoice with us.* (DN 1,27).

**MONDAY, APRIL 23RD 1984**

*There is no need to give more information to the people, they already know what they are supposed to do.* (T. Vlasic, Aug. 12, 1984 VB 1, 861).

**TUESDAY, APRIL 24TH 1984**

With sadness and with tears: *So many people, after they have begun here to pray, to be converted, to fast, and do penitence, quickly forget when they return home, and return to their bad habits.* (DN 1,27). *The information suffices. People already know enough. Tell them this place is a place of prayer. Pray as much as you can, pray however you can, but pray more always. Each of you could pray even four hours a day. But I know that many do not understand because they think only of living for their work.* T. Vlasic then had this conveyed to Our Lady: "If I tell this to the people, then they will go away completely." *Even you do not understand. It is hardly a sixth of your day.* (T. Vlasic, May 26, 1984, VB 1, 30). To Jelena:*Many times, confronting justice and confronting your sins, many times I returned from your home in tears. I could not say a single word. I am your Mother and I do not want to oppose you. But on you, will depend what I wish to do, in you. We must rejoice in Jesus, to make Him happy.* (Tk. Vlasic, Nov. 10, 1984, VB 1, 128).

**THURSDAY, APRIL 26TH 1984**
No message.

**MONDAY, APRIL 30TH 1984**
Maria asks the reason for there not being a message last

**THURSDAY:** *I had a special message for the parish so as to awaken the faith of all the believers. In the meantime, I do not want to force anyone to whatever it may be which would not be felt or desired. Not all have accepted the*
*THURSDAY messages. At the beginning there were more. But now it seems that all that has become common place to them. And recently, some have asked for the message, only out of curiosity, and not with faith and piety to my Son and me.* (F 2,110).

**THURSDAY, MAY 3RD 1984**
No message.

**THURSDAY, MAY 10TH 1984**
The absence of a message, the 26th of April, and again the 3rd of May, had been reported in the same way as the explanation of April 30th. The response was quick in coming: *I address you the words, and I will continue to do so. But listen to these instructions.*

**THURSDAY, MAY 17TH 1984**
To Maria for the parish: *I am happy today because many of you have desired to consecrate yourselves to me. I thank you for it. You have not been mistaken. My Son Jesus Christ wants, through my intercession, to extend the graces of predilection over you. He rejoices that you are consecrating yourselves to Him.*

**SATURDAY, MAY 19TH 1984**
To Jelena:*Dear children, at this time it is especially necessary for you to consecrate yourselves to me and to my heart. Love, pray and fast.*

**MONDAY, MAY 21ST 1984**
To Jelena:*O dear children, how I wish that you would turn to me. Imagine my little children that it is the end of the school year and you have reached halfway That is why now you must become a little more serious.* (Ba 62).

**WEDNESDAY, MAY 23RD 1984**
To Jelena:*I wish that the parish prepare itself through a novena, to receive the sacrament of Confirmation on the day of the feast of the Ascension.* (which will take place May 31). (M. 30).

**THURSDAY, MAY 24TH 1984**
To Maria, for the parish: *Dear children, I have already said it to you; I have chosen you in a special way, just as you are. I am your mother; I love all of you. At every moment, when you have difficulties, do not be afraid because I love you, even when you are far from me and my Son. I ask you not to permit my heart to cry with tears of blood, because of souls who are lost through sin. That is why dear children, pray, pray, pray!*

**FRIDAY, MAY 25TH 1984**
To Jelena:*I truly wish that you would be pure on the day of Pentecost. Pray, pray that your spirit be changed on that day.* (Ba 62).

**SATURDAY, MAY 26TH 1984**
To Jelena:*Dear children, thank you for every prayer Try to pray continuously, and do not forget that I love you and wish that all of you would love one another.* To Jelena, who is requested to ask questions of the Blessed Mother: *For all of these questions, there is an answer: pray to the Holy Spirit so that He may enlighten you, and you will come to know all that you wish.* (Ba 63).

**MONDAY, MAY 28TH 1984**
To Jelena:*Love is a gift from God. Pray then, that God may give you the gift to love.* (Ba 62).

**WEDNESDAY, MAY 30TH 1984**
To Jelena:*The priests should visit families, more particularly those who do not practice anymore, and who have forgotten God. Priests should carry the Gospel of Jesus to the people, and teach them the way of prayer. And the priests themselves, should pray more and even fast. They should give to the poor, what they don 't need.* (T 64).

**THURSDAY, MAY 31ST 1984** (Feast of the Ascension)
To Maria, for the parish: *I will give you the message for the parish,*
*SATURDAY, June 2nd. It should be announced on*
*SUNDAY.*
**MAY 1984**
To Jelena, after inquiring about August 5th, 1984, if they would be celebrating her two thousandth birthday: *Throughout the centuries, I have given myself completely to you. Is it too much to give me, three days? Do not work on those days. Take your rosaries and pray. Fasting has been forgotten during the last quarter of the century, within the Catholic Church.* (T. 57). *Jelena:*"I know that all families can pray four hours a day. But, if I tell that to people, they will back out." *Don 't you understand, that it is only one-sixth of the day?* (F2, 113).

**FRIDAY, JUNE 1ST 1984**
To Jelena:*May the love of God be always in you, because without it, you cannot be fully converted. Let the rosary in your hands make you think of Jesus. Dear children, strive to be absorbed in mass, just as you should. (J).*

**SATURDAY, JUNE 2ND 1984**
To Maria, for the parish (a message which had been anticipated: it will not be given THURSDAY, June 7th) *Dear children, this evening I recommend to you the novena (of Pentecost). Pray for the outpouring of the Holy Spirit on all your families, and on your parish. Pray and you will not be sorry for it. God will bestow His gifts on you, thanks to the fact that you will be glorifying Him until the end of your life.* (F2, 124).
To Jelena:*Thank you for every prayer. Continue to pray, but pray with the heart. Dear children, again it is necessary for you to pray to the Holy Spirit and it would be good for you to pray seven 'Our Fathers,' in the church, as one does it for Pentecost.* (J). During the novena, in preparation for Pentecost, the priest who leads the prayer, makes a brief introduction before each "Our Father" to ask for the seven gifts of the Holy Spirit.

**MONDAY, JUNE 4TH 1984**
*Dear children, I am happy that you have begun to pray as I requested of you. Continue.* (Ba 63).

**FRIDAY, JUNE 8TH 1984**
To Jelena:*Dear children, you need love. Ihave said it to you many times, and I remind you. Continue only to pray and be happy because I am with you.* (J).

**SATURDAY, JUNE 9TH 1984** (Vigil of Pentecost)
*Tomorrow evening, pray to receive the spirit of truth. More particularly, you, members of this parish. The spirit of truth is indispensable to you in order to convey the messages, such as I give them to you, without adding or deleting whatever it may be. Pray, so that the Holy Spirit inspires you, a spirit of prayer, so that you may pray more. I your mother, find that you pray too little.*

**MONDAY, JUNE 11TH 1984**
To Jelena:*I wish that you continue to pray and to fast.* To the group: *I wish that you would become like a flower in the spring. The love which I give you is great, but sometimes you reject it, and thus, it becomes less. Always accept immediately, the gifts which I give you, so that you can profit from them.* (J).

**WEDNESDAY, JUNE 13TH 1984**
*Dear children, I invite you to pray more, you and the entire parish, until the day of the anniversary. Let your prayer become a sign of offering to God. Dear children, I know that you are all tired. You do not know how to offer yourselves to me. Offer yourselves completely to me these days.* (Bl. 141).

**THURSDAY, JUNE 14TH 1984**
No "
THURSDAY message" to the parish. (BN 18, 26 indicated one, though with some confusion). *Pray, Pray!*
**MIDDLE OF JUNE, 1984**
To Jelena:*Prepare yourselves through prayer, for the third anniversary of the beginning of the apparitions. June 25th should be celebrated as the Feast of Mary, 'Queen of Peace.'* (M30).

**THURSDAY, JUNE 21ST 1984**
To Maria, for the parish: *Pray pray, pray! Thank you for having responded to my call.* To Jelena:*If you knew how much I love you, you would cry with joy. When anyone is before you, and asks you something, you will give it to him. lam before so many hearts, but they remain closed. Pray so that the world receives my love.* (BN 18,24). *Each member of the group is like aflower; and if someone tries to crush you, you will grow and will try to grow even more. If someone crushes you a little, you will recover. And if someone pulls a petal, continue to grow as though you were complete.* To Marijana: *My only wish is that you become as joyful and enthusiastic as you were during the first days of my apparitions.* (Ba 64).

**SATURDAY, JUNE 23RD 1984**
*Dear children, lam very happy that there are so many people here this evening. Thank God alone.* (Ba). After Easter, Our Lady does not speak to Jelena or Marijana every day, but specially on
TUESDAY,
WEDNESDAY,
SATURDAY and
SUNDAY.

**SUNDAY, JUNE 24TH 1984** (Feast of Corpus Christi)
Third anniversary of the apparitions. *My Children, I thank you for each sacrifice that you have made during these days. Be converted, forgive each other, fast, pray, pray, pray!* (C. 149).

**MONDAY JUNE 25TH 1984**
*Thank you for all your sacrifices.* (DN 1,27).

**TUESDAY, JUNE 26TH 1984**

*When I say pray, pray, pray, I do not want to say to only increase the number of hours of prayer, but also to reinforce the desire for prayer, and to be in contact with God. Place yourself permanently in a state of spirit bathed in prayer.* (F2, 112).

**THURSDAY, JUNE 28TH 1984**
No
THURSDAY message to the parish.

**THURSDAY, JULY 5TH 1984**
Message to the parish: *Always pray before your work and end it with prayer. If you do that, God will bless you and your work. These last days, you have prayed little and worked very much. Pray more. In prayer, you will find repose.*

**THURSDAY, JULY 12TH 1984**
Message for the Parish: *Dear children, in these days, Satan wants to destroy all my plans. Pray with me so that his design will not be realized. I will pray to my Son, Jesus, so that He may give you the grace to experience His victory over Satan 's temptations.*

**MONDAY, JULY 16TH 1984**
*I pray for the priests and the parishioners, that no one may be troubled. I know the changes which will take place soon,* (in the parish clergy). *At the time of the changes, I will be there. Also, do not be afraid, there will be in the future, signs concerning sinners, unbelievers, alcoholics and young people. They will accept me again.* (T 42).

**THURSDAY, JULY 19TH 1984**
Message for the parish: *Dear children, these last days, you have experienced the work of Satan. I am with you always. Do not be afraid of these temptations. God watches over you always. I am with you in the least of trials.*

**FRIDAY, JULY 20TH 1984**
Late in the evening, on the hill of the apparitions: *Open your hearts to me, come close. Say in a loud voice, your intentions, and your prayers.* The Blessed Virgin paid close attention to the prayers of the seers. When they prayed for the Bishop of Mostar, her eyes were filled with tears. While crying, she tells them: *You are my little flowers. Continue to pray my task is lighter because of it.* She disappeared into Heaven, as she continued to cry, after she had blessed everyone with a crucifix. (T. 43).

**THURSDAY, JULY 26TH 1984**
A message to the parish: *Dear children! Today also I would like to call you to persistent prayer and penance. Especially, let the young people of this parish be more active in their prayers.*
**AT THE BEGINNING OF AUGUST 1984**
To Jelena:*This message is dedicated to the Pope and to all Christians. Prepare the second millennium of my birth which will take place August 5th, 1984 Throughout the centuries, I consecrated my entire life to you. Is it too much for you to consecrate three days for me? Do not work, on that day, but take up the rosary and pray.* (M. 30).

**THURSDAY, AUGUST 2ND 1984**
A message to the parish: *Dear children! Today I am happy and I thank you for your prayers. Pray more these days for the conversion of sinners.* For the presentation of Mary's second millennium. *Dear children! Pray as much as possible. Pray at least the entire rosary every day. Fast on bread and water on*
*WEDNESDAYs and*
*FRIDAYs.* (BN 18, 27). To Jelena:*I am happy for your participation at Mass. Continue as you did this evening. Thank you for having resisted the temptation of Satan.* (DN 1,33).

**SUNDAY, AUGUST 5TH 1984**
The celebration of the second millennium of Mary's birthday was preceded by three days of fasting and continuous prayer. Seventy priests heard confessions without respite; there were conversions in great numbers. *Never in my life have I cried with sorrow, as I have cried this evening with joy. Thank you!* (RN 18,27). In anticipation of this day the Gospa had said: *The priest who will hear confession will have great joy on that day.* During these 3 days of fasting and continuous prayer the seers say the Blessed Virgin was "very joyful," and she repeated: *I am very happy, continue, continue. Continue to pray and to fast.* Her joy seemed to have reached a peak SUNDAY, August 5th. Like a flower when it blooms, and full of joy, she said: *Continue, continue, open your hearts, ask God and I will ask for you.* (T. Vlasic, Aug. 6, 1984, VB. 1,761).

**MONDAY, AUGUST 6TH 1984**
*Continue and make me happy each day.* (T. Vlasic, Aug. 7, 1984, VB 1,79).

**THURSDAY, AUGUST 9TH 1984**
*A message for the parish: Dear children, Satan continues to hinder my plans. Pray, pray, pray! In prayer, abandon yourselves to God. Pray with the heart. Thank you for your response to my call.*

**SATURDAY, AUGUST 11TH 1984**
*Dear children! Pray, because Satan is continually trying to thwart my plans. Pray with your heart and in prayer give yourselves up to Jesus.* (F2, 118).

**TUESDAY, AUGUST 14TH 1984**
To Ivan, at the time of an unexpected apparition, at his home: *I ask the people to pray with me these days, as much as they can. Fast strictly on*
*WEDNESDAYs and*
*FRIDAYs. Every day, at least one rosary, Joyful, Sorrowful and Glorious mysteries.* (C.150).

**THURSDAY, AUGUST 16TH 1984**
A message to the parish: *Dear children! I beg all of you, especially the members of this parish, to live my messages and to tell them to whomever you meet.*

**THURSDAY, AUGUST 23RD 1984**
*To Maria, for the parish: Pray, pray, pray! Besides, Maria said, she asks that everyone, and especially the young people, behave in a worthy manner during holy mass.*

**SATURDAY, AUGUST 25TH 1984**
*To Mirjana: Wait for me September 13th, I will speak to you about the future. (DN 3,12).*

**THURSDAY, AUGUST 30TH 1984**
*Message to the parish, with respect to the cross erected on Mount Krizevac in 1933, for the 1950th anniversary of the death and resurrection of Jesus: Dear children! The cross was in God's plan when you built it. These days especially, go up on the mountain and pray at the foot of the cross. I need your prayers.*

**FRIDAY, AUGUST 31ST 1984**
*I love very specially the cross which you have providentially erected on Mount Krizevac. Go there more often and pray. (Bl.34).*

**THURSDAY, SEPTEMBER 6TH 1984**
*Message to the parish: Dear children! Without prayer there is no peace. For that reason, I say to you; dear children, pray at the foot of the cross for peace.*

**MONDAY, SEPTEMBER 10TH 1984**

*To Jelena:Dear children, you must understand that one has to pray. Prayer is no joke, prayer is a conversation with God. In every prayer you must listen to the voice of God. Without prayer one can not live. Prayer is life. (T. Vlasic, November 10. 1984; VB. 1, 130).*

**THURSDAY, SEPTEMBER 13TH 1984**

*Message for the parish: Dear children! I continually need your prayers. You wonder what all these prayers are for. Look around, dear children, and you will see how much ground sin has gained in this world. Because of that, pray that Jesus conquers.*

**THURSDAY, SEPTEMBER 20TH 1984**

*Message for the parish: Dear children! Today I ask you to start fasting, putting your heart in it. There are many people who fast only because everyone else is fasting. It has become a custom which no one wants to stop. I ask the parish to fast out of gratitude to God for allowing me to remain so long in this parish. Dear children, fast and pray with your heart.*

**THURSDAY, SEPTEMBER 27TH 1984**

*Message for the parish: Dear children! Your prayer has helped my plans to be fulfilled. Pray continually for their complete fulfillment. I beg the families of the parish to pray the family rosary.*

**THURSDAY, OCTOBER 4TH 1984**

*Message for the parish: Dear children! Today I would like to tell you that your prayers delight me, but there are some people in the parish who do not pray and for that my heart is sad. Pray, therefore, that I may bring all your sacrifices and prayers to the Lord.*

**FRIDAY, OCTOBER 5TH 1984**

*To Jelena:I love you. Love me, love one another. (DN 1,33).*

**MONDAY, OCTOBER 8TH 1984**

*Let all the prayers that you say in the evening in your homes, be for the conversion of sinners, because the world is truly in sin. Recite the rosary every evening. (F2, 106). Jakov was sick that day and received this message at his home: Dear children! All the prayers which you recite in the evening in your homes, dedicate them to the conversion of sinners because the world is immersed in a great moral decay. Recite the rosary each evening. (M.36).*

**THURSDAY, OCTOBER 11TH 1984**

*Message for the parish: Dear children! Thank you for offering all your afflictions to God, even at this time when He is trying your patience as you reap your crops. (Our Lady is alluding to prolonged rain which came in the middle of the harvesting and caused great damage.) Be aware, dear children, that He loves you and that it is for that reason that He tests you. Always present your burdens to God and do not worry.*

**SATURDAY, OCTOBER 13TH 1984**

*For the priests of the Marian Movement of Priests: A message to you and to all those who love me. Dear children, pray unceasingly and ask the Holy Spirit to inspire you always. In everything that you ask, in everything that you do, look only for the will of God. (BN 18,27). Live according to your convictions and respect others. (Bl. 221).*

**THURSDAY, OCTOBER 18TH 1984**

*Dear children! Today I ask you to read the Bible in your homes every day. Place it in a visible place there, where it will always remind you to read it and to pray.*

**SATURDAY, OCTOBER 20TH 1984**

*When you pray, you must feel more. Prayer is a conversation with God. To pray means to listen to God. Prayer is useful for you because after prayer everything is clear. Prayer makes one know happiness. Prayer can teach you how to cry. Prayer can teach how to blossom. Prayer is not a joke. Prayer is a dialogue with God. (T. Vlasic, November 10, 1984; VB 1, 125-126).*

**WEDNESDAY, OCTOBER 24TH 1984**
*At 10:00 in the evening at Krizevac: My dear children, I am so happy to see you pray. Pray with me so that God's plan may be realized, thanks to your prayers and to mine. Pray more, and more intensely. (T.45).*

**THURSDAY, OCTOBER 25TH 1984**
*Message for the parish: Dear children! Pray during this month. God has allowed me to help you every day with graces, in order to protect you from evil. This month is mine. I would like to give it to you. Pray and God will give you the graces that you ask for. I will support your requests.*
**OCTOBER 1984**
*I would like to guide you spiritually, but 1 would not know how to help you, if you are not open. It suffices for you to think, for example, where you were with your thoughts yesterday during mass. When you go to mass, your trip from home to church should be a time of preparation for mass. You should also receive Holy Communion with an open and pure heart; purity of heart and openness. Do not leave the church without an appropriate act of thanksgiving. I can help you only if you are accessible to my suggestions; I can not help you if you are not open. (T-59). The most important in spiritual life is to ask for the gift of the Holy Spirit. When the Holy Spirit comes, then peace will be established. When that occurs, everything changes around you. Things will change.* (T. 59).

**THURSDAY, NOVEMBER 1ST 1984**
Message for the parish: *Dear children! Today I call you to renew family prayer in your homes. The field work is over. Now, may all of you devote yourselves to prayer. Let prayer have first place in your families. Thank you for your response to my call.*

**THURSDAY, NOVEMBER 8TH 1984**
Message for the parish: *Dear children! You are not aware of the importance of the messages which God is sending you through me. He is giving you great graces and you do not realize it. Pray to the Holy Spirit for enlightenment. If only you knew how many graces God is giving you, you would pray without ceasing.*

**THURSDAY, NOVEMBER 15TH 1984**
Message for the parish: *Dear children! You are a chosen people and God has given you great graces. You do not realize the importance of every message lam giving you. Now I only wish to say: Pray, pray, pray! I do not know what else to tell you because I love you and wish that in prayer you come to know my love and the love of God.*

**SATURDAY, NOVEMBER 17TH 1984**
To Jelena:*Pray. Do not ask yourself about the reason why I constantly invite you to prayer. Intensify your personal prayer so that it will become a channel for the others.* (BN 18, 30).

**THURSDAY, NOVEMBER 22ND 1984**
To Maria, for the parish: *Dear children! These days, live all of my messages and continue to root them in your hearts this week.*

**THURSDAY, NOVEMBER 29TH 1984**
Message for the parish: *Dear children! You do not yet know how to love, nor do you listen with love to the words I am giving you. Be assured, my beloved ones, that I am your Mother, and that I*

*have come on earth to teach you how to listen with love, how to pray with love, and not be compelled by the cross you are carrying. Through the cross, God is glorified in every person.*

**THURSDAY, DECEMBER 6TH 1984**
Message for the parish: *Dear children! These days, I am calling you to family prayer. Many times, I have given you messages in God's name, but you have not listened. This Christmas will be an unforgettable day for you, provided you accept the messages I am giving you. Dear children, do not allow that day of joy, to be a day of deepest sorrow for me.*

**THURSDAY, DECEMBER 13TH 1984**
To Maria, for the parish: *Dear children! You know that the day of joy is coming near, but without love you will obtain nothing. Therefore, first of all start loving your family and everyone in the parish. Then you will be able to love and accept all those who will come here. Let this week be the week of learning how to love. This Christmas will be unforgettable if you follow me. Disconnect your television sets and your radios, and begin God's programs; meditation, prayer, reading of the Gospel. Prepare yourselves with faith; then you will have understood love, your life will be filled with happiness.* (BN 18, 31).

**MONDAY, DECEMBER 17TH 1984**
Message conveyed by the seers to Monsignor Franic, Archbishop of Split, during a retreat which he is making at Medjugorje: *You will have to suffer more.* (DN 3, 18).

**THURSDAY, DECEMBER 20TH 1984**
To Jelena:*Today I am asking you to do something concrete for Jesus Christ. On the day of joy, I would like every family of the parish to bring a flower as a sign of self offering to Jesus. I would like every member of the family to have a flower next to the crib, so that Jesus can come and see your offering of self to Him.* (VB 2,16). To Maria, for the parish: *Today I invite you to show a concrete gesture for Jesus Christ, I wish that each family in the parish bring each day a flower, as a sign of surrender to Jesus until Christmas which is approaching. Have each member of the family place a flower near the manger; and Jesus, at the time of his ar rival, will see your love for Him there. On December 24th the parishioners carried their flowers near the manger. The whole sanctuary was converted into a flower bed in blossom.*

**FRIDAY, DECEMBER 21ST 1984**
*Dear children! I would like for all of you to be like a flower, which is going to open at Christmas for Jesus; a flower which does not cease to blossom after Christmas. Be the good shepherds of Jesus.* (Bl. 298).

**TUESDAY, DECEMBER 25TH 1984**
*The Virgin did not give a message, but she appeared holding the Child Jesus in her arms. (*DN 5,77).

**THURSDAY, DECEMBER 27TH 1984**
Message for the parish: *Dear children! This Christmas, Satan wanted in a special way to thwart Gods plans. You, dear children, witnessed Satan even on Christmas day. But God conquered in your hearts. Let your hearts continue to rejoice.*

**SATURDAY, DECEMBER 29TH 1984**
To Jelena, the anniversary day of her first apparition. *Today is the feast of the Mother of goodness, of mercy, and of love.* "And she gave us her blessing saying:" *Up until now I have not given it to you.* "And the group felt strongly changed because of it." She motivated them to receive this blessing: *Receive it, do not neglect it as before. I can give you my blessing, but I cannot give it to you if you do not want it.* (T. Vlasic, Mar. 2, 1985, VB 2,381).
To Jelena:*I wish that a great love, a great peace would flourish in you. Thus, pray.* (Bl. 257).

**1985**

**WEDNESDAY, JANUARY 2ND 1985**
At 11:30 at night at Krizevac, the Virgin appeared surrounded by five angels: *I am very happy to have been able to come here for three years, thanks to the prayers of believers. Continue to pray thusly. A part of my plan has been realized. God blesses in a special way, all those who are here. You can return happily to your homes. You do not immediately understand the reasons. Offer your prayers of thanksgiving for next week.* (T, 47).

**THURSDAY, JANUARY 3RD 1985**
To Maria, for the parish: *Dear children! These days, the Lord granted you many graces. Let this week be a week of thanksgiving for all the graces God has granted you. Thank you for having responded to my call.*

**WEDNESDAY, JANUARY 9TH 1985**
*I thank the faithful for having come to church in very bad and cold weather.* (T. 48).

**THURSDAY, JANUARY 10TH 1985**
To Maria, for the parish: *Dear children! Today I want to thank you for all your sacrifices. I thank especially those who come here gladly, and have become dear to my heart. There are parishioners who do not listen to my messages; but because of those who are especially close to my heart, I give messages to the parish. And I will continue giving them, for I love you and want you to spread them with love.*

**THURSDAY, JANUARY 17TH 1985**
To Maria, for the parish: *In these days, Satan is fighting deviously against this parish, and you, dear children, have fallen asleep in (regard to) prayer. Only some of you are going to Mass. Persevere in these days of temptation.*

**THURSDAY, JANUARY 24TH 1985**
To Maria. for the parish: *Dear children! These days you have savored the sweetness of God through the renewal in your parish. Satan plans to work even more energetically to take the joy away from each of you. Through prayer, you can totally disarm him and ensure your happiness.*

**THURSDAY, JANUARY 31ST 1985**
To Maria, for the parish: *Dear children! Today I want to ask you to open your hearts to God, just like the flowers in the spring that yearn for the sun. I am your Mother and I would like you to be ever closer to the Father, so that he pour gifts into your hearts abundantly.*

**JANUARY - FEBRUARY 1985**
To Vicka, at the time of a prayer meeting on the mountain: *My dear children, Satan is strong. He wishes, with all his strength, to destroy my plans. Pray only, and do not stop doing it. I will also pray to my Son, so that all the plans that I have begun will be realized. Be patient and persevere in prayer. Do not permit Satan to take away your courage. He works very hard in the world. Be on your guard.* (DN 3,26).

**SUNDAY, FEBRUARY 3RD 1985**
*I wish for Father Slavko to stay here, for him to guide the life and to assemble all the news, so that when I leave there will be a complete image of everything that has happened here. I am also praying now for Slavko and for all those who work in this parish.* (DN3, 25-26).

**THURSDAY, FEBRUARY 7TH 1985**
To Maria, for the parish: *Dear children! Satan is manifesting himself in this parish in a particular way these days. Pray, dear children, that Gods plan be carried out, and that every work of Satan be turned to the glory of God. I have remained this long to help you in your great trials.*

**THURSDAY, FEBRUARY 14TH 1985**
To Maria, for the parish: *Dear children! Today is the day when I give you the message for the parish, but not everyone in the parish accepts my messages and lives them. I am sad and I want you, dear children, to listen to me and to live my messages. Every family must pray and read the Bible.*

**SUNDAY, FEBRUARY 17TH 1985**
*Pray, dear children, so that God's plan may be accomplished, and all the works of Satan be changed in favor of the glory of God.* (F 2, 158).

**WEDNESDAY, FEBRUARY 20TH 1985** (Ash WEDNESDAY)
To Jelena:*I give you an advice; I would like for you to try to conquer some fault each day. If your fault is to get angry at everything, try each day, to get angry less. If your fault is not to be able to study, try to study. If your fault is not to be able to obey, or if you cannot stand those who do not please you, try on a given day, to speak with them. If your fault is not to be able to stand a proud person, you should try to approach that person. If you desire that person to be humble, be humble yourselves. Show that humility is worth more than pride. Thus, each day, try to go beyond, and to reject every vice from your heart. Find out which are the vices that you most need to reject. During this Lent, you should try and truly desire to spend it in love. Strive as much as possible.* (DN 4bis, 68).

**THURSDAY, FEBRUARY 21ST 1985**
A message to the parish: *Day after day I have been appealing to you for renewal and prayer in the parish. But you are not responding. Today I am appealing to you for the last time. This is the season of Lent, and you, as a parish in Lent, should be moved through love of my appeal to take the first step. If you do not take this step, I do not want to give you any more messages. God will allow me not to give you any more.*

**MONDAY, FEBRUARY 25TH 1985**
To Jelena:*Know that I love you. Know that you are mine. I do not wish to do anything more for anyone, that I do not wish to do for you. Come all of you to me. Remain with me and I will be your Mother always. Come, because I wish to have all of you.* (Bl. 261). To Maria: *For next week, I invite you to say these words: 'I love God in everything.' With love, one obtains everything. You can receive many things, even the most impossible. The Lord wishes for all the parishes to surrender to Him, and I too, in Him. I desire it. Each evening, make your examination of conscience, but only to give thanks in acknowledgment for everything that His love offers us at Medjugorje.* (DN 3, 301).

**THURSDAY, FEBRUARY 28TH 1985**
Message to the parish: *Today I call you to live these words during this week: 'I love God.' Dear children, with love, you can achieve everything, even what appears impossible. God wants this parish to belong to Him completely. And I wish that too.*
**FEBRUARY - MARCH 1985**
*Dear children! You have always prayed that I not abandon you. Now I ask of you, in turn, not to abandon me. Satan wants especially during these days to disperse you. For that, pray very much these days. Dear children, I came again to thank you. You have not yet understood what that means. To give joy to my heart. It is a very great thing. I ask you only to persevere in prayer. As long as you pray I will have words for you. Good-bye, I thank you dear children. My love for you is unlimited; be happy with me, because I am happy with you.* (DN 4 bis, 68).

**THURSDAY, MARCH 7TH 1985**

Message for the parish: *Dear children! Today I invite you to renew prayer in your families. Dear children, encourage the very young to pray and to go to holy Mass.* (BN 19, 30).

**SATURDAY, MARCH 9TH 1985**
*You can receive a grace immediately, or in a month, or in ten years. I do not need a hundred or two hundred 'Our Fathers.' It is better to pray only one, but with a desire to encounter God. You should do everything out of love. Accept all annoyances, all difficulties, everything, with love. Dedi cate yourselves to love.* (BN 19, 30).

**WEDNESDAY, MARCH 13TH 1985**
Message addressed to Vicka, at a time when a mistake by Ivan, who was frightened, caused a stir. (Described in detail in DN 4, p. 17-23). *Pray, pray, pray! It is only with prayer that you will be able to avoid Ivan's error. He should not have written. And after that had to clearly acknowledge it, so as not to plant any doubts.*

**THURSDAY, MARCH 14TH 1985**
To Maria, for the parish: *Dear children! In your life, you have all experienced light and darkness. God gives every person the power to recognize good and evil. lam calling you to light, which you must carry to all those who are in darkness. From day to day, people who are in darkness come into your houses. You, dear children, give them light.*

**MONDAY, MARCH 18TH 1985**
To Mirjana: *The rosary is not an ornament for the home, as one often times limits himself to using it. Tell everyone to pray it.* (DN 4bis, 421). *Right now, many are greatly seeking money, not only in the parish, but in the whole world. Woe to those who seek to take everything from those who come, and blessed are those from whom they take everything. (This relates to the exploitation of some pilgrims.)* (DN 4 bis, 26). *May the priests help you because I have entrusted to you a heavy burden, and I suffer from your difficulties. Ivan did not make a big mistake. I have sufficiently reprimanded him for the error. It is not necessary to scold him anymore.* (BI 111).

**THURSDAY, MARCH 21ST 1985**
To Maria, for the parish:*Dear children! I want to give you the messages. Therefore I ask you to accept these messages. Dear children, I love you. In a special way I have chosen this parish which is more dear to me than any of the others to which I gladly came when the Almighty sent me. Therefore, dear children, I ask you to accept me for your well-being. Live the messages.*

**SUNDAY, MARCH 24TH 1985** (vigil of the Annunciation)
*Today I invite all of you to Confession, even if you have already gone to Confession during the last days. I wish that you would live my feast in your hearts. You are not able to, if you do not abandon yourselves completely to the Lord. It is for this reason that I call all of you to reconciliation with the Lord.* (DN. 4 bis, 64).
**LENT 1985** (February 20-April 6)
*To Jelena:Fast on bread and water during the first week of the Passion and on Holy WEDNESDAY, Holy THURSDAY, and Good FRIDAY.* (Bl. 209).

**MONDAY, MARCH 25TH 1985** (Feast of the Annunciation)
*Through my joy and the joy of this people, I say to all of you this evening, I love you, and I wish you well.* (DN. 4 his, 64). ***Jelena:****"Why are you so beautiful?" I am beautiful because I love. If you want to be beautiful, love. There is no one in the world who does not desire beauty.* (Bl. 263).

**THURSDAY, MARCH 28TH 1985**

Message to the parish: *Dear children! Today, I am asking you to pray, pray, pray. In prayer you will experience great joy and the solution to every hopeless situation. Thank you for making progress in prayer. Each one of you belongs to my heart. I am grateful to all of you who have begun praying in your families.* To Jelena:*You all know the flowers. A flower must blossom and each part of the flower is very important. But there is a moment when the flower must wilt so that the seed can ripen, and after, when the seed is ripe, other flowers will come.* Jelena did not know how to explain this parable. But Tomislav Vlasic explained: One finds in it the whole liturgy of this evening (
SATURDAY, vigil of Palm
SUNDAY); one must die in order to be able to rise again. We say sometimes that it is sad that a flower must wilt. But, if it does not wilt, it is not able to ripen the seed from where the other flowers come. If it does not die, life can not multiply itself. (S. Barbaric, April 6, 1985, VB. 2, 801).

**THURSDAY, APRIL 4TH 1985** (Holy
THURSDAY)
Message to the parish: *Dear children! I am thankful that you have begun to reassure more highly in your hearts the glory of God. Today is the day that I wanted to stop giving messages because certain people do not accept them. The parish has responded and I wish to continue to give messages to a degree, such as has never before been witnessed in the world, since the beginning of history. Try to remain in my heart. Do not remain on the side.* (T. Vlasic, April 29, 1985; VB 2, 135).

**FRIDAY, APRIL 5TH 1985**
*You, the members of this parish, have a large and heavy cross to bear. But do not be afraid to carry it. My Son is here to help you.* (DN 4 bis, 65).

# Apparitions in the Rectory (Apr 11, 1985 To Sep 1987)

On orders from the Bishop (letter of March 25th), the apparitions, forbidden in every room contiguous to the Church itself, were transferred to the rectory.

**THURSDAY, APRIL 11TH 1985**
To Maria, for the parish: *I would like to tell everyone in the parish: pray especially to be enlightened by the Holy Spirit. Beginning today, the Lord wants to try the parish in a special way, in order to strengthen it in faith.*

**MONDAY, APRIL 15TH 1985**
*You must begin to work in your hearts as you work in the field. Work and change your hearts so that the new spirit of God can dwell there.* (C 207)

**THURSDAY, APRIL 18TH 1985**
To Maria, for the parish: *Dear children! Today I thank you for the opening up of your hearts. Joy overwhelms me for every heart that opens to God, especially in the parish. Rejoice with me. Pray all the prayers for the opening of sinful hearts. I desire this. God desires this through me.*

**THURSDAY, APRIL 25TH 1985**

Message for the parish: *Dear children! Today, I invite you to pray with your heart and not only through habit. Some come here but do not pray with their hearts. Therefore, as your mother, I beg you to pray that prayer may prevail in your hearts at every moment.*

**THURSDAY, MAY 2ND 1985**
*Dear children! Today, I invite you to pray with your heart and not only through habit. Some come here but do not pray with their hearts. Therefore, as your mother, I beg you to pray that prayer may prevail in your hearts at every moment.*

**FRIDAY, MAY 3RD 1985**
To Jelena:*Sometimes prayers said in a loud voice keep Jesus at a distance, because when men want to conquer with their own power there is no place for God. Prayers said in a loud voice are good when they come from the heart.* (BN. 19, 33)

**TUESDAY, MAY 7TH 1985**
Ivanka has a vision at home, which lasts about an hour: "the Blessed Virgin was more beautiful than ever and was accompanied by two angels. She asks me what I wished. I prayed to her to let me see my mother. The Blessed Virgin smiled and approved with a nod. My mother appeared to me very soon. She was smiling. Our Lady told me to stand up. My mother embraced me then as she said 'My child, I am so proud of you.' She embraced me again and disappeared. Our Lady said to me then:"
*My dear child, today is our last meeting, do not be sad. I will return to see you at each anniversary of the first apparition (June 25), beginning next year. Dear child, do not think that you have done any thing bad, and that this would be the reason why I'm not returning near to you. No, it is not that. With all your heart you have accepted the plans which my Son and I formulated, and you have accomplished everything. No one in the world has had the grace which you, your brothers and sisters have received. Be happy because I am your Mother and I love you from the bottom of my heart. Ivanka, thank you for the response to the call of my Son, thank you for persevering and remaining always with Him as long as He will ask you. Dear child, tell all your friends that my Son and I are always with them when they call on us. What I have told you during these years on the secrets, do not speak to anyone about them.*
"Dear Gospa, may I embrace you?" "The blessed Virgin gives an affirmative sign with her head. I then embraced her. I asked her to bless me. She did it with a smile and added:" *Go in the peace of God.* Then she left slowly with the two angels. (F 2, 150-152 and VB 3. 149)

**THURSDAY, MAY 9TH 1985**
To Maria, for the parish: *Dear children! You do not know how many graces God is bestowing upon you. You are not willing to get moving in these days when the Holy Spirit is working in a special way; you do not want to advance. Your hearts are turned to earthly things and you are preoccupied by them. Turn your hearts to prayer and ask that the Holy Spirit be poured upon you.*

**THURSDAY, MAY 16TH 1985**
To Maria, for the parish: *Dear children! I am calling you to more attentive prayer and to greater participation in the Mass. I want you to experience God within yourselves at Mass. I want to tell young people especially, to be open to the Holy Spirit, because God desires to draw you to Himself during these days when Satan is active.*

**SUNDAY, MAY 19TH 1985**
To Jelena:*Dear children, at this time I ask you particularly to consecrate yourselves to me and to my Immaculate Heart. Love, pray, and fast.* (BI 304).

**THURSDAY, MAY 23RD 1985** (day before Pentecost)

Message to the parish: *Dear children, I invite you especially these days, open your hearts to the Holy Spirit. The Holy Spirit acts now through you. Open your hearts and offer your life to Jesus, so that he will act in your hearts and strengthen you in the faith. Thank you for your response to my call.*

**TUESDAY, MAY 28TH 1985**
*Love is a gift from God. Pray so that God may grant you the gift to be able to love.* (BI 255)

**THURSDAY, MAY 30TH 1985**
To Maria, for the parish: *Dear children, lam calling you again to prayer of the heart. Let prayer, dear children, be your everyday food, especially when work in the fields is exhausting you, and you cannot pray with your heart. Pray, and then you will overcome every tiredness. Prayer will be your happiness and rest.*

**SATURDAY, JUNE 1 1985**
To Jelena:*Always have the love of God in you, because without this love, you are not able to convert yourselves completely. Let the rosary be in your hands in memory of Jesus. Dear children, strive to deepen your knowledge of the mass as you should.* (J).

**SUNDAY, JUNE 2ND 1985**
*Dear children, this evening I would like to tell you to pray more during the novena for an out pouring of the Holy Spirit, on your families and your parish. Pray, you will not be sorry for it. God will present you with gifts for which you are going to glorify Him all your earthly life.*

**THURSDAY, JUNE 6TH 1985**
*To Maria, for the parish: Dear children! Many people of all nationalities will come to the parish and now I am calling you to love. Love first of all the members of your own family and then you might be able to accept and love all those who are coming.*

**THURSDAY, JUNE 13TH 1985**
To Maria, for the parish: *Dear children: I am begging you, the people of this parish, to pray more until the anniversary of the apparitions. (June 25th). May your prayer be an act of devotion and commitment to God. I know about your tiredness, dear children, but you do not know how to give yourselves to me. These days, I beg you, make an act of total dedication to me.*

**THURSDAY, JUNE 20TH 1985**
To Maria, for the parish: *Dear children! For the coming feast I want to say to you: Open your hearts to the Lord of all hearts! Give me all your feelings and all your problems. I want to console you in all your trials. My wish is to fill you completely with God's peace, joy, and love.*

**SATURDAY, JUNE 22ND 1985**
***Jelena:***The Gospa dictated to me (perhaps, it would be better to say, inspired) this prayer and advised me to recite it in our prayer group:

**PETITION TO GOD**

Oh God, our heart is in deep obscurity, in spite of our union to Your Heart. Our heart is struggling between You and Satan; do not permit it to be in this manner!

Every time that the heart is divided between good and evil, let it be enlightened by Your light and let it be unified.

Never permit, for there to be able to exist in us two loves, that there can never co-exist in us two faiths, and that there can never co-exist in us; lying and sincerity, love and hatred, honesty and dishonesty, humility and pride.

Help us on the contrary, so that our hearts may be elevated toward You just like that of a child. May our heart be ravished with peace and continue to always have the nostalgia of it.

May Your Holy will and Your love find a permanent place in us, that at least sometimes we would really wish to be Your children and when, Oh Lord, we will desire to be Your children, remember our past desires and help us to receive You again.
We open our hearts to you so that Your holy love will remain in us. We open our souls to you, so that they may be touched by Your holy mercy which will help us to see clearly all our sins, and will make us realize, that which makes us impure is sin.
God, we want to be Your children, humble and devout, to the point of becoming your cherished and sincere children, such as only the Father would be able to desire that we be. Help us, Jesus our brother, to obtain the goodness of the Father in our regard, and to be good to Him.
Help us Jesus, to understand well what God gives us, although sometimes we fail to perform a good act, as though it were for us an evil. (VB 3, 218-219).

**PRAYER FOR A SICK PERSON**

Likewise dictated (inspired) to Jelena, with this clause: "Here is the most beautiful prayer that you could recite for a sick person."
O my God behold this sick person before You. He has come to ask You what he wishes and what he considers as the most important thing for him. You, oh my God, make these words enter into his heart: (What is important, is the health of his soul)
Lord, may Your will in everything take place in his regard, if You want for him to be cured, let health be given to him; but if Your will is something else, let him continue to bear his cross.
I also pray to You for us, who intercedes for him; purify our hearts, to make us worthy to convey Your holy Mercy.
Protect him and relieve his pain, that Your holy will be done in him, that Your holy name be revealed through him, help him to bear his cross with courage. (VB 3, 220-221).
Before this prayer and the preceding one, recite three times the "Glory Be."

**TUESDAY, JUNE 25TH 1985**

On this anniversary day of the first apparition on the hill, Maria asks: "What do you wish from the priests?" *I urge you to ask everyone to pray the rosary. With the rosary you will overcome all the troubles which Satan is trying to inflict on the Catholic Church. Let all priests pray the rosary. Give time to the rosary. (F 2, 118). To Jelena:A heart which belongs to the Lord is splendid, even if it is flooded with difficulties and trials. But if the heart engaged in difficulties, strays away from God, it loses its splendor.* (BN 19,34).

**THURSDAY, JUNE 27TH 1985**

To Maria, for the parish: *Today I invite you to humility. These days all of you have felt a great joy because of all the people who came here, and to whom you spoke with love about your experience. With humility and an opening of the heart, continue to speak with all those who come.*

**JUNE - 1985**

To Jelena:*Dear children, if there is someone and he asks you for something, give it to him. I too, ask before many hearts, and they do not open up. Pray so that the world may receive my love.* (Bl. 258).

**MONDAY, JULY 1ST 1985**

On the hill of the apparitions: *I thank all those who have responded to my call. I bless all of you, I bless each of you. These days I ask you to pray for my intentions. Go in the peace of God.* (Bl. 183).

**THURSDAY, JULY 4TH 1985**

Message for the parish: *Dear children, I thank you for each sacrifice you have made. Now I urge you to offer all your sacrifices with love. I want you who are troubled to begin to help pilgrims with confidence and the Lord will give to you in the same manner.*

**THURSDAY, JULY 11TH 1985**

Message to the parish: *Dear children! I love your parish and I protect it under my mantle against every satanic enterprise. Pray that Satan will flee from your parish and from everyone who comes to your parish. In that way you will be able to hear each appeal from God and to respond to it with your life. Thank you for your response to my call.*

**THURSDAY, JULY 18TH 1985**
Message to the parish: *Dear children! Today I invite you to put more blessed objects in your home and may every person carry blessed objects on himself Let everything be blessed. Then, because you are armored against Satan, he will tempt you less.*

**THURSDAY, JULY 25TH 1985**
To Maria, for the parish: *Dear children! I want to shepherd you but you do not want to obey my messages. Today I call you to obey my messages and then you will be able to live everything that God tells me to relate to you. Open yourselves to God, and God will work through you, and give you everything you need.*

**THURSDAY, AUGUST 1ST 1985**
To Maria, for the parish: *Dear children! I wish to tell you that I have chosen this parish. I guard it in my hands like a little flower that does not want to die. I beg you to give yourselves to me so that I can offer you as a gift to God, fresh and without sin. Satan has undertaken one part of my plan and wants to possess it. Pray that he does not succeed because I desire to have you for myself so that I can offer you to God.*

**MONDAY, AUGUST 5TH 1985**
Message to Ivan, during an apparition in the evening, on the mountain of Krizevac, where she came "with vestments of gold." *Praise be Jesus Christ. My children, I'm happy to be with you this evening, and to see you so numerous. I bless you with a special blessing.* After having prayed for a long time and listened to Ivan who recommended the persons present, she concluded: *Make progress in holiness through the messages, I will help you. Give your utmost and we will go together, sensitive to the sweetness of life, light, and joy.* After having blessed them, she left in the sign of the radiant cross while saying: *Go in the peace of God, my children, my little children.*

**THURSDAY, AUGUST 8TH 1985**
Message for the parish: *Dear children! Today lam calling you to begin your struggle against Satan with prayer. Satan wants to work more now that you know he is active. Dress up, dear children, in clothes of armor against Satan; with rosaries in your hands, you will conquer.*

**WEDNESDAY, AUGUST 14TH 1985**
To Ivan: *Observe the complete fasts,*
*WEDNESDAYs and*
*FRIDAYs. Pray at least an entire Rosary: Joyous, Sorrowful, and Glorious mysteries.* (BN. 19, 351).

**THURSDAY, AUGUST 15TH 1985** (Feast of the Assumption)
Message to the parish: *Dear children! Today I bless you and I wish to tell you that I love you. I appeal to you at this moment to live my messages. Today I bless you all with the solemn blessing which the Almighty has granted me.* To Mirjana: *My angel, pray for unbelievers. People will tear their hair, brother will plead with brother, he will curse his past life, lived without God. They will repent, but it will be too late. Now is the time for conversion. I have been exhorting you for the past four years. Pray for them.* (BN 19, 35). *Invite everyone to pray the Rosary.* (Bl. 154).

**THURSDAY, AUGUST 22ND 1985**
To Maria, for the parish: *Dear children! Today I wish to tell you that the Lord wants to put you to the test, which you can overcome by prayer. God puts you to the test in your daily activities. Pray*

*now that you pass every test peacefully. Come through every test from God more open to Him and approach Him with greater love.*

**THURSDAY AUGUST, 29TH 1985**

To Maria, for the parish: *Dear children! I invite you especially to prayer because Satan wants to help himself with the harvests of your vineyards. Pray so that he will not succeed.* (Placed on guard against the materialism which surrounded them, still, certain persons began to sell grapes to the pilgrims more expensively.)

**THURSDAY, SEPTEMBER 5TH 1985**

To Maria, for the parish: *Dear children! I thank you today for all your prayers. Pray continually and pray more so that Satan will go far away from this place. Dear children, the plan of Satan has failed. Pray that every plan of God be realized in this parish. I especially thank young people for the sacrifices they have offered.*

**THURSDAY, SEPTEMBER 12TH 1985**

To Maria, for the parish, before the celebration of the feast of the Holy Cross, day of the largest pilgrimage of the year, at Krizevac: *Dear children! I wish to tell you these days to put the Cross at the center of your life. Pray especially before the Cross which is the origin of great graces. In your homes make a special consecration to the Cross of the Lord. Promise that you will not offend Jesus and that you will not insult Him, nor the Cross.*

**FRIDAY, SEPTEMBER 20TH 1985** (instead of
THURSDAY, 19th)

To Maria, for the parish: *Dear children! Today I am calling you to live in humility all the messages I give you. Dear children, when you live the messages do not glorify yourselves by saying: I live the messages. If you carry the messages in your heart and live them everyone will notice it. So, there is no need for words which serve only those who do not wish to hear. For you it is not necessary to speak. For you, my dear children, it is necessary to live and witness by your lives.* (DN 4 bis, 67).

**THURSDAY, SEPTEMBER 26TH 1985**

To Maria, for the parish: *Dear children! Thank you for all your prayers. Thank you for all your sacrifices. I want you to renew the messages that I am giving you. Heed the call to fasting because by fasting you will ensure that the total plan of God here in Medjugorje will be fulfilled. That will give me great joy. Thank you for having responded to my call.*

**SEPTEMBER 1985**

To Maria: *I have given you my love, so that you may give it to others.*

**THURSDAY, OCTOBER 3RD 1985**

To Maria, for the parish: *Dear children! I want to say to you, be thankful to Godfor every grace that God gave you. For all the fruits of grace, be thankful to the Lord and praise Him. Dear children, learn to be thankful for little things, and then you will be able to be thankful for great things.*

**THURSDAY, OCTOBER 10TH 1985**

To Maria, for the parish: *1 invite you one more time to live the messages in the parish. I invite the young people of this parish particularly, to do it. Dear children, if you live the messages you will develop the seeds of holiness. As Mother, I invite all of you to holiness, so that you will be able to transmit it to others. You are a mirror for others.*

**THURSDAY, OCTOBER 17TH 1985**

To Maria, for the parish: *There is a time for each thing. Today, I invite you to begin to work on your hearts. At present, all the work in the fields has ended. You find the time to clean the most neglected places, but you set your hearts aside. Work more now, with love, to clean each of the recesses of your heart.*

**THURSDAY, OCTOBER 24TH 1985**

To Maria, for the parish: *I wish from day to day, to clothe you with sanctity, goodness, obedience and love of God, so that you may be from day to day, more beautiful and better prepared for your God. Dear children, listen to my messages and live them. 1 want to guide you.*

**FRIDAY, OCTOBER 25TH 1985**

***Mirjana:*** "When she appeared, the Blessed Virgin greeted me, 'Praised be Jesus.' Then she spoke of unbelievers;" *They are my children. I suffer because of them. They do not know what awaits them. You must pray more for them.* "We prayed with her for the weak, the unfortunate, the foresaken. After the prayer, she blessed us. Then she showed me, as in a film, the realization of the first secret. The earth was desolate. *It is the upheaval of a region of the world.* "She was precise. I cried." "Why so soon," I asked? *In the world, there are so many sins. What can I do, if you do not help me. Remember, that I love you.*"How can God have such a hard heart?" *God does not have a hard heart. Look around you and see what men do, then you will no longer say that God has a hard heart. How many people come to church, to the house of God, with respect, a strong faith, and love of God? Very few! Here you have a time of grace and conversion. It is necessary to use it well.* (DN 5, 39). To Mirjana: *Pray very much for Father Pero, to whom I send a special blessing. I am a mother, that is why I come. You must not fear for I am there.* Father Pero Ljubicic had been chosen by Mirjana, to unveil to the world, the first three warnings, three days before the event. (DN 5, 40).

**THURSDAY, OCTOBER 31ST 1985**

To Maria, for the parish: *Dear children, today I love all of you with the same love, and I wish that each one would do all that is possible, according to his own capacity. Dear children, you can do it, I know. But you do not want it, because you feel small and weak. Take courage, and offer little flowers to the Church and to Jesus, so that all of us may be happy* Message to the prayer group: *God loves you very much. He loves you a hundred-fold more than your parents love you.* (and she invited to offer her heart to this love. T. Vlasic, 2 Nov. 1985, VB 3, 179).

**THURSDAY, NOVEMBER 7TH 1985**

To Maria, for the parish: *I invite you to love your neighbor, especially those who do you harm. In this way, you will be able to discern the intentions of the heart with love. Pray and love, dear children. It is with the strength of love, that you will be able to accomplish what seems impossible to you.*

**THURSDAY, NOVEMBER 14TH 1985**

To Maria, for the parish: *I, your Mother, love you. I encourage you to pray. I never get tired. I call you even when you are far from my heart. Ifeel badly for each person who is lost. But lam your Mother; Iforgive easily, and I experience joy for each child who returns to me.*

**THURSDAY, NOVEMBER 21ST 1985**

To Maria, for the parish: *I am anxious to tell you that it is a special time for you and for the parish. During the summer, you say that you have to work very much. At this time, there is no work in the fields. Thus, I invite you to work on yourselves. Come to mass; the time is being provided for you. Dear children, there are many who come; in spite of the bad weather, because they love me, and want to prove their love to me. I ask all of you to prove your love to me by coming to mass. The Lord will reward you generously for it.*

**THURSDAY, NOVEMBER 28TH 1985**

To Maria, for the parish: *I wish to thank all of you for everything you have done for me, especially the young people. I ask you dear children, enter conscientiously into prayer; because it is in prayer, that you will know Gods designs.*

**WEDNESDAY, DECEMBER 4TH 1985**
Gianni Sgreva, an Italian Passionist, was inspired to found a "Community of Consecrated" on the message of Medjugorje, and seeking discernment, submitted his case of conscience to Maria, who questioned the Gospa. *I prefer to answer him personally.* It seems that the message was positive, because the community opened May, 18th, 1987, at Priabona in Italy. (There follows another message, which one will find later: June 7, 1986, Archives Sgreval.)

**THURSDAY, DECEMBER 5TH 1985**
To Maria, for the parish: *I wish io invite you to prepare yourselves for the feast of Christmas; through prayer; penance; and acts of love. Do not worry so much, dear children, about material things, because in this manner, you will not be able to live the feast of Christmas.*

**SATURDAY, DECEMBER 7TH 1985**
To Jelena *I have only one wish for tomorrows feast. I ask of you to find at least a quarter of an hour; for you to come before me and entrust your problems to me. No one will understand you, as I do.* (J).

**THURSDAY, DECEMBER 12TH 1985**
To Maria, for the parish: *I invite you to praise Jesus, with me, at this time of Christmas. On that day; I give Him to you in a special way, and invite you to celebrate Jesus' birth with me. Dear children; on that day, pray more, and think more of Jesus.*

**THURSDAY, DECEMBER 19TH 1985**
To Maria, for the parish: *I invite you to love your neighbor. If you love your neighbor, you will feel more the presence of Jesus, especially on Christmas day. God will fill you with great gifts, if you abandon yourselves to Him. On Christmas Day, I will give a special blessing to all the mothers, my maternal blessing. And Jesus will grant His blessing to everyone.*

**THURSDAY, DECEMBER 26TH 1985**
To Maria, for the parish: *I thank all of you who have listened to my messages, and who have lived, on Christmas Day, what I had told you previously. Beginning now, you are purified of your sins, and I would like to continue to guide you in the love of your heart.*

**TUESDAY, DECEMBER 31ST 1985**
To Jelena, during the eve of December 31st: *Next year is the year of peace; not because men have named it so, but because God has programmed it. You will not have peace through the presidents, but through prayer. Through one of the little seers of the group, during this same vigil, Jesus said: When you hear the clocks at midnight, you will fall on your knees, bow your head to the ground, so that the King of Peace will come. This year, I will offer my peace to the world. But afterwards, I will ask you where you were when I offered you my peace.* (These two messages were reported by T. Vlasic, February, 6th, 1986. VB 4, 34).
**1986**

**THURSDAY, JANUARY 2ND 1986**
Message to the parish: *I invite you to decide totally for God. I beg of you dear children, give yourselves completely, and you will be able to live everything that I have told you. It will not be difficult for you to give yourselves completely to God.*

**MONDAY, JANUARY 6TH 1986**

To Vicka: *If you agree to it, I will not appear to you anymore for 50 days. Vicka accepts this sacrifice.* (DN 5, 107).

**THURSDAY, JANUARY 9TH 1986**

Message to the parish: *I invite you to help Jesus through your prayer, for the realization of all His plans, which He has already begun here. Offer your sacrifices to Jesus, so that He will realize everything that He has planned, and that Satan will not be able to do anything.*

**THURSDAY, JANUARY 16TH 1986**

Message to the parish: *Today, I still invite you to prayer. I need your prayers so that God may be glor fled through all of you. Dear children, I beg of you: Listen to my maternal call, and live it. If I invite you to it, it is only out of love, and in order to be able to help you.*

**TUESDAY, JANUARY 21ST 1986**

It was the second day of retreat for a prayer group, probably that of Jelena, (January 21-24, 1986). *This evening, rest.* (T. Vlasic, 23 Jan. 86, VB 4, 24).

**WEDNESDAY, JANUARY 22ND 1986**

To the same group: *I know that you are tired, but I cannot tell you, rest. Today, I tell you, pray, and do not go to bed before having prayed at least a quarter of a hour, for the group. Tomorrow will be a better day.* (T. Vlasic, 23 Jan. 86, VB 4, 24).

**THURSDAY, JANUARY 23RD 1986**

Message to the parish: *I invite you, again, to prayer of the heart. If you pray with the heart, dear children, the eyes of your brothers will melt, and every barrier will disappear. Conversion will be easy for all those who want to receive it. It is a gift which you must implore for your neighbor.*

**THURSDAY, JANUARY 30TH 1986**

To Maria, for the parish: *I invite all of you to pray, so that all of Gods designs on you, may be realized, and all that God pursues through you. Help all the others to be converted, especially all those who come to Medjugorje. Dear children, do not permit Satan to become the master of your heart, because in that case, you will become the image of Satan, and not mine. I invite you to pray, in order to become witnesses of my presence. Without you, the Lord cannot realize what He wishes. The Lord has given each one a free will, and you can dispose of it.*

**THURSDAY, FEBRUARY 6TH 1986**

To Maria, for the parish: *This parish, which I have chosen, is a special parish which distinguishes itself from others. I offer some special graces to all those who pray with the heart. Dear children, I give these messages first to the parishioners, and then to all the others. You will be responsible for these messages before my Son, Jesus, and me.*

**THURSDAY, FEBRUARY 13TH 1986**

To Maria, for the parish: *This Lent is for you, a special stimulant to change your life. Begin from this moment. Unplug the television and put aside so many other useless things. Dear children, I invite you to individual conversion. This time belongs to you.*

**THURSDAY, FEBRUARY 20TH 1986**

To Maria, for the parish: *Here is my second message for Lent. Renew your prayer before the cross. Dear children, I offer you special graces and Jesus, the extraordinary merits of the cross. Accept them, and live them. Meditate on the passion of Jesus. Unite your life to Jesus.*

**SATURDAY, FEBRUARY 22ND 1986**

At the end of the meeting of the prayer group, before the blessing: *Dear children, you will be able to receive Divine love, only in proportion to when you understand that, on the cross, God offers you His immense love.* (God's punishment is a sign of love, observes T. Vlasic, March 31, 86. VB 45, 59).

**THURSDAY, FEBRUARY 27TH 1986**
To Maria, for the parish: *Dear children, live in humility, the messages which I give you.*

**THURSDAY, MARCH 6TH 1986**
To Maria, for the parish: *Even today, I invite you to open up more to God, so that He can work through you. It is in proportion to how you open yourselves, that you will harvest the fruits. I invite you again to prayer.*

**THURSDAY, MARCH 13TH 1986**
To Maria, for the parish: *Today I invite you to live Lent with your small sacrifices. Thank you for each sacrifice which you have brought me. Dear children, continue to live in this way. With love, help me to present your offerings. God will reward you.*

**THURSDAY, MARCH 20TH 1986**
To Maria, for the parish: *Today, I invite you to actively enter into prayer. You wish to live all that I tell you, but, you are not successful in it because you do not pray enough. Dear children, I beseech you, open yourselves and begin to pray. Prayer will be a joy for you. If you begin, you will not be uncomfortable, because you will pray in joy*

**MONDAY, MARCH 24TH 1986**
To the prayer group: *Dear children, receive all that the Lord offers you. Do not have your hands paralyzed and do not repeat: 'Jesus, give me.' But open your hands, and take everything that the Lord offers you.* (T. Vlasic, April 27, 86, VB 4, 64).

**THURSDAY, MARCH 27TH 1986**
To Maria, for the parish: *Thank you for all the sacrifices , but I invite you to a greater sacrifice: the sacrifice of love. Without love, you cannot receive neither my Son, nor me. Without love, you are not able to convey to others, your experience. For that, I invite you dear children, to begin to live love in your hearts.*

**THURSDAY, APRIL 3RD 1986**
To Maria, for the parish: *Dear children, I am calling you to live the holy Mass. There are many of you who have experienced the beauty of the Mass, but there are others who go unwillingly. I have chosen you, dear children, and Jesus is giving you His graces in the holy Mass. Let everyone who comes to Mass be joyful. Come with love and rejoice in the holy Mass.*

**THURSDAY, APRIL 10TH 1986**
To Maria, for the parish: *Dear children, I invite you to grow in love. A flower cannot grow without water. Neither can you grow without God's blessing. Everyday, you should ask for God's blessing so that you can grow normally, and carry out your works.*

**THURSDAY, APRIL 17TH 1986**
To Maria, for the parish: *Dear children, you are preoccupied with material things, and you lose, thus, everything that God wants to give you. Pray then, dear children, for the gifts of the Holy Spirit. They are necessary for you, in order that you may give witness to my presence here, and to everything that I give you. Dear children, abandon yourselves to me so that I can guide you fully. Do not worry so much about material things.*

**THURSDAY, APRIL 24TH 1986**
To Maria, for the parish: *Dear children , today I invite you to prayer. You have forgotten that you are all important, especially the elderly in the families. Invite them to pray. Let all the young*

*people, by their lives, be an example for others. Let them be witnesses for Jesus. Dear children, I beseech you to begin to convert yourselves through prayer, then you will know what you must do.*

**THURSDAY, MAY 1ST 1986**

To Maria, for the parish: *Begin to change your lives in your families. Let your family be a harmonious flower, which I can offer to Jesus. Dear children, let each family be active in prayer. It is my wish that one day, one will be aware of the fruits of prayer in the family. It is only thus, that I will offer you all, as petals to Jesus in fulfillment of God's plan.*

**THURSDAY, MAY 8TH 1986**

To Maria, for the parish: *Dear children, you are responsible for the messages that I give here. Here one finds the fountain of grace, and you are the vessels which convey these gifts. That is why I invite you, dear children, to carry out this work, which is yours, with responsibility. Each one in the measure of his ability. Dear children, I invite you to carry these gifts to others with love. Do not keep them for yourselves.*

**THURSDAY, MAY 15TH 1986**

To Maria, for the parish: *Dear children, today I invite you to offer to me your hearts so that I can convert them, and make them similar to mine. You ask yourselves why you are not able to satisfy my requests? You are not able to because you have not entrusted your hearts to me, so that I can change them. You say, but you do not do it. Do then, everything that I tell you. Only in that way, can I be with you.*

**THURSDAY, MAY 22ND 1986**

To Maria, for the parish: *Today I wish to give you my love. You do not realize, dear children, how great my love is, and you do not know how to receive it. I wish to manifest it to you in many ways dear children , but you do not recognize it. You do not understand my words with your hearts, and because of that you do not understand my love. Dear children, accept me in your life. Thus, you will be able to accept everything that I tell you , and everything to which I invite you.*

**THURSDAY, MAY 29TH 1986**

To Maria, for the parish: *Dear children, live the love of God, and toward your neighbor. I invite you to it. Without love, dear children, you are not able to do anything. That is why I invite you to live a mutual love. Only in that way will you be able to love, and to receive me, and all those who are around you and come to your parish. Everyone will feel my love through you. Thus, I beg you to start, as of today, to love with a burning love, the love with which I love you.*

**THURSDAY, JUNE 6TH 1986**

To Maria, for the parish: *Dear children! I invite you to decide whether or not you want to live the messages which I give you. I wish that you live and actively convey my messages to others. In a very particular way, dear children, I wish that all of you become a reflection of Jesus, and bear witness to this unfaithful world. I desire that you become a light to all, that all of you will testify to the light. Dear children, you are not called to darkness, but to light. So be a light, by the way you live your life.*

**JUNE 7TH 1986** (First
FRIDAY of the month)

Fr. Pere Gianni Sgreva, who wanted to found a new community on the messages of Medjugorje, had questioned Maria on June 6th. On the 7th of June she tells him: "This is what the Gospa answered." *Yes, one must pray. What you are doing pleases me. For the time being, keep a very active prayer life, and God will then light up the other plans.* "Since the Gospa said that, we are sure that the road is a good one. She was happy when I asked her about it." The community which opened in 1987, in Italy, is prospering so well, that before the end of the year, it had to move, since the large house at Priabona had become too small.

**THURSDAY, JUNE 12TH 1986**

To Maria, for the parish: *Dear children! Today I invite you to begin to pray the rosary with a living faith. Only in that way will I be able to help you. You wish to receive graces, but you do not pray. I am not able to help you if you do not decide to begin. I invite you, dear children, to pray the rosary in such a way that it will be a commitment for you, achieved in joy. In this way, you will understand the reason for which I have been with you, for such a long time. I want to teach you to pray*

**THURSDAY, JUNE 19TH 1986**

Message for the parish: *These days, Our Lord has permitted me to intercede more for you. I invite you then, to again, pray. Pray without ceasing. In this way, I can give you the joy which Our Lord gives me. Through His graces, dear children, let your sufferings be transformed into joy. I am your Mother, and want to help you.*

**TUESDAY, JUNE 24TH 1986**

Maria and Ivan met with the prayer group on Mt. Krizevac: *You are on a Thabor. You receive blessings, strength and love. Carry them into your families, and into your homes. To each one of you, I grant a special blessing. Continue in joy, prayer, and reconciliation.* (DN 5, 14-15). To the prayer group: *I beseech you, withdraw in silence. Your obligation is not so much to do, but to adore God, to stay with Him.* (T. Vlasic,26 June 86 VB 4, 115).

**THURSDAY, JUNE 26TH 1986**

To Maria, for the parish: *Dear children, God has given me permission to realize with Him, this oasis of peace. I invite you to keep it intact. Through their indifference, some people destroy prayer and peace. I beseech you, testify and help by your lives to preserve it.*

**THURSDAY, JULY 3RD 1986**

To Maria, for the parish: *Dear children! Today I invite all of you to prayer. Without prayer, dear children, you are not able to perceive neither God, nor me, nor the graces which I give you. Therefore, I ask you to always begin and end each day with prayer. Dear children, I desire to lead you day after day, as much as possible toward prayer, but you cannot grow, if you do not wish to. I exhort you, dear children, let prayer have the first place.*

**THURSDAY, JULY 10TH 1986**

To Maria, for the parish: *Today I invite you to holiness. You cannot live without holiness. That is why you must, with love, be victorious over every sin. Overcome all difficulty with love. I beseech you, dear children, live love within yourselves.*

**THURSDAY, JULY 17TH 1986**

To Maria, for the parish: *Dear children! Today I invite you to ask yourselves why I have been with you such a long time. I am the intercessor between you and God. For that reason, dear children, I invite you to always live with love, everything that God asks of you. Live all the messages that I give you in complete humility.*

**THURSDAY, JULY 24TH 1986**

To Maria, for the parish: *What joy you give me; you are on the road to holiness. I beg you, help by your witness, all those who do not know how to live in holiness. That is why your family must be the place where holiness is born. Help everyone to live in holiness, especially the members of your own family.*

**THURSDAY, JULY 31ST 1986**

To Maria, for the parish: *Hatred gives rise to division and blinds one to everything and everybody. I invite you to spread harmony and peace, more specially, there where you live. Dear children, act with love. May love be your only tool. With love, convert into good, all that Satan is trying to destroy and take to himself It is only thus, that you will be completely mine, and that I will be able to help you.*

**THURSDAY, AUGUST 7TH 1986**

To Maria, for the parish: *You know that I promised you an oasis of peace , but you do not know that around this oasis is a desert, where Satan watches and tries to tempt each one of you. Dear children, it is only through prayer, that you will be able to overcome every influence of Satan, wherever you may be. I am with you, but I cannot deprive you of your free will.*

**THURSDAY, AUGUST 14TH 1986**

To Maria, for the parish: *May your prayer be the joy of a meeting with the Lord. I cannot guide you there, if you yourselves do not feel the joy of prayer. I wish to guide you every day, more deeply into prayer, but I cannot force you.*

**THURSDAY, AUGUST 21ST 1986**

To Maria, for the parish: *I am grateful for the love that you show me. You know, dear children, I love you immensely, and each day I pray to the Lord to help you to understand the love which I bear for you. That is why, dear children, pray, pray, pray*

**THURSDAY, AUGUST 28TH 1986**

To Maria, for the parish: *I invite you to be, in everything, an example for others, especially in prayer and bearing witness. Without you, dear children, I cannot help the world. I want your cooperation with me in everything, even the smallest things. Therefore, dear children, help me. May your prayer be a prayer of the heart, and abandon yourselves completely to me. In this way, I will be able to teach you and to guide you on the path, upon which I have set you.*

**THURSDAY, SEPTEMBER 4TH 1986**

To Maria, for the parish: *Again today, I invite you to prayer and fasting. Be assured, dear children, that with your help, I can do everything and prevent Satan from leading you into sin, and to force him to leave this place. Dear children, Satan lies in wait for each of you. He tries, each day, to plant doubts in each of you. Therefore, dear children, make each day a prayer and total abandonment to God.*

**THURSDAY, SEPTEMBER 11TH 1986**

To Maria, for the parish: *During these days, when you joyfully celebrate the Feast of the Cross, I wish that your own cross become a source of joy. Especially, dear children, pray in order to be able to accept sickness and suffering with love, as Jesus did. It is only in this way, that I can experience the joy of giving you the graces and the cures, which Jesus permits me to grant you.*

**THURSDAY, SEPTEMBER 18TH 1986**

To Maria, for the parish: *Again today, I thank you for everything you have done for me in recent days. I thank you more particularly, dear children, in the name of Jesus, for the sacrifices you have offered this last week. Dear children , you forget that I rely on your sacrifices to help you, and to keep Satan away from you. It is for that reason, that I again invite you to offer your sacrifices to God with a deep reverence.*

**THURSDAY, SEPTEMBER 25TH 1986**

To Maria, for the parish: *I invite you to help others through your peace, so that they see it, and begin to look for peace within themselves. Because you are in peace, dear children, you cannot understand the absence of it. That is why I invite you to help through your prayers and your life, to destroy every evil among men, and to unmask Satan 's deceptions. Pray, so that truth may prevail in your hearts.*

**THURSDAY, OCTOBER 2ND 1986**

To Maria, for the parish: *Even today, I invite you to pray. You do not realize, dear children, the value of prayer, so you do not tell yourselves: 'Now is the time for prayer; nothing is more important to me. No one is more important for me than God. ' Dear children, dedicate yourselves to prayer with a special love. In this way, God will be able to give you His graces. Thank you for your response to my call.*

**THURSDAY, OCTOBER 9TH 1986**

To Maria, for the parish: *You know that I wish to lead you on the road to holiness. But I cannot compel you by force to become saints. I wish that everyone of you helps me, and himself, by your small sacrifices. In this way I will be able to guide you, and make you more holy, day by day Dear children, I do not want to force you to live my messages, but this long time I have spent with you is the sign of the immense love I bear for you. I wish that each one of you become holy*

**THURSDAY, OCTOBER 16TH 1986**

To Maria, for the parish: *Today, I wish to show you again, how much I love you. I am sad that I am unable to help each of you to understand my love. That is why, dear children, I invite you to pray and to consecrate yourselves completely to God, because Satan wants to conquer you in daily affairs, and to take first place in your lives. For that, dear children, you must pray without ceasing.*

**THURSDAY, OCTOBER 23RD 1986**

To Maria, for the parish: *Again today, I call you to prayer More particularly, dear children, I invite you to pray for peace. Without your prayer, I cannot help you to understand the messages that my Lord has permitted me to give you. That is why, dear children , you must pray, in order to know through prayer, the peace that God gives you.*

**THURSDAY, OCTOBER 30TH 1986**

To Maria, for the parish: *Today, again, I invite you accept and live seriously the messages which I give you. It is for you, dear children, that I have stayed here for such a long time. It is so that I might be able to help you to realize these messages which I give you.*

**THURSDAY, NOVEMBER 6TH 1986**

To Maria, for the parish: *Dear children, today I invite you to pray everyday for the souls in Purgatory. Every soul needs prayer and grace in order to reach God and His love. By this way, dear children, you will gain new intercessors, who will help you during your life to discern that nothing on earth is more important for you, than longing for Heaven. For that dear children, pray without respite, so that you may be able to help yourselves and others, to whom your prayers will bring joy*

**THURSDAY, NOVEMBER 13TH 1986**

To Maria, for the parish: *Even today, I invite all of you to pray with all your heart, as well as to reform your life from day to day. I am especially calling you, dear children, to live righteously through prayer and sacrifice. I wish that each one of you, near this source of grace, (Medjugorje), come to paradise with this special gift which He will give - holiness. Pray and reform your life, dear children, so as to become saintly. I will always be near you.*

**THURSDAY, NOVEMBER 20TH 1986**

To Maria, for the parish: *Today I invite you to live, and to follow all the messages which I give you with my special love. Dear children, God does not want you to be restless and indecisive, but totally abandoned to Him. You know that I love you, and that I burn with love for you. For that reason, dear children, decide also in favor of love. May love prevail in all of you so that daily, you may burn with the love of God and experience it for yourselves. Not human love, but God's love.*

**THURSDAY, NOVEMBER 27TH 1986**

To Maria, for the parish: *Dear children, today I invite you again, to dedicate your life to me with love, so that I may be able to guide it lovingly. It is a very special love that I bear for you, dear children, and it is my desire to lead all of you to Heaven and near to God. Understand that this life lasts a short time, in comparison with that of Heaven. That is why, dear children, again today, decide in favor of God. In this way only, can I show you, how dear you are to me, and how much I desire that all of you be saved, and be with me in Heaven.*

**THURSDAY, DECEMBER 4TH 1986**
To Maria, for the parish: *I invite you still today, to prepare your hearts for these days when the Lord wants above all, to purify you from all the sins of your past. You cannot do it alone, dear children, and for that reason, I am here to help you. Pray, dear children, because it is only in this way that you will be able to know all the evil that dwells in you, and abandon it to the Lord, so that He may purify your hearts completely. So, dear children, pray constantly and prepare your hearts through pen ance and fasting.*

**THURSDAY, DECEMBER 11TH 1986**
To Maria, for the parish: *Dear children, I invite you to pray during this special time, so that you may taste the joy of meeting with the newborn Jesus. Dear children, I wish that you live these days as I lived them. I want to guide you and show you this joy, to which I want to bring all of you. That is why, dear children, pray and abandon yourselves totally to me.*

**THURSDAY, DECEMBER 18TH 1986**
To Maria, for the parish: *Today I call you again, to prayer. When you pray, you are so much more beautiful. You are like flowers, which after the snows, are bursting with beauty in their indescribable colors. In the same way, dear children, after prayer, display more before God, all that is beautiful, in order to please Him. That is why dear children, pray and open your life to the Lord, so that He may make of you a beautiful and harmonious flower for paradise.*

**THURSDAY, DECEMBER 25TH 1986**
To Maria, for the parish: *I thank the Lord today for all that He does, and especially for the gift of permitting me to remain with you. Dear children, these are the days when the Lord grants special graces to all those who open their hearts to Him. I bless you and I wish that you also know these graces. Place yourselves at the disposition of the Lord, so that He may be glorified through you. My heart follows attentively, your progress.*
**1987**

**THURSDAY, JANUARY 1ST 1987**
To Maria, for the parish: *Dear Children! Today, the day of the new year, I invite all of you to live the messages which I give you. You know, dear children, that because of you, I have stayed here this long, in order to teach you to walk on the road to holiness. Therefore, dear children , pray constantly, and live all the messages which I give you. I do it with a great love for God, and for you.*

**THURSDAY, JANUARY 8TH 1987**
To Maria, for the parish: *I would like to thank you for your response to my messages; especially, dear children, thank you for all the sacrifices and all the prayers you have presented to me. I wish to continue to give you messages, no longer each*
*THURSDAY, but on the 25th of each month. The time has come when, what my Lord wanted, has been accomplished. From now on, I will give you fewer messages, but I will remain with you. Also, I ask you dear children, to listen to my messages and to live them so that I can guide you.*

**SUNDAY, JANUARY 25TH 1987**
The first apparition of the 25th of the month, (the anniversary day of the month of the first apparition on the hill), given to Maria, for the parish: *Today I want to appeal to all of you to start*

*living a new life from this day on. Dear Children, I wish that you would understand that God has chosen each one of you to have a part in the great plan for the salvation of mankind. You cannot fully understand how great your role is in God's design. For that reason, pray, dear children, so that through prayer, you may be able to know your role in God's plan. I am with you, so that you may be able to realize it fully.* Beginning January 25th, the messages are now monthly, each 25th of the month, monthly anniversary date of the first apparition. As in the case of the THURSDAY messages, we do not give any reference. These messages have been transmitted by benevolent organizations to the whole world.

**WEDNESDAY, JANUARY 28TH 1987**

To Mirjana, at Sarajevo:

*My dear children! I came to you in order to lead you to purity of soul, and then to God. How did you receive me? At the beginning you were fearful, suspicious of the children I had chosen. Later on, the majority received me in their heart. They began to put into practice, my maternal recommendation. Unfortunately, that did not last a long time. Whatever be the place where I appear, and with me also my Son, Satan also comes. You permitted him to subdue you without realizing that you were being led by him. It is up to you to realize that your behavior is not permitted by God, but you immediately stifle the thought. Do not give in dear children. Wipe away from my face, the tears which I shed on seeing you act in this manner. Look around you. Take the time to come to God in the Church. Come into your Father's house. Take the time to meet for family prayer, in order to obtain the grace from God. Remember your deceased; make them happy by offering the Mass. Do not look with scorn on the poor man who is begging a morsel of bread. Do not send him away from your abundant table. Help him and God will help you. It could very well happen that the blessing he leaves you as a sign of gratitude, will be fulfilled for you. God may listen to him. You have forgotten all that my children. Satan has influenced you in that. Do not give in. Pray with me! Do not deceive yourselves in thinking, I am good, but my brother, who lives next to me is not good. You will be mistaken. I love you because I am your mother, and I warn you. There are the secrets my children. One does not know what they are; when they learn, it will be too late. Return to prayer! Nothing is more necessary. I would like it if the Lord would have permitted me to show you just a little about the secrets, but, He already gives you enough graces. Think! What do you offer to Him in return. When was the last time you gave up something for the Lord? I will not blame you further, but once again call you to prayer, fasting, and to penance. If you wish to obtain a grace from the Lord by fasting, then let no one know that you are fasting. If you wish to obtain the grace of God through a gift to the poor, let no one know it, except you and the Lord. Listen to me, my children! Meditate on my message in prayer.*

**WEDNESDAY, FEBRUARY 25TH 1987**

Message to the parish: *Dear children! I wish to cover all of you with my mantle,and to lead all of you on the road to conversion. I beg you, dear children, entrust all your past to the Lord, with all the evil that has accumulated in your hearts. I wish each one of you to be happy, but with sin, that is never possible. Pray, dear children, and in prayer you will know the new road of joy. Joy will shine forth in your hearts, and in joy, you will be the witnesses of what my Son and I expect of each one of you. I bless you.*

**WEDNESDAY, MARCH 25TH 1987** (Feast of the Annunciation)

Message to the parish: *Today I thank you for your presence in this place where I give you special graces. I call each of you to begin to live, starting today, the life which God desires of you, and to start doing good deeds of love and mercy. I do not wish, dear children, that you live the message while at the same time displeasing me by committing sins. Also, dear children, I wish that each of you live a new life, without destroying all that God has done in you, and what He gives to you. I give you my special blessing, and I remain with you on your road to conversion.*

**SATURDAY, APRIL 25TH 1987**

Message for the parish: *Dear children! Today I once again invite all of you to pray. You know that God grants special graces through prayer. Therefore, dear children, try to pray so that you will be able to understand all that I give you here. I invite you, dear children, to prayer of the heart. You know that without prayer you cannot comprehend all that God has planned through each one of you. So Pray! It is my wish that God's plan be fulfilled in and through each of you, and that all He has placed in your hearts will increase. Pray that God 's blessing may protect you from all the evil that threatens you. I give you my blessing.*

**MONDAY, MAY 25TH 1987**

Message to the parish: *I call on each of you to begin to live in God 's love. Dear children, you are ready to commit sin, and to place yourselves in Satan 's hands without reflection. I call you so each of you will decide knowingly for God, and against Satan. I am your mother, and I desire to lead all of you to complete holiness. I wish for each of you to be happy on earth and then to be with me in Heaven. This, dear children, is my purpose in coming here, and my desire. Thank you for having responded to my call.*

**WEDNESDAY, JUNE 24TH 1987**

Sixth anniversary of the prelude to the apparitions: Maria invited the pilgrims to climb Krizevac at 11:30 at night. A crowd of thousands of people climbed the rocky foot path, without accident, (One wonders how!). After reciting the rosary, toward midnight, Maria confided in those who surrounded her. "The Blessed Virgin was joyful. First of all, she prayed over all of us. We asked her to bless us. She did. Then she gave us, in substance, this message:" *Dear children! I want to lead you on the road to conversion. I desire that you convert the world and that your life be a conversion for others. Do not full into infidelity. Let each one of you be completely submitted to my will and to the will of God. Beginning this day, I give you special graces, and in particular the gift of conversion. Let each one of you take home my blessing, and motivate the others to a real conversion. "Through her," Maria concluded, "God gives us this gift this evening. Before leaving us, Our Lady prayed again over all of us for a moment. We prayed with her for all our needs, for all your needs, for each of you here present. Finally the Blessed Virgin said:" Go in the peace of God! (Transcribed the same day at Medjugorje.)*

**THURSDAY, JUNE 25TH 1987**

Message to the parish: *Dear children! Today I thank you all, and wish to call all of you to the peace of God. I wish that each one of you may know, in his heart, this peace which God gives. Today, I bless all of you. I bless you with God's blessing, and ask you, dear children, to follow and to live my way. I love you all, dear children. That is why I have called you so many times. I thank you for all that you have done according to my intentions. Please help me, so that I may be able to present you to God, and guide you on the path to salvation. Thank you for having responded to my call.*

**SATURDAY, JULY 25TH 1987**

Message to the parish: *Dear children! I beseech you from this day on, take up the way of holiness. I love you and therefore, I wish you to be holy. Do not let Satan block you on the way. Dear children, pray and accept all that God is offering you on this way which is bitter, but to whomever is engaged in it, God reveals joy and the sweetness to respond in good heart, to His calls. Do not measure the importance of little things, but long for Heaven and holiness.*

**TUESDAY, AUGUST 25TH 1987**

Message to the parish: *Dear children! Today also I call upon you again to decide to live the messages. God has permitted me, in this year which the Church has dedicated to me, to be able to speak to you and to encourage you on the way to holiness. Dear children, ask God for the graces which He wants to give you through me. I am ready to intercede with God for all that you ask, so that your holiness may be complete. There fore, dear children, do not forget to ask, because God has permitted me to obtain graces for you.*

# The Apparitions, Forbidden in the Rectory In Search of A Discreet Place

*A solution: The choir loft in the church, without eyewitnesses, starting the beginning of September, 1987.*

**FRIDAY, SEPTEMBER 25TH 1987**
Message to the parish: *Dear children! Today, I wish to invite all of you to prayer. Let prayer be LIFE for you. Dear children, devote your time to Jesus only, and He will give you everything that you search for. He will reveal Himself to you completely. Dear children, Satan is strong, and he watches over each of you in order to tempt you. Pray, and this way he will not be able to harm you nor to block your way on the road to holiness. Dear children, make progress as much as possible, toward God and in prayer, from day to day. Thank you for having responded to my call.*

**SUNDAY, OCTOBER 25TH 1987**
Message to the parish: *Today I invite all of you to decide for paradise. The way is difficult for those who have not decided for God. Dear children, decide and believe. God offers Himself to you in His fullness. You are called and you need to respond to the call of the Father, who is calling you, through me. Pray, because in prayer, each one of you will be able to achieve perfect love. I am blessing you and I want to help each one of you, so that you will be under my motherly mantle.*

**WEDNESDAY, NOVEMBER 25TH 1987**
Message to the parish: *Even today again, I invite you. May each of you decide to abandon yourself completely to me. Only thus, can I in turn, present each of you to God. Dear children, you know that I love you immeasurably, and I wish for each one of you to be mine. But God gives everyone freedom, which I lovingly respect, and to which I humbly submit.Dear children, I wish that God's plan regarding this parish be realized. But, if you do not pray, you will not be able to recognize my love, nor God 's plan for this parish, and for each of you. Pray that Satan does not entice you with his pride and deceptive strength. I am with you and want you to believe that I love you.*

**FRIDAY, DECEMBER 25TH 1987**
Message to the parish: *Rejoice with me. My heart is rejoicing because of Jesus, and it is He, whom I want to present to you today. Dear children, I want each one of you to open your heart to Jesus, and I will give Him to you with love. It is He who transforms you, teaches you and protects you. Today I pray for each one of you in a special way, and I present you to God that He may manifest Himself to you.I invite you to sincere prayer with the heart. Let each one of your prayers be an encounter with God. In your work,and in your everyday life, put God in the first place. I ask you with great seriousness to obey me, I beseech you.*
**1988**
**JANUARY, 25TH 1988**
Message to the parish: *Dear children, today I again am calling you to complete conversion, which is difficult for those who have not chosen God. I am inviting you, dear children, to convert fully to God. God can give you everything that you seek from Him. But you seek God only when sicknesses, problems and difficulties come to you, and you think that God is far from you and is not listening and does not hear your prayers. No, dear children, that is not the truth. When you are far from God, you cannot receive graces, because you do not seek them with a firm faith. Day by day, I am praying for you, and I want to draw you evermore near to God. I cannot, if you do not*

*desire it. Therefore, dear children, put your life in God's hands. I bless you all. Thank you for responding to my call.*

**FEBRUARY 25TH 1988,**

Message to the parish: *Dear children, I am calling you to prayer and complete surrender to God. You know that I love you and am coming here out of love, so I could show you the path of peace and salvation for your souls. I want you to obey me and not permit Satan to seduce you. Satan is very strong and therefore I wish you to dedicate your prayers to me, so that those who are under his influence may be saved. Give witness by your life; sacrifice your life for the salvation of the world. I am with you and am grateful to you, but in Heaven you shall receive the Father's reward, which He has promised to you. Therefore, dear children, do not be afraid. If you pray, Satan cannot injure you even a little, because you are God's children and He is watching over you. Pray and let the rosary always be in your hands as a sign to Satan that you belong to me.*

**MARCH 25TH 1988,**

Message to the parish: *Today, I invite you dear children, to complete surrender to God. You are not conscious of how God loves you with such a great love. He permits me to be with you so I can instruct you and help you to find the way of Peace. This way, however, you cannot discover if you do not pray. Dear children, forsake everything to consecrate your time to God; and then God will bestow gifts upon you and bless you. Little children, do not forget that your life is fleeting like a spring flower, which today is wondrously beautiful but tomorrow has vanished. Therefore, pray in such a way that your prayer, your surrender to God, may become like a road sign. That way, your witness will not only have value for yourself, but for others, and for all eternity.*

**APRIL 25TH 1988**

Message for the parish: *Dear children, God wants to make you holy. Through me, He is inviting you to complete surrender. Let Holy Mass be your life. Understand that the Church is God's palace, the place in which I gather you and want to show you the way to God. Come and pray! Neither look at others, nor slander them. Rather let your life be a testimony on the way of holiness. Churches deserve respect and are set apart as holy because God, who became man, dwells in them day and night. Little children, believe and pray that the Father will in crease your faith; then you can ask for whatever you need. I am with you and I am rejoicing because of your conversion; and I am protecting you with my motherly mantle. Thank you for your response to my call.*

# Messages Undated or Approximated *Gathered by Different Authors*

We give in an appendix, the messages which have been gathered by authors, who had made inquiry into the messages of Medjugorje. These messages, which they generally did not date, (nor give the means for dating) are presented in a chronological order, per each book. This provides a "date limit." As an exception, we group at the end, the four volumes of homilies of Father T. Vlasic and Father Slavko Barbaric, which are remarkable for the quality of their information.

**APOCALYPTIC MESSAGES**

Received by Mirjana before December 26, 1982, confided on November 5, 1983 to Tomislav Vlasic, who conveyed them to the Pope on December 16, 1983. In his letter of December 16,

1983, to the Pope, and published in "Is The Virgin Mary Appearing at Medjugorje?" (Paris, 1984), Tomislav Vlasic reports some revelations received by Mirjana in 1982, and confided to him November 5, 1983, with this significant introduction: "During the apparition of December 25, 1982, according to Mirjana, the Madonna confided to her the tenth and last secret, and revealed to her, the dates in which the different secrets will be realized. The Blessed Virgin revealed to Mirjana some aspects of the future, up to this point, in greater detail than to the other seers. For this reason, I am reporting here what Mirjana told me in a conversation of November5, 1983. I summarized the essentials of her account, without literal quotation. Mirjana told me:"
Before the visible sign is given to humanity, there will be three warnings to the world. The warnings will be in the form of events on earth. Mirjana will be a witness to them. Ten days before one of the admonitions, Mirjana will notify a priest of her choice. The witness of Mirjana will be a confirmation of the apparitions and a stimulus for the conversion of the world. After the admonitions, the visible sign will appear on the site of the apparitions in Medjugorje for all the world to see. The sign will be given as a testimony to the apparitions and in order to call people back to faith. The ninth and tenth secrets are serious. They concern chastisement for the sins of the world. Punishment is inevitable, for we cannot expect the whole world to be converted. The punishment can be diminished by prayer and penance, but it cannot be eliminated. Mirjana says that one of the evils that threatened the world, the one contained in the seventh secret,has been averted thanks to prayer and fasting. That is why the Blessed Virgin continues to encourage prayer and fasting: *You have forgotten that through prayer and fasting you can avert wars and suspend the laws of nature.* After the first admonition, the others will follow in a rather short time. Thus, people will have some time for conversion. That interval will be a period of grace and conversion. After the visible sign appears, those who are still alive will have little time for conversion. For that reason, the Blessed Virgin invites us to urgent conversion and reconciliation. The invitation to prayer and penance is meant to avert evil and war, but most of all to save souls. According to Mirjana, the events predicted by the Blessed Virgin are near. By virtue of this experience, Mirjana proclaims to the world: "Convert as quickly as possible. Open your hearts to God."

"In addition to this basic message, Mirjana related an apparition she had in 1982 which we believe sheds some light on some aspects of Church history. She spoke of an apparition in which Satan appeared to her. Satan asked Mirjana to renounce the Madonna and follow him. That way she could be happy in love and in life. He said that following the Virgin, on the contrary, would only lead to suffering. Mirjana rejected him, and immediately the Virgin arrived and Satan disappeared. Then the Blessed Virgin gave her the following message, in substance:"
*Excuse me for this, but you must realize that Satan exists. One day he appeared before the throne of God and asked permission to submit the Church to a period of trial. God gave him permission to try the Church for one century. This century is under the power of the Devil, but when the secrets confided to you come to pass, his power will be destroyed. Even now he is beginning to lose his power and has become aggressive. He is destroying marriages, creating division among priests and is responsible for obsessions and murder You must protect yourselves against these things through fasting and prayer, especially community prayer. Carry blessed objects with you. Put them in your house, and restore the use of holy water.*

**KRALJEVIC (1983)**
The Virgin tells the children: *I know that many will not believe you, and that many who have an impassioned faith will cool off You remain firm , and motivate people to instant prayer, penance and conversion. At the end, you will be happier.* (K.56).
Messages approximately grouped on Ecumenism (see annex#2): *In God differences do not exist among his people; religion need not separate people. Every person must be respected, despite his or her particular profession of faith. God presides over all religions, as a king controls his subjects, through his priests and ministers. The sole mediator of salvation is Jesus Christ.* Do differences exist among the believers of different churches? (A question asked in reference to a certain Protestant community.) *It is not equally efficacious to belong to or pray in any church or*

*community, because the Holy Spirit grants his power differently among the churches and ministers. All believers do not pray the same way. It is intentional that all apparitions are under the auspices of the Catholic Church.* (K.59).
To the seers: *When you will suffer difficulties, and need something, come to me.* (K.72). *I cannot cure. God alone cures. Pray! I will pray with you. Believe firmly. Fast, do penance. I will help you as long as it is in my power to do it. God comes to help everyone. I am not God. I need your sacrifices and your prayers to help me.* (K.86, and F.1,45). *Faith cannot be alive without prayer.* (K.86). *The Mass is the greatest prayer of God. You will never be able to understand its greatness. That is why you must be perfect and humble at Mass, and you should prepare yourselves there.* (K.86).
For a Priest who questions: "Is it preferable to pray to you or to pray to Jesus?" *I beseech you, pray to Jesus! I am His Mother, and I intercede for you with Him. But all prayers go to Jesus. I will help, I will pray, but everything does not depend solely on me. but also on your strength, and the strength of those who pray (K.87).*
With respect to the souls in Purgatory: *These persons wait for your prayers and your sacrifices.*(K.87).
*The most beautiful prayer is the "Creed. "* (K.94). *The most important thing, is to believe.* (K.94). *All prayers are good, if they are said with faith.* (K.95). *My Son wants to win all souls to Him, but the Devil strives to obtain something. The Devil makes a great effort to infiltrate among you, at all costs.* (K.116).

***JOURNAL OF JELENA***
Questioned on the similarity between the signs announced at Medjugorje, and the third secret of Fatima, Jelena responds, "Toward these things the Gospa told us: *Do not fear anything. You must forget what is behind you in your life. I only want that from now on, you be new people. Do not fear anything when I am near you. I love you.*
Conversation with Fr. Bonifacio and Fr. Petar Ljubicic: *It does not suffice to pray. You must change your life, your heart. Love the others, have love for others. Love what you do and always think about Jesus and you will understand what is good, and what is bad. (ibid).*

**FATHER BUBALO (1981)**
**Vicka:**'At the very beginning, the Gospa tells us:" *You may leave, but let little Jakov stay with me.* And **Vicka** adds: "Jakov is an extraordinary boy; the Gospa knew it." (Bu.52).
During the times of the first apparitions: To Mirjana: *My Son struggles for each of you, but Satan fights Him also. He prowls around you, sets traps for you. He tries to divide you, you the seers, to plant discord among you; to confuse you so you will detest yourselves, and will abandon yourselves to him.*
**Vicka** adds: "Our Lady has said it to us on several occasions." (Bu.71).
BOTTA-FRIGERIO (1984)
*The world can only be saved through peace. But it will only have peace in its meeting with God.* (Bo.75). *The world lives amidst very strong tensions. It is on the edge of catastrophe.* (Bo.75). *I have come here because there are many believers. I want to remain with you in order to convert many and to bring peace to everyone. Begin by loving your enemies. Do not judge, do not slander, and do not despise, but give only love. Bless your adversaries and pray for them. I know well that you are not capable of doing it; I advise you to pray each day at least five minutes to the Sacred Heart, so that you can receive the gift of Divine Love, with which you will be able to love your enemies.* (Bo.75). *It is necessary to convert oneself to God, in order to obtain peace. Tell the whole world; tell it without delay, that I ardently wish conversion. Be converted, do not wait. I will ask my Son that He not chastise the world. Convert yourselves, renounce everything, and be ready for everything.*
*Do not go in search of extraordinary ways, take rather, the Gospel and read it. There, everything will be clear.* (Bo.76). *You only learn to pray, through praying.* (Bo.76). *Offer your time to God and let yourself be guided by the Holy Spirit. Then, your work will go well and you will have free time. Those who abandon themselves to God, do not have place in their hearts for fear. The difficulties*

*which you will face, will contribute to your growth and to the glory of the Lord. For that, reject fear.* (Bo.77). *Prayer always leads to peace and serenity. (Bo.78, cf Bl 298). No one is dispensed from fasting, except those who are gravely ill. Prayer and works of charity cannot replace fasting. I recommend to you in a special way, to attend Holy Mass every day*(Bo.79). *Mass represents the highest form of prayer. You must be humble and respectful during Holy Mass, and prepare yourself for it with care.* (Bo.79, cf Bl 238). *May the Holy Father announce with courage, peace and love to the world. May He not consider Himself the Father of Catholics, but of all mankind.* (Bo.80).

**CASTELLA - LJUBIC (1984-85)**

Reported by ***Mirjana:*** *Tell the faithful that I need their prayers, and prayers from all the people. It is necessary to pray as much as possible and do penance because very few people have been converted up until now There are many Christians who live like pagans. There are always so few, true believers.* (C.49, cf. Bl 213).

To the priest who asked what they should do: *Carry out well your responsibility, and do what the Church asks you to do.* (C52).

One day the Gospa reproached Jakov for his behavior at school towards his friends: *You must love them all.* "I love them all. But they are so annoying to me." *Then accept it as a sacrifice, and offer it.* (C.64).

A group of seminarians from Zagreb and Djakovo, attended an apparition. ***Maria:*** "The Gospa looked at each one of us, and told us with a smile:" *Tell them, that with prayer, one obtains everything.* (C.68).

The Blessed Virgin received a young nun with open arms, while she kept her hands joined before the others. Questioned by ***Mirjana***, she said: *I will take with me very soon, all those to whom I extended my arms.* (C.69).

To a nun who asked about her brother, who had died in an accident: *I understand the question,* answered the Blessed Virgin. *He died in the state of grace. He needs Masses and prayers.* (C.70).

Asked by the seers why her choice had fallen upon them, the Blessed Virgin replied: *I do not choose the best. Are you angry with my choice, my angels?* (C.75).

Mirjana reports to a religious, a close friend, this word from the Gospa: *The hour has come when the demon is authorized to act with all his force and power The present hour, is the hour of Satan.* (C.99). *Many pretend to see Jesus and the Mother of God, and to understand their words, but they are, in fact, lying. It is a very grave sin, and it is necessary to pray very much for them.* (C.123). *lam anxious for people to know what is happening in Medjugorje. Speak about it, so that all will be converted.* (C. 134).

To Mirjana, who asks the Gospa on her insistence in saying, "It presses me to. . . :" *When you will be in Heaven, you will understand why I am so pressed.* (C.214).

To the seers who ask regarding the apparitions and their purpose: *Is it, after all, that I bore you? Everything passes exactly according to God's plan. Have patience, persevere in prayer and in penance. Everything happens in its own time.* (C.215).

On the matter of a Catholic priest, confused because of the cure of an Orthodox child: *Tell this priest, tell everyone, that it is you who is divided on earth. The Muslims and the Orthodox, for the same reason as Catholics, are equal before my Son and me. You are all my children. Certainly, all religions are not equal, but all men are equal before God, as St. Paul says. It does not suffice to belong to the Catholic Church to be saved, but it is necessary to respect the commandments of God in following one's conscience. Those who are not Catholics, are no less creatures made in the image of God, and destined to rejoin someday, the House of the Father. Salvation is available to everyone, without exception. Only those who refuse God deliberately, are condemned. To him, who has been given little, little will be asked for. To whomever has been given much (to Catholics) , very much will be required. It is God alone, in His infinite justice, Who determines the degree of responsibility and pronounces judgment.* (C 128).

**FR. ROBERT FARICY (1985)**

On the subject of Christ: *I am His Mother, and I intercede for you, near to Him.*(F2,134).

**TUTTO (1985)**
*Let the faithful meditate each day on the life of Jesus, while praying the rosary.* (T.43). *Every prayer, which comes from the heart, is agreeable to God.* (T.58). *You do not celebrate the Eucharist, as you should. If you would know what grace, and what gifts you receive, you would prepare yourselves for it each day, for an hour at least. You should go to confession once a month. You should consecrate three days to reconciliation, each month: the first FRIDAY of the month, followed by SATURDAY, and SUNDAY* The parish at Medjugorje had established an hour of adoration, before the Most Blessed Sacrament, the first FRIDAY of the month. On the SATURDAY which followed, an hour of devotion before the cross, with prayers for sinners. And on SUNDAY, the Holy Mass was followed by a meal of reconciliation. (T.58).

**BLAIS (1986)**
*I do not have the right to impose on anyone, what they should do. You have reason, and a will. You should, after having prayed, reflect and decide.* (B1.37). *Receive the peace of my Son. Live it, and spread it.* (Bl.90).*Permit Jesus to perform great works in you. The door of your heart, the lock is rusted. Permit Him to open it. May it be open through your prayer, your fasting, your conversion.* (B1.143). *Pray slowly, and meditate while saying the prayers of the rosary. Take a quarter of an hour to recite: 5 Our Father's, Hail Mary* **'s,** *and Glory Be's.* (Bl.173). *I love you so much. And if you love me, you will be able to feel it. I bless you in the name of the Most Holy Trinity, and in my name. Remain in peace.* (Bl.183). *You will find everything in the Gospels.* (Bl.244). *Let the word of God begin to speak in your heart.* (Bl.245). *Begin to love your enemies. Do not judge or slander. Do not scorn. Do not curse. Only give your adversaries love. Bless them, and pray for them. I know that you are not capable of doing it, but I advise you to pray each day at least five minutes, to the Sacred Heart, so that He can give you Divine love, with which you will be able to love, even your enemies.* (Bl.301). (Another version of the message previously shown in Botta.) *You can direct your prayers not only to those who are already in Heaven, but also to those who are in Purgatory, because with their prayer, they can help you to reach eternal happiness.* (Bi .326). *One must follow the authority of the Church with certainty. Yet, before she expresses an opinion, it is necessary to advance spiritually, because she will not be able to express a judgment in a vacuum, but in a confirmation which presupposes growth of the child. First comes birth, followed by Baptism, then Confirmation. The Church comes to confirm him, who is born of God. We must walk and advance in the spiritual life, affected by these messages.* (Bl.330).

**MIRAVALLE (1986)**
Before December, 1983: *So many believers never pray. Have the people pray! Faith cannot be alive without prayer.* (M 8). *I am not able to cure you. God alone, can cure you. Pray! I will pray with you. Believe firmly, fast, do penance. God comes to help each one. I am not God. I need your prayers and your sacrifices to help me.* (M 8). *You do not need a sign; you yourselves must be a sign.* (M 9). *Peace is necessary for prayer. Peace should be present before prayer, and while one is praying. Prayer should, of course, lead to peace and reflection.* (M 30). *Why ask so many questions? The answer is found in the Gospels.* (M 31).
To Jelena:*The subject on the certainties of catastrophes comes from false prophets. They say, on such a day, at such an hour, there will be a catastrophe. I have always said: Punishment will come about, if the world is not converted. Call all mankind to conversion. Everything depends on your conversion. (M 31).* To Jelena:*When others cause you some difficulty, do not defend it, rather, pray* (M 31).
To Jelena:*I desire that you be a flower, which blossoms for Jesus at Christmas. A flower which does not cease to bloom when Christmas has passed. I wish that you have a shepherd's, heart for*

*Jesus.* (M 31). *Dear children, when someone comes to you and asks you a favor, answer by giving. Ifind myself before so many hearts which do not open themselves to me. Pray, so that the world willingly wants to accept my love.* (M 39).
Between June and December, 1984: *Dear children, the love of God has not spread over all the earth. That is why, pray!* (M 40). *Dear children, I wish that the whole world become my children, but they do not want to. I want to give them all things. That is why, pray!* (M 40). *Dear children, I love you so much. When you love me, you will be able to feel it. I bless you in the name of the Most Holy Trinity, and in my name. Go in peace.* (M 40).

**BOA NOVA**
*These are my last apparitions to mankind. With the events which are preparing themselves, and which are near, the power which Satan still holds, will be withdrawn from him. The present century has been under his power. Now that he is consciousof losing the battle, he is becoming more aggressive. He attacks the family, separates husband and wife. He creates divisions among the priests, and even gives himself to physical attacks. Protect yourselves, above all through prayer, through blessed sacred objects, through community prayer.* (BN 20, 10).

**LATEST NEWS (1987)**
*Love your Serbian, Orthodox and Muslim brothers, and the atheists who persecute you.* (DN 2, 73). (Concerning information from Bishop Franic. *All your prayers touch me very much, especially your daily rosary.* (DN 6, 15).

**FR'S. TOMISLAV VLASIC AND SLAVKO BARBARIC (VB)**
The weekly information given by Fr. Tomislav Vlasic and Fr. Slavko Barbaric, to Italian pilgrims, have been edited, in four volumes which we have designated through the abbreviations: VB 1, VB 2, VB 3, VB 4. Here, we re-group the messages, which are not dated, in these four volumes. Each volume gives way to a "limit date"as follows. The first gives some communication from May 24 to December 29, 1984. The second, January 4 to June25, 1985; the third from July to December, 1985; and the fourth, from January 4, 1986, to January 8, 1987.
VB 1 (1984)

*I've already said many times, that peace in the world is in a state of crisis. Become again, brothers to one another Pray and fast more, in order to be saved.* (Sept. 1983, VB 1, 15). *Pray, fast, and let God act. If you want to be very happy, lead a simple, humble life, pray very much, and do not sink into problems. Let God resolve them.* (message also in M 30). *Peace should follow your prayer. Often , prayer said in a loud voice keeps Jesus at a distance, because men want to conquer with their own strength. Then there is no more place for God. Prayers said in a loud voice are good, but they must come from peace in the heart. Even joy and songs can hinder the rise of the groups, if the people deliver themselves only to emotion.* (T. Vlasic, May 24, 1984; collects these teachings as a rule of life, given by Our Lady, VB 133). *When I tell you, pray, pray, do not understand it only as an increase in quantity. What I want is to carry you to a profound continuous desire of God.* (T. Vlasic, VB 1, 39). *The most important thing is to believe. That is, to open one's self to God; pray and fast.* (T. Vlasic, June 1,1984, VB 1, 41).
Response from Our Lady to two questions from Tomislav Vlasic: "Have you come to purify the new renewal movements, which are multiplying?" *It is exactly so.*
"How could Jesus pray all night, without getting tired. What was His method?" *He had a great desire for God, and for the salvation of souls. Prayer is a dialogue with God, a meeting with the Gospel.*

"What do you say about Oriental meditations?" (Zen, Transcendental meditation): *Why do you call them 'meditations,' when it deals with human works? The true meditation is a meeting with Jesus. When you discover joy, interior peace, you must know there is only one God, and only one Mediator, Jesus Christ.* (VB 1, 45). *Your days will not be the same according to whether you pray, or you do not pray* (VB 1 51).

Responses to questions asked by the seers at the request of Tomislav Vlasic: What do you tell the priests and religious? *Be strong in faith and protect the faith of your people.* What do you advise us for advent? *Do what the Church tells you.* Do you want to give a sign for priests? *Have them take the Gospel and they will understand everything.* (T. Vlasic, June 20, 1984. VB 1, 51). *Go to the heart. Words are not sufficient. Go to the heart.* (VB 1, 52).
In the past autumn (1983), Our Lady said: *I would be happy for people, families, to pray a minimum of half-an-hour, in the morning and in the evening.* The people shook their heads at this, stated Fr. Vlasic.

But in the spring of 1984, Our Lady said: *I know that in the parish and in all the parishes, you can pray four hours a day, but you do not understand it yet because you live only for your work. One does not live from work alone, but also from prayer.* As I objected to her: "If one asks so much, people will go away." She replied: *Not even you understand. That makes hardly a sixth of your day* (T. Vlasic, July 31, 1984. VB 1, 55). *You, do not think of wars, of evil, of chastisements. If you think about evil, you are on the road where one meets it. Your role is to accept Divine peace, to live it and spread it.* (VB 1, 61).
To Jelena:*Christians make a mistake in considering the future because they think of wars and of evil. For a Christian, there is only one attitude toward the future. It is hope of salvation.* (ibid). *Your responsibility is to accept Divine peace, to live, and to spread it not through words, but through your life.* (Same communication of T. Vlasic Aug. 2, 1984. VB 1, 63).
To Jelena:*The only attitude of the Christian toward the future is hope of salvation. Those who think only of wars, evils, punishment, do not do well. If you think of evil, punishment, wars, you are on the road to meeting them. Your responsibility is to accept Divine peace, live it and spread it.* (A more ample transmission of the word already cited in VB 1, 61. T. Vlasic, Aug. 12, 1984. VB 1, 81). *If you have not listened to my messages, the day of joy will become for me, a day of sadness.* (S. Barbaric, Dec. 8, 1985. VB 1, 135).
VB 2 (1985)

To Ivan's prayer group: *Even the little things, entrust them to me. Consecrate them to my mission.* (S. Barbaric, Mar. 2, 1985. VB 2, p.40).
To the question: How does one behave before Satan? *Fervent prayer, humility, reciprocal love will prevent Satan from approaching you.*To a question conveyed through Tomislav Vlasic at the beginning of Lent, 1985: What do you most wish for the fast? The Gospa responds insisting on something else: *Honesty, love, humility and sincerity will lead you to me.* (T. Vlasic, Mar. 9, 1985. VB 2, 45).

What should one do in the midst of so many discussions and publications on Medjugorje? *See! Now I am there, in each family, in each home. I am everywhere because I love. Do the same. The world lives from love.* After having repeated a song three times: *Excuse me for making you repeat, but I wish you to sing with the heart. You must really do everything with the heart.* And afterwards, (the seers continue, quoted by T. Vlasic) , she made us know this at the beginning of prayer: *One has to be already prepared. If there are some sins, one must pull them out, otherwise, one will not be able to enter into prayer. If one has concerns, he should submit them to God.* That same evening she said: *Take off your jackets. Here it is warm. Remember what Jesus said: Have faith. You must abandon yourselves to God.* (All that in preparation for prayer.). *You must not preoccupy yourselves during prayer. During prayer, you must not be preoccupied with your sins. Sins must remain behind.* (Words at the beginning of Lent, at the end of Feb. or the beginning of Mar. 1985, reported by T. Vlasic, VB 2, 66). *Many come to pray, but do not enter into prayer.* (T. Vlasic, Apr. 5, 1985. VB 2, 74). *When you have entered into prayer, then you are able to pray for God's plans, because when God is there, he inspires your plans. Do not ask for the blessing, just as you have done the last time. You asked for it and you did not obtain it.* (Because it is not a magic thing, she crowns what God has inspired in you in prayer, observes T. Vlasic, Apr. 5, 1985. VB 2, 75). *Prayer must be enjoyment in God, blossoming in God, be full of peace, be full of joy* (T. Vlasic, Apr. 10, 1985. VB 2, 107). *Many Christians do not ever enter into prayer. They arrive at the beginning, but they remain there.* (ibid). (If you enter into prayer after you have been relieved of all your concerns, remorse, analysis), *then you will be able to ask God to inspire your plans from within. You will feel what God wants,* (inside of you, yourself and your group)*, and then ask for the blessing.* (T. Vlasic, Apr. 10, 1985. VB 2, 112). *Your work will not go well without prayer in the morning. Pray then in the morning, and pray in the evening. Understand that your work cannot be done well without prayer* (Message of autumn 1983, T. Vlasic, Apr. 29, 1985. VB 2, 137). *Come early to church. Sometimes it is better not to come to Mass than to come in a hurry and to return home in a hurry,* (S. Barbaric, May 18,1985, VB 2, 147). *These apparitions are the last for humanity* (T. Vlasic, May31, 1985, VB 2, 165).

To Jelena, message of 1983: *Take me seriously. When God comes among men, he does not come to joke, but to say serious things. It is better to stay in church and pray with faith than to gather together with onlookers near the seers during an apparition.* (Which had then taken place in the presbytery).

Message to the prayer group which had received many messages during Lent and was surprised not to receive any more after Easter: *Thank you to all those who pray and feel my presence. I regret that some individuals say the Gospa is no longer among us. Pray, and you will feel that I am present.* In a meeting of her prayer group, Jelena saw the desert, and in the desert, a tree, and under the tree, where the sun was shining. In this sun, she recognized Jesus Christ. The Gospa told her, among other things: *To this group, many graces have been given, but you must not reject them.* (T. Vlasic, June 15, 1985, VB 2, 18).
VB 3 (1986)

To Jelena's group, toward the beginning of July 1985: *I cannot speak to you. Your hearts are closed. You have not done what I told you, I cannot speak to you. I cannot give you graces as long as you remain closed.* (T.Vlasic, July 13, 1985, VB 3, 15). To Jelena for her group: *Each of you has a special gift which is your own, and can alone understand it interiorly.* To Jelena's prayer group: *It seems when you carry my messages, be on your guard that they are not lost. Carry my messages with humility, in such a way that on seeing happiness in you, persons will desire to be like you. Do not carry my messages to simply throw them to others.* T. Vlasic, July 15, 1985 comments: "Don't go to the cities: Milan, Rome or Turin to cry: 'The Madonna has appeared.' Have them understand it through what you are. " In the middle of June, 1985, Jelena saw a splendid pearl which divided itself, and each part glittered, then it faded. And she heard this explanation: *Jelena, man's heart is like this splendid pearl. When he belongs completely to the Lord, he shines even in the dark ness. But when he is divided, a little to Satan, a little to sin, a little to everything, he fades and is no longer worth any thing.* (S. Barbaric, Aug. 4, 1985, VB 3, 37). To Jelena, during the week of July 28th to August the 4th: *During these days, I wish that you consider this idea: After so long and so much time, I have not met Jesus, my friend. After so long and so much time, I have not encountered my Mother, Mary. In these days, I want to encounter them.* (T. Vlasic, Aug. 5, 1985, VB 3, 39). *Do not be afraid of Satan. That isn 't worth the trouble, because with a humble prayer, and an ardent love, one can disarm him.* (S. Barbaric, Aug. 8, 1985, VB 3, 57).

Prayer given to Jelena for her group: *My soul is full of love like the sea. My heart is full of peace like the river. I am not a saint, but I am invited to be one.* (T. Vlasic, Sept. 10, 1985, VB 3, 97). Against temptations of analysis, which are temptations from the devil: *With respect to sin, it suffices to give it serious consideration, and soon, move ahead and correct the sin. Your humility must be proud* (high minded). *Your pride should be humble. If you have received a gift from God, you must be proud but do not say that it is yours. Say, rather, that it is God's.* (T. Vlasic, Sept. 10, 1985, VB 3, 98).

To Mirjana, in 1984 (Probably Aug. - Sept.): *Every adult is capable of knowing God. The sin of the world lies in this: It does not look for God.* (T. Vlasic, Sept. 10, 1985, VB 3, 98).

To Maria, during her retreat of one week, beginning of September, in response to her question: Have you anything concrete for me? *Yes. I give you my love so that you can give it to others.* (S. Barbaric, Oct. 7, 1985, VB 3, 121).
The Gospa said with sadness: *Those who say, 'I do not believe in God, ' how difficult it will be for them when they will approach the Throne of God and hear the voice: Enter into Hell.* (T. Vlasic, Oct. 8, 1985, VB 3, 127).
To Jelena, three evenings in succession, toward October 10th to 15th: *If you wanted to accept my love, you would never sin.*
On the following evening (the fourth day) **, *Jelena*** asks: Why do you always repeat the same message? *But I don't have anything else to say to you.* And she cries. (T. Vlasic, Oct. 19, 1985, VB 3, 151). *There are many who finish their prayers, even without entering into them.* (ibid 3, 158).
A question from the pilgrims of Milan to Jelena:We have come to you, Dear Mother. When will you come to Milan?
The Gospa's answer through Jelena:*When you open your hearts to me. (T. Vlasic, Oct. 25, 1985, 3, 167).*
Tomislav Vlasic, whom the Blessed Virgin had entrusted with a responsibility through Jelena, asks through the seer, Maria: How should I do it? *Do not worry, I will help you. If you want to be stronger than evil, and grow in goodness, then develop an active conscience.* (T. Vlasic, Nov. 2, 1985, VB 3, 179).
To a prayer group, after an hour in which prayer of petition had prevailed: *Have you forgotten that you are in my hands?* (T. Vlasic, Nov. 16, 1985, VB 3, 201).
VB 4 (1987)

To Jelena and Marijana, a little before February 25th: *Understand that you are nothing, incapable, really nothing. It is the Father who will do everything.* (T. Vlasic, Feb. 25, 1986, VB 4, 39).
To Jelena, for her prayer group, after prayer and fasting: *I have listened to your prayer and yet you will not receive what you have wished. You will receive other things because it is not up to you to glorify yourself but to me to glorify myself in you.* (ibid VB 4, 39). *Do not be afraid. Confide yourself to the Father. Pray, until you are sure that He guides everything. In difficulties, when you carry the cross, sing, be full of joy*

To a group who was praying for a person in crisis: *You cannot do anything. I can change her. You must only love her. Do not create any barriers in her life, because as long as there are barriers, the river foams and rises. Leave her free, like the river. Do not build any more bridges because as long as one builds bridges, the river is restricted and does not flow freely. Leave her free to flow like the river flows.*

A month later the group, frustrated in its prayer, asks: "But how is it that this girl (in Crisis) does not change?" Answer, after a long moment of prayer: *Let her run like the river. Do not create any barriers. Do not build any bridges. Consider well and see how many barriers you have already created, how many bridges you have built. Be attentive not to close her. This young girl is at the point of opening up. She has confidence in you. Be patient still. Understand that you can do nothing. You must only love and leave everything to me.*

To Jelena:*When people ask you to speak about the apparition, say: 'Let us pray together to understand the apparitions of the Gospa. '*
In the prayer group which found the advice from the Gospa too rigid: Why shut down the television? Why not even read the newspaper? *If you look at the programs, if you look at the newspapers,your heads are filled with news, then there is no longer any place for me in your hearts. Pray. Fast. Let God act! Pray for the gift of love, for the gift of faith, for the gift of prayer, for the gift of fasting.* (T. Vlasic, Apr. 17, 1986, VB 4, 63).
To Jelena, for her group: *I beg you, destroy your house made of cardboard which you have built on desires. Thus I will be able to act for you.* (T. Vlasic, Apr. 17, 1986, VB 4, 63).

To Maria , for her prayer group: *Dear Children, seek to make your hearts happy through the means of prayer. Dear Children, be the joy for all mankind, be the hope of mankind. You will only be able to obtain it through the means of prayer. Pray, pray!* (T. Vlasic, May 3, 1986, VB 4, 82).
To the prayer group during the week preceding May 3rd: *I give you the best that I can give anyone. I give myself and my Son.*
To the group on March 25th, on the Feast of the Annunciation: *Today, before God, I say my 'Fiat ' for all of you. I repeat it: I say my 'Fiat ' for all of you. Dear Children, pray, so that in the whole world may come the Kingdom of Love. How mankind would be happy if love reigned!*
To Jelena, during the autumn of 1983: *Dear Children, one lives not only from work, one lives also from prayer.*

Toward May 12th (at the beginning of the Novena of Pentecost) **to** the prayer group: *You will be happy if you do not judge yourselves according to your faults, but if you understand that in your faults even graces are offered to you.* (T. Vlasic, May 18, 1986, VB 4, 93). *Love. If you do not love, you are not able to transmit the testimony. You are not able to witness, neither for me, nor for Jesus.* (S. Barbaric, June 6, 1986, VB 4, 105). *I wish for all of you to be the reflection of Jesus. He will thus illuminate this unfaithful world which moves in darkness* (ibid VB 4, 105). *Pray before the Cross. Special graces come from the Cross. Consecrate yourselves to the Cross. Do not blaspheme neither Jesus nor the Cross.* (S. Barbaric, June 20, 1986, VB 4, 109). *You will have as many graces as you want. That depends on you. You will have love when you want it, as long as you want it. That depends on you.* (T. Vlasic, June 26, 1986, VB 4, 110).
To the prayer group (July 10, 1986), before giving her blessing, at the end of an evaluation of the group: *I thank you for that. You have done well, but do not forget* ***(. .. )****; basically, God's will is decisive.* (T. Vlasic, July 20, 1986, VB 4, 121). *I wish only that for you the Rosary become your life.* (T. Vlasic, Aug. 4, 1986, VB 4, 134). *Read each*
*THURSDAY the Gospel of Matthew, where it is said: No one can serve two masters (...). You cannot serve God and money.* (Mt. 6, 24-34. - T. Vlasic, Aug. 5, 1986, VB 4, 14).
To Jelena, for her group: *I wish only that you would be happy, that you would be filled with joy, that you be filled with peace and announce this joy.* (ibid).
To the prayer group: ***if*** *you would abandon yourselves to me, you will not even feel the passage from this life to the next life. You will begin to live the life of Heaven from this earth.* (T. Vlasic, Aug, 7, 1986, VB 4, 142).
To Jelena, the beginning of September 1986: *Today it is not words nor deeds which are important. The important thing is only to pray, to remain in God.* (T. Vlasic, Sept. 9, 1986, VB 4, 156).
*Many have begun to pray for healing here at Medjugorje, but, when they have returned to their homes, they abandon prayer, forget, and also lose many graces.* (S. Barbaric, Sept. 12, 1986 VB 4, 158).
Message of Jesus through Jelena:*I am joyful, but my joy is not complete until you are filled with joy. You are not yet filled with joy because you are not yet at the stage of understanding my immense love.* (T. Vlasic, Oct. 8, 1986, VB 4, 167). Answer from the Gospa through a seer, to Tomislav Vlasic, who was confronted with problems dealing with truth: "Should I write, answer these injustices, these lies?" *Do not waste your time. Pray and love. You cannot even imagine how powerful God is.* (T. Vlasic, Dec. 29, 1986, VB 4, 213).
To Vicka: *Do you want to offer yourself, also, for the salvation of the world? I need your sacrifices. To a group from the parish of Medjugorje: Come at 11 o 'clock at night to the place of the apparitions (...). Come at three o'clock in the morning to pray at the place of the Apparition. Come at one o'clock in the morning to Krizevac. Come and pray all night.* It is to Ivan's group that these messages of nocturnal prayer were addressed on the hill of the first apparitions, or at Krizevac. (T. Vlasic, Dec. 31, 1986, VB 4, 220).

# Prayer Intentions
# Given By The Gospa At Medjugorje

We group these intentions according to the principal focus of interest: God, His plan, His word, the pastors, prayer and fasting, Medjugorje, peace, and resurrection.

## LET US PRAY

**GOD**
For the triumph of Jesus (Sept. 9, 1984). For the glorification of God through us (Jan. 16, 1986). For a knowledge of the glory of the Lord (Nov. 28, 1985). For the experience of joy, caused by a meeting with Jesus (Dec. 11, 1986) For God's blessing (Nov. 6, 1986). For the outpouring of the Holy Spirit (Mar. - Apr., 1983; May 9, 1985). For the coming of the Spirit of Truth (June 9, 1984). For parish renewal by the Holy Spirit (Mar. 30, 1984). For obtaining the gifts of the Holy Spirit (Apr. 17, 1986).
**HIS PLAN** For the realization of God's plan (Oct. 24, 1984). For the knowledge of our role in God's plan (Jan. 25, 1987). For the accomplishment of all the plans which God wants to realize through us (Jan. 30, 1986). For the conversion of Satan's trials, to the glory of God (Feb. 7, 1985).
**HIS WORD**
For anchoring the word of God in our hearts, through daily meditation of Holy Scriptures (Apr. 19, 1984). For learning to pray and to read the Bible in the family (Feb. 14, 1985).
**PASTORS OF THE CHURCH**
For the Pope (Nov. 1981). For the Bishop (May 25, 1983, a frequent intention.). For the authorities of the Church (Mar. - Apr., 1983).
**PRAYER AND FASTING**
For learning to pray with love (Nov. 29, 1984). To pray without ceasing (Nov. 13, 1983). For our prayer to become a channel for others (Nov. 17, 1984). For learning in prayer, the path of joy. (Feb. 25, 1987). For prayer to lead us to humility (Feb. 10, 1984). For the world's understanding that prayer is the only road to peace (Oct. 29, 1983). For our learning to fast through love and not only through habit (Sept. 20, 1984). For the avoidance of wars and catastrophes, through our prayer and our fasting (July 27, 1982).
**CONVERSION AND RECONCILIATION**
For the conversion and reconciliation of the world (October 15, 19 83). For the conversion of sinners (Aug. 2, 1984). For the world to become aware of sin, in which it is floundering (Feb. 17, 1984). For the conversion of all mankind (Apr. 4, 1984). For world understanding of the last call of Mary to conversion (May 2, 19 82). For receiving, each month, the Sacrament of Reconciliation (Transfiguration 1982). For the reconciliation of mankind with God, and with one another (June 26, 1981).
**PURGATORY**
For the souls in Purgatory, our future intercessors (Nov. 6, 1985). For concerned souls, who are in Purgatory (July 21, 1982). For the souls of Purgatory who do not receive prayers of intercession (Ju ly 21, 1982).
**MEDJUGORJE**
For the realization of all of Mary's plans at Medjugorje (Sept. 27, 1984) 2E For the continuation of Mary's presence at Medjugorje (Jan. 2, 1985). For the understanding of all that Mary gives us at Medjugorje (Apr.25, 1987). For defeating Satan's objectives in the parish (Aug. 1, 1985). The Church recognition of the supernatural character of Medjugorje (June 3, 1983).
**LOVE AND PEACE**

For obtaining the gift of love (May 28, 1985). For our understanding of the love-sacrifice, by loving those who harm us (Oct. 7, 1985). For our conversion into good, through love, that which Satan seeks to destroy and have for himself (July 31, 1986). For our understanding of Mary's love for us (Mar. 1, 1982). For the peace granted to those who pray to God (Oct. 23, 1986). For peace and humility of heart (Feb. 11, 1984). For the growth of a great peace and a great love in us (Sept. 29, 1983).

---

**ABBREVIATIONS**

Ba Barbaric, Slavko: (Account of the inner locutions of Jelena Vasilj and Marijana Vasilj.)

Bl Blais, Yves-Maria: (Apparitions of Medjugorje, 500 Messages to Live) Montreal, Queen of Peace, 1986

BN (Boa Nova), Sameiro, 4700 Braga, Portugal.

Bo Botta, M. and Frigerio: (The Apparitions of Medjugorje), Pessano, 1984.

Bu Bubalo, Janko: (A Thousand Encounters With the Blessed Virgin), Paris, O.E.I.L. 1984.

C Castella, Andre, and Ljubic: (Medjugorje, Invitation for Prayer and Conversion), Hauteville, Paris, 1986. Reference to book of Ljubic Lj.

CP (Parish Chronicle), from Fr. Tomislav Vlasic, 1981.

D Dugandzic, Ivan: (Chronological Study of the Apparitions).

DN (Is the Virgin Mary Appearing at Medjugorje?) and supplemental update s by Fr. Rene Laurentin, December 1984 through July 1987.[1]

DV Diaries of Vicka: July 1981 through March, 1982. (DV #1, #2, #3.)

EM (Medical and Scientific Studies of the Apparitions of Medjugorje), H. = Joyeux and R. Laurentin, O.E.I.L. Paris, 1985)

Fl Faricy, Robt. and Rooney, Lucy: (Medjugorje, Mary the Queen of Peace) = Tequi, Paris, 1984.

F2 Faricy, R. (The Heart of Medjugorje; Mary speaks to the World). Prefac e by R. Laurentin, Fayard, 1986.

Fr Fr. Frigerio: (Scientific Study of Medjugorje) Como, Mescat, 1986.

G (Gebetsaktion Medjugorje) Wien. (German text: "Action of Prayer in Medjugorje")

J Jelena:(Journal), as transmitted to Fr. Tomislav Vlasic.

K Kraljevic, Svetozar: (The Apparitions of Medjugorje) Fayard, 1984.

L1 Laurentin, Rene: (Is the Virgin Mary Appearing at Medjugorje?) 1984

L2 Laurentin, Rene: (Medjugorje, The Story and Messages of the Apparition s) O.E.I.L. Paris, 1986

L3 (Medjugorje) presented by R. Laurentin, DDB, Paris, 1987.

Lj Ljubic, Marija: (The Virgin Appears in Yugoslavia), Hauteville, Parvis , January, 1985.

M Miravalle, Mark: (The Message of Medjugorje), Doctorate Thesis, University Press of America, 1986.

MG (Messages of
THURSDAY), Lecco, Ruscomviaggi, 1987. (In Italian)

MM (Messages of Mary) 15 rue du Champ du Pardon, 76000 Rouen, France.

T Totto, George: (Medjugorje, Our Lady's Parish) Medjugorje Information Service, St. Leonard's on the Sea, England, 1985.

VB Vlasic, Tomislav and Barbaric, Slavko: Four volumes of meditations on Our Lady's messages, 1984 through 1987. (In the United States, the first two volumes are known as the Grey Book and Blue Book). Friends of Medjugorje, West, Texas.

[1]. In the United States, these supplemental updates include: "The Apparitions at Medjugorje Prolonged" and, "Latest News of Medjugorje" published by The Riehle Foundation.

# CHAPTER II.
# MESSAGES FOLLOWING (1987-2014)

**Monthly Messages**
Following the main body of the messages (1981 to 1987), Our Lady's messages quickly reduced in frequency, both for private and public messages. From this point forward, many of the public messages only occur on a monthly basis. Perhaps one of the reasons for this is because Our Lady had already said everything She intended to say, and now focusses mostly on messages of encouragement. From here on out, the messages will be organized by visionary, beginning with Marija.

## Part I.
## Monthly Messages to Marija Pavlovic
## (1987-2013)

On January 8, 1987, Our Lady began giving public messages on the 25th of each month. These messages are given entirely through Marija Pavlovic, and were obtained from the parish in Medjugorje (Information Center MIR Medjugorje, http://www.medjugorje.hr).

***January 25, 1987*** *The first apparition of the 25th of the month, given to Marija, for the parish: "Today I want to appeal to all of you to start living a new life from this day on. Dear children, I wish that you would understand that God has chosen each one of you to have a part in the great plan for the salvation of mankind. You cannot fully understand how great your role is in God's design. For that reason, pray, dear children, so that through prayer, you may be able to know your role in God's plan. I am with you, so that you may be able to realize it fully."*

***January 28, 1987*** *To Mirjana in Sarajevo: "My dear children! I came to you in order to lead you to purity of soul, and then to God. How did you receive me? At the beginning you were fearful, suspicious of the children I had chosen. Later on, the majority received me in their heart. They began to put into practice, my maternal recommendation. Unfortunately, that did not last a long time. Whatever be the place where I appear, and with me also my Son, satan also comes. You permitted him to subdue you without realizing that you were being led by him."*

*"It is up to you to realize that your behavior is not permitted by God, but that you immediately stifle the thought. Do not give in dear children. Wipe away from my face, the tears which I shed on seeing you act in this manner. Look around you. Take the time to come to God in the Church. Come into your Father's house. Take the time to meet for family prayer, in order to obtain the grace from God. Remember your deceased; make them happy by offering the Mass. Do not look with scorn on the poor man who is begging a morsel of bread. Do not send him away from your abundant table. Help him and God will help you. It could very well happen that the blessing he leaves you as a sign of gratitude will be fulfilled for you. God may listen to him."*
*"You have forgotten all of that, my children. Satan has influenced you in that. Do not give in. Pray with me! Do not deceive yourselves in thinking, I am good, but my brother, who lives next to me is not good. You will be mistaken. I love you because I am your mother, and I warn you. There are the secrets my children. One does not know what they are; when they learn, it will be too late. Return to prayer! Nothing is more necessary. I would like it if the Lord would have permitted me to show you just a little about the secrets, but, He already gives you enough graces."*
*"Think! What do you offer to Him in return. When was the last time you gave up something for the Lord? I will not blame you further, but once again call you to prayer, fasting, and to penance. If you wish to obtain a grace from the Lord by fasting, then let no one know that you are fasting. If you wish to obtain the grace of God through a gift to the poor, let no one know it, except you and the Lord. Listen to me, my children! Meditate on my message in prayer."*

**February 25, 1987** *"Dear children! Today I want to wrap you all in my mantle and lead you all along the way of conversion. Dear children, I beseech you, surrender to the Lord your entire past, all the evil that has accumulated in your hearts. I want each one of you to be happy, but in sin nobody can be happy. Therefore, dear children, pray, and in prayer you shall realize a new way of joy. Joy will manifest in your hearts and thus you shall be joyful witnesses of that which I and My Son want from each one of you. I am blessing you. Thank you for having responded to my call."*

**March 25, 1987** *"Dear children! Today I am grateful to you for your presence in this place, where I am giving you special graces. I call each one of you to begin to live as of today that life which God wishes of you and to begin to perform good works of love and mercy. I do not want you, dear children, to live the message and be committing sin which is displeasing to me. Therefore, dear children, I want each of you to live a new life without destroying all that God produces in you and is giving you. I give you my special blessing and I am remaining with you on your way of conversion. Thank you for having responded to my call."*

**April 25, 1987** *"Dear children! Today also I am calling you to prayer. You know, dear children, that God grants special graces in prayer. Therefore, seek and pray in order that you may be able to comprehend all that I am giving here. I call you, dear children, to prayer with the heart. You know that without prayer you cannot comprehend all that God is planning through each one of you. Therefore, pray! I desire that through each one of you God's plan may be fulfilled, that all which God has planted in your heart may keep on growing. So pray that God's blessing may protect each one of you from all the evil that is threatening you. I bless you, dear children. Thank you for having responded to my call."*

**May 25, 1987** *"Dear children! I am calling every one of you to start living in God's love. Dear children, you are ready to commit sin, and to put yourselves in the hand of satan without reflecting. I call on each one of you to consciously decide for God and against satan. I am your Mother and, therefore, I want to lead you all to perfect holiness. I want each one of you to be happy here on earth and to be with me in Heaven. That is, dear children, the purpose of my coming here and it's my desire. Thank you for having responded to my call."*

**June 24, 1987** - The prelude to the sixth anniversary of the apparitions: Marija invited the pilgrims to climb Krizevac at 11:30pm at night. A crowd of thousands of people climbed the rocky foot path, without accident. After reciting the Rosary, toward midnight, Marija confided to those who surrounded her: The Blessed Virgin was joyful. First of all, she prayed over all of us. We asked her to bless us. She did. Then she gave us, in substance, this message:
*"Dear children! I want to lead you on the road to conversion. I desire that you convert the world and that your life be a conversion for others. Do not full into infidelity. Let each one of you be completely submitted to my will and to the will of God. Beginning this day, I give you special graces, and in particular the gift of conversion. Let each one of you take home my blessing, and motivate the others to a real conversion."*
Through Our Lady, Marija concluded, God gives us this gift this evening. Before leaving us, Our Lady prayed again over all of us for a moment. We prayed with her for all our needs, for all your needs, for each of you here present. Finally the Blessed Virgin said: *"Go in the peace of God!"*

**June 25, 1987** *"Dear children! Today I thank you and I want to invite you all to God's peace. I want each one of you to experience in your heart that peace which God gives. I want to bless you all today. I am blessing you with God's blessing and I beseech you, dear children, to follow and to live my way. I love you, dear children, and so not even counting the number of times, I go on calling you and I thank you for all that you are doing for my intentions. I beg you, help me to present you to God and to save you. Thank you for having responded to my call."*

**July 25, 1987** *"Dear children! I beseech you to take up the way of holiness beginning today. I love you and, therefore, I want you to be holy. I do not want satan to block you on that way. Dear children, pray and accept all that God is offering you in a way which is bitter. But at the same time, God will reveal every sweetness to whomever begins to go on that way, and He will gladly answer every call of God. Do not attribute importance to petty things. Long for Heaven. Thank you for having responded to my call."*

**August 25, 1987** *"Dear children! Today also I am calling you all in order that each one of you decides to live my messages. God has permitted me also in this year, which the Church has dedicated to me, to be able to speak to you and to be able to spur you on to holiness. Dear children, seek from God the graces which He is giving you through me. I am ready to intercede with God for all that you seek so that your holiness may be complete. Therefore, dear children, do not forget to seek, because God has permitted me to obtain graces for you. Thank you for having responded to my call."*

## The Apparitions are Forbidden in the Rectory,In Search of a Discreet Place (Beginning Sep 1987-1989) The solution: The choir loft in the church.

**September 25, 1987** *"Dear children! Today also I want to call you all to prayer. Let prayer be your life. Dear children, dedicate your time only to Jesus and He will give you everything that you are seeking. He will reveal Himself to you in fullness. Dear children, satan is strong and is waiting to test each one of you. Pray, and that way he will neither be able to injure you nor block you on the way of holiness. Dear children, through prayer grow all the more toward God from day to day. Thank you for having responded to my call."*
**October 25, 1987** *"My dear children! Today I want to call all of you to decide for Paradise. The way is difficult for those who have not decided for God. Dear children, decide and believe that God is offering Himself to you in His fullness. You are invited and you need to answer the call of the Father, who is calling you through me. Pray, because in prayer each one of you will be able to achieve complete love. I am blessing you and I desire to help you so that each one of you might be under my motherly mantle. Thank you for having responded to my call."*
**November 25, 1987** *"Dear children! Today also I call each one of you to decide to surrender again everything completely to me. Only that way will I be able to present each of you to God. Dear children, you know that I love you immeasurably and that I desire each of you for myself, but God has given to all a freedom which I lovingly respect and humbly submit to. I desire, dear children that you help so that everything God has planned in this parish shall be realized. If you do not pray, you shall not be able to recognize my love and the plans which God has for this parish and for each individual. Pray that satan does not entice you with his pride and deceptive strength. I am with you and I want you to believe me, that I love you. Thank you for having responded to my call."*

**December 25, 1987** *"Dear children! Rejoice with me! My heart is rejoicing because of Jesus and today I want to give Him to you. Dear children, I want each one of you to open your heart to Jesus and I will give Him to you with love. Dear children, I want Him to change you, to teach you and to protect you. Today I am praying in a special way for each one of you and I am presenting you to God so He will manifest Himself in you. I am calling you to sincere prayer with the heart so that every prayer of yours may be an encounter with God. In your work and in your everyday life, put God in the first place. I call you today with great seriousness to obey me and to do as I am calling you. Thank you for having responded to my call."*

**January 25, 1988** *"Dear children! Today again I am calling you to complete conversion, which is difficult for those who have not chosen God. God can give you everything that you seek from Him. But you seek God only when sicknesses, problems and difficulties come to you and you think that God is far from you and is not listening and does not hear your prayers. No, dear children, that is not the truth. When you are far from God, you cannot receive graces because you do not seek them with a firm faith. Day by day, I am praying for you, and I want to draw you ever more near to God, but I cannot if you don't want it. Therefore, dear children put your life in God's hands. I bless you all. Thank you for having responded to my call."*

**February 25, 1988** *"Dear children! Today again I am calling you to prayer to complete surrender to God. You know that I love you and am coming here out of love so I could show you the path to peace and salvation for your souls. I want you to obey me and not permit satan to seduce you. Dear children, satan is very strong and, therefore, I ask you to dedicate your prayers to me so that those who are under his influence can be saved. Give witness by your life. Sacrifice your lives for the salvation of the world. I am with you, and I am grateful to you, but in heaven you shall receive the Father's reward which He has promised to you. Therefore, dear children, do not be afraid. If you pray, satan cannot injure you even a little bit because you are God's children and He is watching over you. Pray and let the rosary always be in your hand as a sign to satan that you belong to me. Thank you for having responded to my call."*

**March 25, 1988** *"Dear children! Today also I am inviting you to a complete surrender to God. Dear children, you are not conscious of how God loves you with such a great love because He permits me to be with you so I can instruct you and help you to find the way of peace. This way, however, you cannot discover if you do not pray. Therefore, dear children, forsake everything and consecrate your time to God and God will bestow gifts upon you and bless you. Little children, don't forget that your life is fleeting like a spring flower which today is wondrously beautiful but tomorrow has vanished. Therefore, pray in such a way that your prayer, your surrender to God, may become like a road sign. That way, your witness will not only have value for yourselves but for all eternity. Thank you for having responded to my call."*

**April 25, 1988** *"Dear children! God wants to make you holy. Therefore, through me He is inviting you to complete surrender. Let holy mass be your life. Understand that the church is God's palace, the place in which I gather you and want to show you the way to God. Come and pray. Neither look at others nor slander them, but rather, let your life be a testimony on the way of holiness. Churches deserve respect and are set apart as holy because God, who became man, dwells in them day and night. Therefore, little children, believe and pray that the Father increase your faith, and then ask for whatever you need. I am with you and I am rejoicing because of you conversion and I am protecting you with my motherly mantle. Thank you for having responded to my call."*

**May 25, 1988** *"Dear children! I am inviting you to a complete surrender to God. Pray, little children, that satan may not carry you about like the branches in the wind. Be strong in God. I desire that through you the whole world may get to know the God of joy. By your life bear witness for God's joy. Do not be anxious nor worried. God himself will help you and show you the way. I desire that you love all men with my love. Only in that way can love reign over the world. Little children, you are mine. I love you and want you to surrender to me so that I can lead you to God. Never cease praying so that satan cannot take advantage of you. Pray for the knowledge that you are mine. I bless you with blessings of joy. Thank you for having responded to my call."*

**June 25, 1988** *"Dear children! I am calling you to that love which is loyal and pleasing to God. Little children, love bears everything bitter and difficult for the sake of Jesus who is love. Therefore, dear children, pray that God come to your aid, not however according to your desire, but according to His love. Surrender yourself to God so that He may hear you, console you and forgive everything inside you which is a hindrance on the way of love. In this way God can move your life, and you will grow in love. Dear children, glorify God with a hymn of love so that God's love may be able to grow in you day by day to its fullness. Thank you for having responded to my call."*

**July 25, 1988** *"Dear children! Today I am calling you to a complete surrender to God. Everything you do and everything you possess give over to God so that He can take control in your life as the King of all that you possess. That way, through me, God can lead you into the depths of the spiritual life. Little children, do not be afraid, because I am with you even if you think there is no way out and that satan is in control. I am bringing peace to you I am your mother, the Queen of Peace. I am blessing you with the blessings of joy so that for you God may be everything in your life. Thank you for having responded to my call."*

**August 25, 1988** *"Dear children! Today I invite you all to rejoice in the life which God gives you. Little children, rejoice in God, the Creator, because He has created you so wonderfully. Pray that your life be joyful thanksgiving which flows out of your heart like a river of joy. Little children, give thanks unceasingly for all that you possess, for each little gift which God has given you, so that a joyful blessing always comes down from God upon your life. Thank you for having responded to my call."*

**September 25, 1988** *"Dear children! Today I am inviting all of you, without exception, to the way of holiness in your life. God gave you the grace, the gift of holiness. Pray that you may, more and more, comprehend it, and in that way, you will be able, by your life, to bear witness for God. Dear children, I am blessing you and I intercede to God for you so that your way and your witness may be a complete one and a joy for God. Thank you for having responded to my call."*

**October 25, 1988** *"Dear children! My invitation that you live the messages which I am giving you is a daily one, specially, little children, because I want to draw you closer to the Heart of Jesus. Therefore, little children, I am inviting you today to the prayer of consecration to Jesus, my dear Son, so that each of you may be His. And then I am inviting you to the consecration of my Immaculate Heart. I want you to consecrate yourselves as parents, as families and as parishioners so that all belong to God through my heart. Therefore, little children, pray that you comprehend the greatness of this message which I am giving you. I do not want anything for myself, rather all for the salvation of your soul. Satan is strong and therefore, you, little children, by constant prayer, press tightly against my motherly heart. Thank you for having responded to my call."*

**November 25, 1988** *"Dear children! I call you to prayer, to have an encounter with God in prayer. God gives Himself to you, but He wants you to answer in your own freedom to his invitation. That is why little children during the day, find yourself a special time when you could pray in peace and humility, and have this meeting with God the creator. I am with you and I intercede for you in front of God, so watch in vigil, so that every encounter in prayer be the joy of your contact with God. Thank you for having responded to my call."*

**December 25, 1988** *"Dear children! I call you to peace. Live it in your heart and all around you, so that all will know peace, peace that does not come from you but from God. Little children, today is a great day. Rejoice with me. Glorify the Nativity of Jesus through the peace that I give you. It is for this peace that I have come as your Mother, Queen of Peace. Today I give you my special blessing. Bring it to all creation, so that all creation will know peace. Thank you for having responded to my call."*

# Private Messages to Marija
# *1989-2014*

**January 25, 1989** *"Dear children! Today I am calling you to the way of holiness. Pray that you may comprehend the beauty and the greatness of this way where God reveals himself to you in a special way. Pray that you may be open to everything that God does through you that in your life you may be enabled to give thanks to God and to rejoice over everything that He does through each individual. I give you my blessing. Thank you for having responded to my call."*

**February 25, 1989** *"Dear children! Today I invite you to prayer of the heart. Throughout this season of grace I wish each of you to be united with Jesus, but without unceasing prayer you cannot experience the beauty and greatness of the grace which God is offering you. Therefore, little children, at all times fill your heart with even the smallest prayers. I am with you and unceasingly keep watch over every heart which is given to me. Thank you for having responded to my call."*

**March 25, 1989** *"Dear children! I am calling you to a complete surrender to God. I am calling you to great joy and peace which only God can give. I am with you and I intercede for you every day before God. I call you, little children, to listen to me and to live the messages that I am giving you. Already for years you are invited to holiness but you are still far away. I am blessing you. Thank you for having responded to my call."*

**April 25, 1989** *"Dear children! I am calling you to a complete surrender to God. Let everything that you possess be in the hands of God. Only in that way shall you have joy in your heart. Little children, rejoice in everything that you have. Give thanks to God because everything is God's gift to you. That way in your life you shall be able to give thanks for everything and discover God in everything even in the smallest flower. Thank you for having responded to my call."*

**May 25, 1989** *"Dear children! I invite you now to be open to God. See, children, how nature is opening herself and is giving life and fruits. In the same way I invite you to live with God and to surrender completely to him. Children, I am with you and I want to introduce you continuously to the joy of life. I desire that everyone may discover the joy and love which can be found only in God and which only God can give. God doesn't want anything from you only your surrender. Therefore, children, decide seriously for God because everything else passes away. Only God doesn't pass away. Pray to be able to discover the greatness and joy of life which God gives you. Thank you for having responded to my call."*

**June 25, 1989** *"Dear children! Today I am calling you to live the messages I have been giving you during the past eight years. This is the time of grace and I desire the grace of God be great for every single one of you. I am blessing you and I love you with a special love. Thank you for having responded to call."*

**July 25, 1989** *"Dear children! Today I am calling you to renew your hearts. Open yourselves to God and surrender to him all your difficulties and crosses so, God may turn everything into joy. Little children, you cannot* *open yourselves to God if you do not pray. Therefore, from today, decide to consecrate a time in the day only for an encounter with God in silence. In that way you will be able, with God, to witness my presence here. Little children, I do not wish to force you. Rather freely give God your time, like children of God. Thank you for having responded to my call."*

**August 25, 1989** *"Dear children! I call you to prayer. By means of prayer, little children, you obtain joy and peace. Through prayer you are richer in the mercy of God. Therefore, little children, let prayer be the life of each one of you. Especially I call you to pray so that all those who are far away from God may be converted. Then our hearts shall be richer because God will rule in the hearts of all men. Therefore, little children, pray, pray, pray! Let prayers begin to rule in the whole world. Thank you for having responded to my call."*

**September 25, 1989** *"Dear children! Today I invite you to give thanks to God for all the gifts you have discovered in the course of your life and even for the least gift that you have perceived. I give thanks with you and want all of you to experience the joy of these gifts. And I want God to be everything for each one of you. And then, little children, you can grow continuously on the way of holiness. Thank you for responding to my call."*

**October 25, 1989** *"Dear children! Today also I am inviting you to prayer. I am always inviting you, but you are still far away. Therefore, from today, decide seriously to dedicate time to God. I am with you and I wish to teach you to pray with the heart. In prayer with the heart you shall encounter God. Therefore, little children, pray, pray, pray! Thank you for having responded to my call."*

**November 25, 1989** *"Dear children! I am inviting you for years by these messages which I am giving you. Little children, by means of the messages I wish to make a very beautiful mosaic in your hearts, so I may be able to present each one of you to God like the original image. Therefore, little children, I desire that your decisions be free before God, because He has given you freedom. Therefore pray, so that, free from any influence of satan, we may decide only for God. I am praying for you before God and I am seeking your surrender to God. Thank you for responding to my call."*

**December 25, 1989** *"Dear children! Today I bless you in a special way with my motherly blessing and I am interceding for you before God that He gives you the gift of conversion of the heart. For years I am calling you and exhorting you to a deep spiritual life in simplicity, but you are so cold. Therefore, little children, I ask you to accept and live the messages with seriousness, so that your soul will not be sad when I will no longer be with you, and when I will no longer lead you like insecure children in their first steps. Therefore, little children, every day read the messages that I have given you and transform them into life. I love you and therefore I am calling you all to the way of salvation with God. Thank you for having responded to my call."*

**January 25, 1990** *"Dear children! Today I invite you to decide for God once again and to choose Him before everything and above everything, so that He may work miracles in your life and that day by day your life may become joy with Him. Therefore, little children, pray and do not permit satan to work in your life through misunderstandings, the non-understanding and non-acceptance of one another. Pray that you may be able to comprehend the greatness and the beauty of the gift of life. Thank you for having responded to my call."*

**February 25, 1990** *"Dear children! I invite you to surrender to God. In this season I specially want you to renounce all the things to which you are attached but which are hurting your spiritual life. Therefore, little children, decide completely for God, and do not allow satan to come into your life through those things that hurt both you and your spiritual life. Little children, God is offering Himself to you in fullness, and you can discover and recognize Him only in prayer. Therefore make a decision for prayer. Thank you for having responded to call."*

**March 25, 1990** *"Dear children! I am with you even if you are not conscious of it. I want to protect you from everything that satan offers you and through which he wants to destroy you. As I bore Jesus in my womb, so also, dear children, do I wish to bear you into holiness. God wants to save you and sends you messages through men, nature, and so many things which can only help you to understand that you must change the direction of your life. Therefore, little children, understand also the greatness of the gift which God is giving you through me, so that I may protect you with my mantle and lead you to the joy of life. Thank you for having responded to my call."*

**April 25, 1990** *"Dear children! Today I invite you to accept with seriousness and to live the messages which I am giving you. I am with you and I desire, dear children, that each one of you be ever closer to my heart. Therefore, little children, pray and seek the will of God in your everyday life. I desire that each one of you discover the way of holiness and grow in it until eternity. I will pray for you and intercede for you before God that you understand the greatness of this gift which God is giving me that I can be with you. Thank you for having responded to my call."*

**May 25, 1990** *"Dear children! I invite you to decide with seriousness to live this novena. Consecrate the time to prayer and to sacrifice. I am with you and I desire to help you to grow in renunciation and mortification, that you may be able to understand the beauty of the life of people who go on giving themselves to me in special way. Dear children, God blesses you day after day and desires a change of your life. Therefore, pray that you may have the strength to change your life. Thank you for having responded to my call."*

**June 25, 1990** *"Dear children! Today I desire to thank you for all your sacrifices and for all your prayers. I am blessing you with my special motherly blessing. I invite you all to decide for God, so that from day to day you will*

*discover His will in prayer. I desire, dear children, to call all of you to a full conversion so that joy will be in your hearts. I am happy that you are here today in such great numbers. Thank you for having responded to my call."*
**July 25, 1990** *"Dear children! Today I invite you to peace. I have come here as the Queen of Peace and I desire to enrich you with my motherly peace. Dear children, I love you and I desire to bring all of you to the peace which only God gives and which enriches every heart. I invite you to become carriers and witnesses of my peace to this unpeaceful world. Let peace reign in the whole world which is without peace and longs for peace. I bless you with my motherly blessing. Thank you for having responded to my call."*
**August 25, 1990** *"Dear children! I desire to invite you to take with seriousness and put into practice the messages which I am giving you. You know, little children, that I am with you and I desire to lead you along the same path to heaven, which is beautiful for those who discover it in prayer. Therefore, little children, do not forget that those messages which I am giving you have to be put into your everyday life in order that you might be able to say: "There, I have taken the messages and tried to live them." Dear children, I am protecting you before the heavenly Father by my own prayers. Thank you for having responded to my call."*
**September 25, 1990** *"Dear children! I invite you to pray with the heart in order that your prayer may be a conversation with God. I desire each one of you to dedicate more time to God. Satan is strong and wants to destroy and deceive you in many ways. Therefore, dear children, pray every day that your life will be good for yourselves and for all those you meet. I am with you and I am protecting you even though satan wishes to destroy my plans and to hinder the desires which the Heavenly Father wants to realize here. Thank you for having responded to my call."*
**October 25, 1990** *"Dear children! Today I call you to pray in a special way that you offer up sacrifices and good deeds for peace in the world. Satan is strong and with all his strength, desires to destroy the peace which comes from God. Therefore, dear children, pray in a special way with me for peace. I am with you and I desire to help you with my prayers and I desire to guide you on the path of peace. I bless you with my motherly blessing. Do not forget to live the messages of peace. Thank you for having responded to my call."*
**November 25, 1990** *"Dear children! Today I invite you to do works of mercy with love and out of love for me and for your and my brothers and sisters. Dear children, all that you do for others, do it with great joy and humility towards God. I am with you and day after day I offer your sacrifices and prayers to God for the salvation of the world. Thank you for having responded to my call."*
**December 25, 1990** *"Dear children! Today I invite you in a special way to pray for peace. Dear children, without peace you cannot experience the birth of the little Jesus neither today nor in your daily lives. Therefore, pray the Lord of Peace that He may protect you with His mantle and that He may help you to comprehend the greatness and the importance of peace in your heart. In this way you shall be able to spread peace from your heart throughout the whole world. I am with you and I intercede for you before God. Pray, because satan wants to destroy my plans of peace. Be reconciled with one another and by means of your lives help peace reign in the whole earth. Thank you for having responded to my call."*

---

**January 25, 1991** *"Dear children! Today, like never before, I invite you to prayer. Let your prayer be a prayer for peace. Satan is strong and desires to destroy not only human life, but also nature and the planet on which you live. Therefore, dear children, pray that through prayer you can protect yourselves with God's blessing of peace. God has sent me among you so that I may help you. If you so wish, grasp for the rosary. Even the rosary alone can work miracles in the world and in your lives. I bless you and I remain with you for as long as it is God's will. Thank you for not betraying my presence here and I thank you because your response is serving the good and the peace."*
**February 25, 1991** *"Dear children! Today, I invite you to decide for God, because distance from god is the fruit of the lack of peace in your hearts. God is only peace. Therefore, approach Him through your personal prayer and then live peace in your hearts and in this way peace will flow from your hearts like a river into the whole world. Do not talk about peace, but make peace. I am blessing each of you and each good decision of yours. Thank you for having responded to my call."*
**March 25, 1991** *"Dear children! Again today I invite you to live the passion of Jesus in prayer, and in union with Him. Decide to give more time to God who gave you these days of grace. Therefore, dear children, pray and in a special way renew the love for Jesus for in your hearts. I am with you and I accompany you with my blessing any my prayers. Thank you for having responded to my call."*
**April 25, 1991** *"Dear children! Today I invite you all so that your prayer be prayer with the heart. Let each of you find time for prayer so that in prayer you discover God. I do not desire you to talk about prayer, but to pray. Let your everyday be filled with prayer of gratitude to God for life and for all that you have. I do not desire your life to pass by in words but that you glorify God with deeds. I am with you and I am grateful to God for every moment spent with you. Thank you for having responded to my call."*
**May 25, 1991** *"Dear Children! Today I invite all of you who have heard my message of peace to realize it with seriousness and with love in your life. There are many who think that they are doing a lot by talking about the messages, but do not live them. Dear children, I invite you to life and to change all the negative in you, so that it all turns into the positive and life. Dear children, I am with you and I desire to help each of you to live and by*

*living, to witness the good news. I am here, dear children, to help you and to lead you to heaven, and in heaven is the joy through which you can already live heaven now. Thank you for having responded to my call!"*
**June 25, 1991** *"Dear children! Today on this great day which you have given to me, I desire to bless all of you and to say: these days while I am with you are days of grace. I desire to teach you and help you to walk the way of holiness. There are many people who do not desire to understand my messages and to accept with seriousness what I am saying. But you I therefore call and ask that by your lives and by your daily living you witness my presence. If you pray, God will help you to discover the true reason for my coming. Therefore, little children, pray and read the Sacred Scriptures so that through my coming you discover the message in Sacred Scripture for you. Thank you for having responded to my call."*
**July 25, 1991** *"Dear Children! Today I invite you to pray for peace. At this time peace is being threatened in a special way, and I am seeking from you to renew fasting and prayer in your families. Dear children, I desire you to grasp the seriousness of the situation and that much of what will happen depends on your prayers and you are praying a little bit. Dear children, I am with you and I am inviting you to begin to pray and fast seriously as in the first days of my coming. Thank you for having responded to my call."*
**August 25, 1991** *"Dear Children! Today also I invite you to prayer, now as never before when my plan has begun to be realized. Satan is strong and wants to sweep away my plans of peace and joy and make you think that my Son is not strong in His decisions. Therefore, I call all of you, dear children, to pray and fast still more firmly. I invite you to self-renunciation for nine days so that, with your help, everything that I desire to realize through the secrets I began in Fatima, may be fulfilled. I call you, dear children, to now grasp the importance of my coming and the seriousness of the situation. I want to save all souls and present them to God. Therefore, let us pray that everything I have begun be fully realized. Thank you for having responded to my call."*
**September 25, 1991** *"Dear children! Today in a special way I invite you all to prayer and renunciation. For now as never before satan wants to show the world his shameful face by which he wants to seduce as many people as possible onto the way of death and sin. Therefore, dear children, help my Immaculate Heart to triumph in the sinful world. I beseech all of you to offer prayers and sacrifices for my intentions so I can present them to God for what is most necessary. Forget your desires, dear children, and pray for what God desires, and not for what you desire. Thank you for having responded to my call."*
**October 25, 1991** *"Dear children! Pray! Pray! Pray!"*
**November 25, 1991** *"Dear Children! This time also I am inviting you to prayer. Pray that you might be able to comprehend what God desires to tell you through my presence and through the messages I am giving you. I desire to draw you ever closer to Jesus and to His wounded heart that you might be able to comprehend the immeasurable love which gave itself for each one of you. Therefore, dear children, pray that from your heart would flow a fountain of love to every person both to the one who hates you and to the one who despises you. That way you will be able through Jesus' love to overcome all the misery in this world of sorrows, which is without hope for those who do not know Jesus. I am with you and I love you with the immeasurable love of Jesus. Thank you for all your sacrifices and prayers. Pray so I might be able to help you still more. Your prayers are necessary to me. Thank you for having responded to my call."*
**December 25, 1991** *"Dear children! Today in a special way I bring the little Jesus to you, that He may bless you with His blessing of peace and love. Dear children, do not forget that this is a grace which many people neither understand nor accept. Therefore, you who have said that you are mine, and seek my help, give all of yourself. First of all, give your love and example in your families. You say that Christmas is a family feast. Therefore, dear children, put God in the first place in your families, so that He may give you peace and may protect you not only from war, but also in peace protect you from every satanic attack. When God is with you, you have everything. But when you do not want Him, then you are miserable and lost, and you do not know on whose side you are. Therefore, dear children, decide for God. Then you will get everything. Thank you for having responded to my call."*

---

**January 25, 1992** *"Dear Children! Today, I am inviting you to a renewal of prayer in your families so that way every family will become a joy to my son Jesus. Therefore, dear children, pray and seek more time for Jesus and then you will be able to understand and accept everything, even the most difficult sicknesses and crosses. I am with you and I desire to take you into my heart and protect you, but you have not yet decided. Therefore, dear children, I am seeking for you to pray, so through prayer you would allow me to help you. Pray, my dear little children, so prayer becomes your daily bread. Thank you for having responded to my call."*
**February 25, 1992** *"Dear children! Today I invite you to draw still closer to God through prayer. Only that way will I be able to help you and to protect you from every attack of satan. I am with you and I intercede for you with God, that He protect you. But I need your prayers and your - "Yes." You get lost easily in material and human things, and forget that God is your greatest friend. Therefore, my dear little children, draw close to God so He may protect you and guard you from every evil. Thank you for having responded to my call!"*
**March 25, 1992** *"Dear children! Today as never before I invite you to live my messages and to put them into practice in your life. I have come to you to help you and, therefore, I invite you to change your life because you have taken a path of misery, a path of ruin. When I told you: convert, pray, fast, be reconciled, you took these*

*messages superficially. You started to live them and then you stopped, because it was difficult for you. No, dear children, when something is good, you have to persevere in the good and not think: God does not see me, He is not listening, He is not helping. And so you have gone away from God and from me because of your miserable interest. I wanted to create of you an oasis of peace, love and goodness. God wanted you, with your love and with His help, to do miracles and, thus, give an example. Therefore, here is what I say to you: Satan is playing with you and with your souls and I cannot help you because you are far away from my heart. Therefore, pray, live my messages and then you will see the miracles of God's love in your everyday life. Thank you for having responded to my call."*

**April 25, 1992** *"Dear children! Today also I invite you to prayer. Only by prayer and fasting can war be stopped. Therefore, my dear little children, pray and by your life give witness that you are mine and that you belong to me, because satan wishes in these turbulent days to seduce as many souls as possible. Therefore, I invite you to decide for God and He will protect you and show you what you should do and which path to take. I invite all those who have said "yes" to me to renew their consecration to my Son Jesus and to His Heart and to me so we can take you more intensely as instruments of peace in this unpeaceful world. Medjugorje is a sign to all of you and a call to pray and live the days of grace that God is giving you. Therefore, dear children, accept the call to prayer with seriousness. I am with you and your suffering is also mine. Thank you for having responded to my call."*

**May 25, 1992** *"Dear children! Today also I invite you to prayer, so that through prayer you come still nearer to God. I am with you and I desire to lead you on the path to salvation that Jesus gives you. From day to day, I am nearer to you although you are not aware of it and you do not want to admit that you are only linked to me in a small way with your few prayers. When trials and problems arise, you say, "O God! O Mother! Where are you?" As for me, I only wait for your "Yes" to present to Jesus for Him to fill you with His grace. That is why, once more, please accept my call and start to pray in a new way until prayer becomes joy to you. Then you will discover that God is all-powerful in your daily life. I am with you and I am waiting for you. Thank you for having responded to my call."*

**June 25, 1992** *"Dear children! Today I am happy, even if in my heart there is still a little sadness for all those who have started on this path and then have left it. My presence here is to take you on a new path, the path to salvation. This is why I call you, day after day to conversion. But if you do not pray, you cannot say that you are on the way to being converted. I pray for you and I intercede to God for peace; first peace in your hearts and also peace around you, so that God may be your peace. Thank you for having responded to my call."*

**July 25, 1992** *"Dear children! Today also I invite you to prayer, a prayer of joy so that in these sad days no one amongst you may feel sadness in prayer, but a joyful meeting with God His Creator. Pray, little children, to be able to come closer to me and to feel through prayer what it is I desire from you. I am with you and each day I bless you with my maternal blessing so that Our Lord may fill you abundantly with His grace for your daily life. Give thanks to God for the grace of my being able to be with you because I assure you it is a great grace. Thank you for having responded to my call."*

**August 25, 1992** *"Dear children! Today I desire to tell you that I love you. I love you with my maternal love and I invite you to open yourselves completely to me so that, through each one of you, I can convert and save this world which is full of sin and bad things. That is why, my dear little children, you should open yourselves completely to me so that I may carry you always further toward the marvelous love of God the Creator who reveals Himself to you from day to day. I am with you and I wish to reveal to you and show you the God who loves you. Thank you for having responded to my call."*

**September 25, 1992** *"Dear children! Today again I would like to say to you that I am with you also in these troubled days during which satan wishes to destroy all that my Son Jesus and I are building. He desires especially to destroy your souls. He wants to take you away as far as possible from the Christian life and from the commandments that the Church calls you to live. Satan wishes to destroy everything that is holy in you and around you. This is why, little children, pray, pray, pray to be able to grasp all that God is giving you through my coming. Thank you for having responded to my call."*

**October 25, 1992** *"Dear children! I invite you to prayer now when satan is strong and wishes to make as many souls as possible his own. Pray, dear children, and have more trust in me because I am here in order to help you and to guide you on a new path toward a new life. Therefore, dear little children, listen and live what I tell you because it is important for you when I shall not be with you any longer that you remember my words and all that I told you. I call you to begin to change your life from the beginning and that you decide for conversion not with words but with your life. Thank you for having responded to my call."*

**November 25, 1992** *"Dear Children! Today, more than ever, I am calling you to pray. May your life become a continuous prayer. Without love you cannot pray. That is why I am calling you to love God, the Creator of your lives, above everything else. Then you will come to know God and will love Him in everything as He loves you. Dear children, it is a grace that I am with you. That is why you should accept and live my messages for your own good. I love you and that is why I am with you, in order to teach you and to lead you to a new life of conversion and renunciation. Only in this way will you discover God and all that which now seems so far away from you. Therefore, my dear children, pray. Thank you for having responded to my call."*

**December 25, 1992** *"Dear children! I desire to place all of you under my mantle and protect you from all satanic attacks. Today is a day of peace, but in the whole world there is a great lack of peace. That is why I call you all to build a new world of peace with me through prayer. This I cannot do without you, and this is why I call all of you with my motherly love and God will do the rest. So, open yourselves to God's plan and to His designs to be able to cooperate with Him for peace and for everything that is good. Do not forget that your life does not belong to you, but is a gift with which you must bring joy to others and lead them to eternal life. May the tenderness of the little Jesus always accompany you. Thank you for having responded to my call."*

**January 25, 1993** *"Dear children! Today I call you to accept and live my messages with seriousness. These days are the days when you need to decide for God, for peace and for the good. May every hatred and jealousy disappear from your life and your thoughts, and may there only dwell love for God and for your neighbor. Thus, and only thus shall you be able to discern the signs of the time. I am with you and I guide you into a new time, a time which God gives you as grace so that you may get to know him more. Thank you for having responded to my call."*

**February 25, 1993** *"Dear children! Today I bless you with my motherly blessing and I invite you all to conversion. I wish that each of you decide for a change of life and that each of you works more in the Church not through words and thoughts but through example, so that your life may be a joyful testimony for Jesus. You cannot say that you are converted, because your life must become a daily conversion. In order to understand what you have to do, little children, pray and God will give you what you completely have to do, and where you have to change. I am with you and place you all under my mantle. Thank you for having responded to my call."*

**March 25, 1993** *"Dear children! Today like never I call you to pray for peace, for peace in your hearts, peace in your families and peace in the whole world, because satan wants war, wants lack of peace, wants to destroy all which is good. Therefore, dear children, pray, pray, pray. Thank you for having responded to my call."*

**April 25, 1993** *"Dear children! Today I invite you all to awaken your hearts to love. Go into nature and look how nature is awakening and it will be a help to you to open your hearts to the love of God, the Creator. I desire you to awaken love in your families so that where there is unrest and hatred, love will reign and when there is love in your hearts then there is also prayer. And, dear children, do not forget that I am with you and I am helping you with my prayer that God may give you the strength to love. I bless and love you with my motherly love. Thank you for having responded to my call."*

**May 25, 1993** *"Dear children! Today I invite you to open yourselves to God by means of prayer so the Holy Spirit may begin to work miracles in you and through you. I am with you and I intercede before God for each one of you because, dear children, each one of you is important in my plan of salvation. I invite you to be carriers of good and peace. God can give you peace only if you convert and pray. Therefore, my dear little children, pray, pray, pray and do that which the Holy Spirit inspires you. Thank you for having responded to my call."*

**June 25, 1993** *"Dear children! Today I also rejoice at your presence here. I bless you with my motherly blessing and intercede for each one of you before God. I call you anew to live my messages and to put them into life and practice. I am with you and bless all of you day by day. Dear children, these are special times and, therefore, I am with you to love and protect you; to protect your hearts from satan and to bring you all closer to the heart of my Son, Jesus. Thank you for having responded to my call."*

***July 25, 1993*** *"Dear children! I thank you for your prayers and for the love you show toward me. I invite you to decide to pray for my intentions. Dear children, offer novenas, making sacrifices wherein you feel the most bound. I want your life to be bound to me. I am your Mother, little children, and I do not want satan to deceive you for He wants to lead you the wrong way, but he cannot if you do not permit him. Therefore, little children, renew prayer in your hearts, and then you will understand my call and my live desire to help you. Thank you for having responded to my call."*

**August 25, 1993** *"Dear children! I want you to understand that I am your Mother, that I want to help you and call you to prayer. Only by prayer can you understand and accept my messages and practice them in your life. Read Sacred Scripture, live it, and pray to understand the signs of the times. This is a special time, therefore, I am with you to draw you close to my heart and the heart of my Son, Jesus. Dear little children, I want you to be children of the light and not of the darkness. Therefore, live what I am telling you. Thank you for having responded to my call."*

**September 25, 1993** *"Dear children! I am your Mother and I invite you to come closer to God through prayer because only He is your peace, your savior. Therefore, little children, do not seek comfort in material things, but rather seek God. I am praying for you and I intercede before God for each individual. I am looking for your prayers that you accept me and accept my messages as in the first days of the apparitions and only then when you open your hearts and pray will miracles happen. Thank you for having responded to my call."*

**October 25, 1993** *"Dear children! These years I have been calling you to pray, to live what I am telling you, but you are living my messages a little. You talk, but do not live, that is why little children, this war is lasting so long. I invite you to open yourselves to God and in your hearts to live with God, living the good and giving witness to my messages. I love you and wish to protect you from every evil, but you do not desire it. Dear children, I cannot help you if you do not live God's commandments, if you do not live the mass, if you do not give up sin. I invite you to be apostles of love and goodness. In this world of unrest give witness to God and God's love, and God will bless you and give you what you seek from Him. Thank you for having responded to my call."*

**November 25, 1993** *"Dear children! I invite you in this time like never before to prepare for the coming of Jesus. Let little Jesus reign in your hearts and only then when Jesus is your friend will you be happy. It will not be difficult for you either to pray or offer sacrifices or to witness Jesus' greatness in your life because He will give you strength and joy in this time. I am close to you by my intercession and prayer and I love and bless all of you. Thank you for having responded to my call."*
**December 25, 1993** *"Dear children! Today I rejoice with the little Jesus and I desire that Jesus' joy may enter into every heart. Little children, with the message I give you a blessing with my son Jesus, so that in every heart peace may reign. I love you, little children, and I invite all of your to come closer to me by means of prayer. You talk and talk but do not pray. Therefore, little children, decide for prayer. Only in this way will you be happy and God will give you what you seek from Him. Thank you for having responded to my call."*
**January 25, 1994** *"Dear children! You are all my children. I love you. But, little children, you must not forget that without prayer you cannot be close to me. In these times satan wants to create disorder in your hearts and in your families. Little children, do not give in. You should not allow him to lead you and your life. I love you and intercede before God for you. Little children, pray. Thank you for having responded to my call."*
**February 25, 1994** *"Dear children! Today I thank you for your prayers. All of you have helped me so that this war may end as soon as possible. I am close to you and I pray for each one of you and I beg you: pray, pray, pray. Only through prayer can we defeat evil and protect all that satan wants to destroy in your lives. I am your Mother and I love you all equally, and I intercede for you before God. Thank you for having responded to my call."*
**March 25, 1994** *"Dear children! Today I rejoice with you and I invite you to open yourselves to me, and become an instrument in my hands for the salvation of the world. I desire, little children, that all of you who have felt the odor of holiness through these messages which I am giving you to carry, to carry it into this world, hungry for God and God's love. I thank you all for having responded in such a number and I bless you all with my motherly blessing. Thank you for having responded to my call."*
**April 25, 1994** *"Dear children! Today I invite you to decide to pray according to my intention. Little children, I invite each one of you to help my plan to be realized through this parish. Now I invite you in a special way, little children, to decide to go along the way of holiness. Only this way will you be close to me. I love you and I desire to conduct you all with me to Paradise. But, if you do not pray and if you are not humble and obedient to the messages which I am giving you, I cannot help you. Thank you for having responded to my call."*
**May 25, 1994** *"Dear children! I invite you all to have more trust in me and to live my messages more deeply. I am with you and I intercede before God for you but also I wait for your hearts to open up to my messages. Rejoice because God loves you and gives you the possibility to convert every day and to believe more in God the Creator. Thank you having responded to my call."*
**June 25, 1994** *"Dear children! Today I rejoice in my heart in seeing you all present here. I bless you and I call you all to decide to live my messages which I give you here. I desire, little children, to guide you all to Jesus because He is your salvation. Therefore, little children, the more you pray the more you will be mine and of my Son, Jesus. I bless you all with my motherly blessing and I thank you for having responded to my call."*
**July 25, 1994** *"Dear children! Today I invite you to decide to give time patiently for prayer. Little children, you cannot say you are mine and that you have experienced conversion through my messages if you are not ready to give time to God every day. I am close to you and I bless you all. Little children, do not forget that if you do not pray you are not close to me, nor are you close to the Holy Spirit who leads you along the path to holiness. Thank you for having responded to my call."*
**August 25, 1994** *"Dear children! Today I am united with you in prayer in a special way, praying for the gift of the presence of my most beloved son in your home country. Pray, little children, for the health of my most beloved son, who suffers, and whom I have chosen for these times. I pray and intercede before my Son, Jesus, so that the dream that your fathers had may be fulfilled. Pray, little children, in a special way, because satan is strong and wants to destroy hope in your heart. I bless you. Thank you for having responded to my call."*
**September 25, 1994** *"Dear children! I rejoice with you and I invite you to prayer. Little children, pray for my intention. Your prayers are necessary to me, through which I desire to bring you closer to God. He is your salvation. God sends me to help you and to guide you towards paradise, which is your goal. Therefore, little children, pray, pray, pray. Thank you for having responded to my call."*
**October 25, 1994** *"Dear children! I am with you and I rejoice today because the Most High has granted me to be with you and to teach you and to guide you on the path of perfection. Little children, I wish you to be a beautiful bouquet of flowers which I wish to present to God for the day of All Saints. I invite you to open yourselves and to live, taking the saints as an example. Mother Church has chosen them, that they may be an impulse for your daily life. Thank you for having responded to my call!"*
**November 25, 1994** *"Dear children! Today I call you to prayer. I am with you and I love you all. I am your Mother and I wish that your hearts be similar to my heart. Little children, without prayer you cannot live and say that you are mine. Prayer is joy. Prayer is what the human heart desires. Therefore, get closer, little children, to my Immaculate Heart and you will discover God. Thank you for having responded to my call."*
**December 25, 1994** *"Dear children! Today I rejoice with you and I am praying with you for peace: peace in your hearts, peace in your families, peace in your desires, peace in the whole world. May the King of Peace bless*

*you today and give your peace. I bless you and I carry each one of your in my heart. Thank you for having responded to my call."*

**January 25, 1995** *"Dear children! I invite you to open the door of your heart to Jesus as the flower opens itself to the sun. Jesus desires to fill your hearts with peace and joy. You cannot, little children, realize peace if you are not at peace with Jesus. Therefore, I invite you to confession so Jesus may be your truth and peace. So, little children, pray to have the strength to realize what I am telling you. I am with your and I love you. Thank you for having responded to my call."*

**February 25, 1995** *"Dear children! Today I invite you to become missionaries of my messages, which I am giving here through this place that is dear to me. God has allowed me to stay this long with you and therefore, little children, I invite you to live with love the messages I give and to transmit them to the whole world, so that a river of love flows to people who are full of hatred and without peace. I invite you, little children, to become peace where there is no peace and light where there is darkness, so that each heart accepts the light and the way of salvation. Thank you for having responded to my call."*

**March 25, 1995** *"Dear Children! Today I invite you to live the peace in your hearts and families. There is no peace, little children, where there is no prayer and there is no love, where there is no faith. Therefore, little children, I invite you all, to decide again today for conversion. I am close to you and I invite you all, little children, into my embrace to help you, but you do not want and in this way, satan is tempting you, and in the smallest thing, your faith disappears. This is why little children, pray and through prayer, you will have blessing and peace. Thank you for having responded to my call."*

**April 25, 1995** *"Dear children! Today I call you to love. Little children, without love you can neither live with God nor with brother. Therefore, I call all of you to open your hearts to the love of God that is so great and open to each one of you. God, out of love for man, has sent me among you to show you the path of salvation, the path of love. If you do not first love God, then you will neither be able to love neighbor nor the one you hate. Therefore, little children, pray and through prayer you will discover love. Thank you for having responded to my call."*

**May 25, 1995** *"Dear Children! I invite you, little children, to help me through your prayers so that as many hearts as possible come close to my Immaculate Heart. Satan is strong and with all his forces wants to bring closer the most people possible to himself and to sin. That is why he is on the prowl to snatch more every moment. I beg you, little children, pray and help me to help you. I am your mother and I love you and that is why I wish to help you. Thank you for having responded to my call."*

**June 25, 1995** *"Dear Children! Today I am happy to see you in such great numbers, that you have responded and have come to live my messages. I invite you, little children, to be my joyful carriers of peace in this troubled world. Pray for peace so that as soon as possible a time of peace, which my heart waits impatiently for, may reign. I am near to you, little children, and intercede for every one of you before the Most High. I bless you with my motherly blessing. Thank you for having responded to my call."*

**July 25, 1995** *"Dear children! Today I invite you to prayer because only in prayer can you understand my coming here. The Holy Spirit will enlighten you to understand that you must convert. Little children, I wish to make of you a most beautiful bouquet prepared for eternity but you do not accept the way of conversion, the way of salvation that I am offering you through these apparitions. Little children, pray, convert your hearts and come closer to me. May good overcome evil. I love you and bless you. Thank you for having responded to my call."*

**August 25, 1995** *"Dear children! Today I invite you to prayer. Let prayer be life for you. A family cannot say that it is in peace if it does not pray. Therefore, let your morning begin with morning prayer, and the evening end with thanksgiving. Little children, I am with you, and I love you and I bless you and I wish for every one of you to be in my embrace. You cannot be in my embrace if you are not ready to pray every day. Thank you for having responded to my call."*

**September 25, 1995** *"Dear Children! Today I invite you to fall in love with the Most Holy Sacrament of the Altar. Adore Him, little children, in your Parishes and in this way you will be united with the entire world. Jesus will become your friend and you will not talk of Him like someone whom you barely know. Unity with Him will be a joy for you and you will become witnesses to the love of Jesus that He has for every creature. Little children, when you adore Jesus you are also close to me. Thank you for having responded to my call."*

**October 25, 1995** *"Dear Children! Today I invite you to go into nature because there you will meet God the Creator. Today I invite you, little children, to thank God for all that He gives you. In thanking Him you will discover the Most High and all the goods that surround you. Little children, God is great and His love for every creature is great. Therefore, pray to be able to understand the love and goodness of God. In the goodness and the love of God the Creator, I also am with you as a gift. Thank you for having responded to my call."*

**November 25, 1995** *"Dear Children! Today I invite you that each of you begin again to love, in the first place, God who saved and redeemed each of you, and then brothers and sisters in your proximity. Without love, little children, you cannot grow in holiness and cannot do good deeds. Therefore, little children, pray without ceasing that God reveals His love to you. I have invited all of you to unite yourselves with me and to love. Today I am with you and invite you to discover love in your hearts and in the families. For God to live in your hearts, you must love. Thank you for having responded to my call."*

**December 25, 1995** *"Dear Children! Today I also rejoice with you and I bring you little Jesus, so that He may bless you. I invite you, dear children, so that your life may be united with Him. Jesus is the King of Peace and only He can give you the peace that you seek. I am with you and I present you to Jesus in a special way, now in this new time in which one should decide for Him. This time is the time of grace. Thank you for having responded to my call."*
**January 25, 1996** *"Dear Children! Today I invite you to decide for peace. Pray that God give you the true peace. Live peace in your hearts and you will understand, dear children, that peace is the gift of God. Dear children, without love you cannot live peace. The fruit of peace is love and the fruit of love is forgiveness. I am with you and I invite all of you, little children, that before all else forgive in the family and then you will be able to forgive others. Thank you for having responded to my call."*
**February 25, 1996** *"Dear children! Today I invite you to conversion. This is the most important message that I have given you here. Little children, I wish that each of you become a carrier of my messages. I invite you, little children, to live the messages that I have given you over these years. This time is a time of grace. Especially now, when the Church also is inviting you to prayer and conversion. I also, little children, invite you to live my messages that I have given you during the time since I appear here. Thank you for having responded to my call."*
**March 25, 1996** *"Dear children! I invite you to decide again to love God above all else. In this time when due to the spirit of consumerism one forgets what it means to love and to cherish true values, I invite you again, little children, to put God in the first place in your life. Do not let satan attract you through material things but, little children, decide for God who is freedom and love. Choose life and not death of the soul, little children, and in this time when you meditate upon the suffering and death of Jesus I invite you to decide for life which blossomed through the Resurrection, and that your life may be renewed today through conversion that shall lead you to eternal life. Thank you for having responded to my call."*
**April 25, 1996** *"Dear children! Today I invite you again to put prayer in the first place in your families. Little children, when God is in the first place, then you will, in all that you do, seek the will of God. In this way your daily conversion will become easier. Little children, seek with humility that which is not in order in your hearts, and you shall understand what you have to do. Conversion will become a daily duty that you will do with joy. Little children, I am with you, I bless you all and I invite you to become my witnesses by prayer and personal conversion. Thank you for having responded to my call."*
**May 25, 1996** *"Dear children! Today I wish to thank you for all your prayers and sacrifices that you, during this month which is consecrated to me, have offered to me. Little children, I also wish that you all become active during this time that is through me connected to heaven in a special way. Pray in order to understand that you all, through your life and your example, ought to collaborate in the work of salvation. Little children, I wish that all people convert and see me and my son, Jesus, in you. I will intercede for you and help you to become the light. In helping the other, your soul will also find salvation. Thank you for having responded to my call."*
**June 25, 1996** *"Dear children! Today I thank you for all the sacrifices you have offered me these days. Little children, I invite you to open yourselves to me and to decide for conversion. Your hearts, little children, are still not completely open to me and therefore, I invite you again to open to prayer so that in prayer the Holy Spirit will help you, that your hearts become of flesh and not of stone. Little children, thank you for having responded to my call and for having decided to walk with me toward holiness."*
**July 25, 1996** *"Dear children! Today I invite you to decide every day for God. Little children, you speak much about God, but you witness little with your life. Therefore, little children, decide for conversion, that your life may be true before God, so that in the truth of your life you witness the beauty God gave you. Little children, I invite you again to decide for prayer because through prayer, you will be able to live the conversion. Each one of you shall become in the simplicity, similar to a child which is open to the love of the Father. Thank you for having responded to my call."*
**August 25, 1996** *"Dear children! Listen, because I wish to speak to you and to invite you to have more faith and trust in God, who loves you immeasurably. Little children, you do not know how to live in the grace of God, that is why I call you all anew, to carry the word of God in your heart and in thoughts. Little children, place the Sacred Scripture in a visible place in your family, and read and live it. Teach your children, because if you are not an example to them, children depart into godlessness. Reflect and pray and then God will be born in your heart and your heart will be joyous. Thank you for having for responded to my call."*
**September 25, 1996** *"Dear children! Today I invite you to offer your crosses and suffering for my intentions. Little children, I am your mother and I wish to help you by seeking for you the grace from God. Little children, offer your sufferings as a gift to God so they become a most beautiful flower of joy. That is why, little children, pray that you may understand that suffering can become joy and the cross the way of joy. Thank you for having for responded to my call."*
**October 25, 1996** *"Dear children! Today I invite you to open yourselves to God the Creator, so that He changes you. Little children, you are dear to me. I love you all and I call you to be closer to me and that your love towards my Immaculate Heart be more fervent. I wish to renew you and lead you with my Heart to the Heart of Jesus, which still today suffers for you and calls you to conversion and renewal. Through you, I wish to renew the world. Comprehend, little children, that you are today the salt of the earth and the light of the world. Little*

*children, I invite you and I love you and in a special way implore: Convert!" Thank you for having responded to my call."*

**November 25, 1996** *"Dear children! Today, again, I invite you to pray, so that through prayer, fasting and small sacrifices you may prepare yourselves for the coming of Jesus. May this time, little children, be a time of grace for you. Use every moment and do good, for only in this way will you feel the birth of Jesus in your hearts. If with your life you give an example and become a sign of God's love, joy will prevail in the hearts of men. Thank you for having responded to my call."*

**December 25, 1996** *"Dear children! Today I am with you in a special way, holding little Jesus in my lap and I invite you, little children, to open yourselves to His call. He calls you to joy. Little children, joyfully live the messages of the Gospel, which I am repeating in the time since I am with you. Little children, I am your Mother and I desire to reveal to you the God of love and the God of peace. I do not desire for your life to be in sadness but that it be realized in joy for eternity, according to the Gospel. Only in this way will your life have meaning. Thank you for having responded to my call."*

**January 25, 1997** *"Dear children! I invite you to reflect about your future. You are creating a new world without God, only with your own strength and that is why you are unsatisfied and without joy in the heart. This time is my time and that is why, little children, I invite you again to pray. When you find unity with God, you will feel hunger for the word of God and your heart, little children, will overflow with joy. You will witness God's love wherever you are. I bless you and I repeat to you that I am with you to help you. Thank you for having responded to my call."*

**February 25, 1997** *"Dear children! Today I invite you in a special way to open yourselves to God the Creator and to become active. I invite you, little children, to see at this time who needs your spiritual or material help. By your example, little children, you will be the extended hands of God, which humanity is seeking. Only in this way will you understand, that you are called to witness and to become joyful carriers of God's word and of His love. Thank you for having responded to my call."*

**March 25, 1997** *"Dear children! Today, in a special way, I invite you to take the cross in the hands and to meditate on the wounds of Jesus. Ask of Jesus to heal your wounds, which you, dear children, during your life sustained because of your sins or the sins of your parents. Only in this way, dear children, you will understand that the world is in need of healing of faith in God the Creator. By Jesus' passion and death on the cross, you will understand that only through prayer you, too, can become true apostles of faith; when, in simplicity and prayer, you live faith which is a gift. Thank you for having responded to my call."*

**April 25, 1997** *"Dear children! Today I call you to have your life be connected with God the Creator, because only in this way will your life have meaning and you will comprehend that God is love. God sends me to you out of love, that I may help you to comprehend that without Him there is no future or joy and, above all, there is no eternal salvation. Little children, I call you to leave sin and to accept prayer at all times, that you may in prayer come to know the meaning of your life. God gives Himself to him who seeks Him. Thank you for having responded to my call."*

**May 25, 1997** *"Dear children! Today I invite you to glorify God and for the Name of God to be holy in your hearts and in your life. Little children, when you are in the holiness of God, He is with you and gives you peace and joy which come from God only through prayer. That is why, little children, renew prayer in your families and your heart will glorify the holy Name of God and heaven will reign in your heart. I am close to you and I intercede for you before God. Thank you for having responded to my call."*

**June 25, 1997** *"Dear children! Today I am with you in a special way and I bring you my motherly blessing of peace. I pray for you and I intercede for you before God, so that you may comprehend that each of you is a carrier of peace. You cannot have peace if your heart is not at peace with God. That is why, little children, pray, pray, pray, because prayer is the foundation of your peace. Open your heart and give time to God so that He will be your friend. When true friendship with God is realized, no storm can destroy it. Thank you for having responded to my call."*

**July 25, 1997** *"Dear children! Today I invite you to respond to my call to prayer. I desire, dear children, that during this time you find a corner for personal prayer. I desire to lead you towards prayer with the heart. Only in this way will you comprehend that your life is empty without prayer. You will discover the meaning of your life when you discover God in prayer. That is why, little children, open the door of your heart and you will comprehend that prayer is joy without which you cannot live. Thank you for having responded to my call."*

**August 25, 1997** *"Dear children! God gives me this time as a gift to you, so that I may instruct and lead you on the path of salvation. Dear children, now you do not comprehend this grace, but soon a time will come when you will lament for these messages. That is why, little children, live all of the words which I have given you through this time of grace and renew prayer, until prayer becomes a joy for you. Especially, I call all those who have consecrated themselves to my Immaculate Heart to become an example to others. I call all priests and religious brothers and sisters to pray the rosary and to teach others to pray. The rosary, little children, is especially dear to me. Through the rosary open your heart to me and I am able to help you. Thank you for having responded to my call."*

**September 25, 1997** *"Dear children! Today I call you to comprehend that without love you cannot comprehend that God needs to be in the first place in your life. That is why, little children, I call you all to love, not with a* *human but with God's love. In this way, your life will be more beautiful and without an interest. You will comprehend that God gives Himself to you in the simplest way out of love. Little children, so that you may comprehend my words which I give you out of love, pray, pray, pray and you will be able to accept others with love and to forgive all who have done evil to you. Respond with prayer; prayer is a fruit of love towards God the Creator. Thank you for having responded to my call."*

**October 25, 1997** *"Dear children! Also today I am with you and I call all of you to renew yourselves by living my messages. Little children, may prayer be life for you and may you be an example to others. Little children, I desire for you to become carriers of peace and of God's joy to today's world without peace. That is why, little children, pray, pray, pray! I am with you and I bless you with my motherly peace. Thank you for having responded to my call."*

**November 25, 1997** *"Dear children! Today I invite you to comprehend your Christian vocation. Little children, I led and am leading you through this time of grace, that you may become conscious of your Christian vocation. Holy martyrs died witnessing: I am a Christian and love God over everything. Little children, today also I invite you to rejoice and be joyful Christians, responsible and conscious that God called you in a special way to be joyfully extended hands toward those who do not believe, and that through the example of your life, they may receive faith and love for God. Therefore, pray, pray, pray that your heart may open and be sensitive for the Word of God. Thank you for having responded to my call."*

**December 25, 1997** *"Dear children! Also today I rejoice with you and I call you to the good. I desire that each of you reflect and carry peace in your heart and say: I want to put God in the first place in my life. In this way, little children, each of you will become holy. Little children, tell everyone, I want the good for you and he will respond with the good and, little children, good will come to dwell in the heart of each man. Little children, tonight I bring to you the good of my Son who gave His life to save you. That is why, little children, rejoice and extend your hands to Jesus who is only good. Thank you for having responded to my call."*

**January 25, 1998** *"Dear children! Today again I call all of you to prayer. Only with prayer, dear children, will your heart change, become better, and be more sensitive to the Word of God. Little children, do not permit satan to pull you apart and to do with you what he wants. I call you to be responsible and determined and to consecrate each day to God in prayer. May Holy Mass, little children, not be a habit for you, but life. By living Holy Mass each day, you will feel the need for holiness and you will grow in holiness. I am close to you and intercede before God for each of you, so that He may give you strength to change your heart. Thank you for having responded to my call."*

**February 25, 1998** *"Dear children! Also today I am with you and I, again, call all of you to come closer to me through your prayers. In a special way, I call you to renunciation in this time of grace. Little children, meditate on and live, through your little sacrifices, the passion and death of Jesus for each of you. Only if you come closer to Jesus will you comprehend the immeasurable love He has for each of you. Through prayer and your renunciation you will become more open to the gift of faith and love towards the Church and the people who are around you. I love you and bless you. Thank you for having responded to my call."*

**March 25, 1998** *"Dear children! Also today I call you to fasting and renunciation. Little children, renounce that which hinders you from being closer to Jesus. In a special way I call you: Pray, because only through prayer will you be able to overcome your will and discover the will of God even in the smallest things. By your daily life, little children, you will become an example and witness that you live for Jesus or against Him and His will. Little children, I desire that you become apostles of love. By loving, little children, it will be recognized that you are mine. Thank you for having responded to my call."*

**April 25, 1998** *"Dear children! Today I call you, through prayer, to open yourselves to God as a flower opens itself to the rays of the morning sun. Little children, do not be afraid. I am with you and I intercede before God for each of you so that your heart receives the gift of conversion. Only in this way, little children, will you comprehend the importance of grace in these times and God will become nearer to you. Thank you for having responded to my call."*

**May 25, 1998** *"Dear children! Today I call you, through prayer and sacrifice, to prepare yourselves for the coming of the Holy Spirit. Little children, this is a time of grace and so, again, I call you to decide for God the Creator. Allow Him to transform and change you. May your heart be prepared to listen to, and live, everything which the Holy Spirit has in His plan for each of you. Little children, allow the Holy Spirit to lead you on the way of truth and salvation towards eternal life. Thank you for having responded to my call."*

**June 25, 1998** *"Dear children! Today I desire to thank you for living my messages. I bless you all with my motherly blessing and I bring you all before my Son Jesus. Thank you for having responded to my call."*

**July 25, 1998** *"Dear children! Today, little children, I invite you, through prayer, to be with Jesus, so that through a personal experience of prayer you may be able to discover the beauty of God's creatures. You cannot speak or witness about prayer, if you do not pray. That is why, little children, in the silence of the heart, remain with Jesus, so that He may change and transform you with His love. This, little children, is a time of grace for you. Make good use of it for your personal conversion, because when you have God, you have everything. Thank you for having responded to my call."*

**August 25, 1998** *"Dear children! Today I invite you to come still closer to me through prayer. Little children, I am your mother, I love you and I desire that each of you be saved and thus be with me in Heaven. That is why, little children, pray, pray, pray until your life becomes prayer. Thank you for having responded to my call."*
**September 25, 1998** *"Dear children! Today, I call you to become my witnesses by living the faith of your fathers. Little children, you seek signs and messages and do not see that, with every morning sunrise, God calls you to convert and to return to the way of truth and salvation. You speak much, little children, but you work little on your conversion. That is why, convert and start to live my messages, not with your words but with your life. In this way, little children, you will have the strength to decide for the true conversion of the heart. Thank you for having responded to my call."*
**October 25, 1998** *"Dear children! Today I call you to come closer to my Immaculate Heart. I call you to renew in your families the fervor of the first days when I called you to fasting, prayer and conversion. Little children, you accepted my messages with open hearts, although you did not know what prayer was. Today, I call you to open yourselves completely to me so that I may transform you and lead you to the heart of my son Jesus, so that He can fill you with His love. Only in this way, little children, will you find true peace - the peace that only God gives you. Thank you for having responded to my call."*
**November 25, 1998** *"Dear children! Today I call you to prepare yourselves for the coming of Jesus. In a special way, prepare your hearts. May holy Confession be the first act of conversion for you and then, dear children, decide for holiness. May your conversion and decision for holiness begin today and not tomorrow. Little children, I call you all to the way of salvation and I desire to show you the way to Heaven. That is why, little children, be mine and decide with me for holiness. Little children, accept prayer with seriousness and pray, pray, pray. Thank you for having responded to my call."*
**December 25, 1998** *"Dear children! In this Christmas joy I desire to bless you with my blessing. In a special way, little children, I give you the blessing of little Jesus. May He fill you with His peace. Today, little children, you do not have peace and yet you yearn for it. That is why, with my Son Jesus, on this day I call you to pray, pray, pray, because without prayer you do not have joy or peace or a future. Yearn for peace and seek it, for God is true peace. Thank you for having responded to my call."*
**January 25, 1999** *"Dear children! I again invite you to prayer. You have no excuse to work more because nature still lies in deep sleep. Open yourselves in prayer. Renew prayer in your families. Put Holy Scripture in a visible place in your families, read it, reflect on it and learn how God loves His people. His love shows itself also in present times because He sends me to call you upon the path of salvation. Thank you for having responded to my call."*
**February 25, 1999** *"Dear children! Also today I am with you in a special way contemplating and living the passion of Jesus in my heart. Little children, open your hearts and give me everything that is in them: joys, sorrows and each, even the smallest pain, that I may offer them to Jesus; so that with His immeasurable love, He may burn and transform your sorrows into the joy of His resurrection. That is why, I now call you in a special way, little children, for your hearts to open to prayer, so that through prayer you may become friends of Jesus. Thank you for having responded to my call."*
**March 25, 1999** *"Dear children! I call you to prayer with the heart. In a special way, little children, I call you to pray for conversion of sinners, for those who pierce my heart and the heart of my Son Jesus with the sword of hatred and daily blasphemies. Let us pray, little children, for all those who do not desire to come to know the love of God, even though they are in the Church. Let us pray that they convert, so that the Church may resurrect in love. Only with love and prayer, little children, can you live this time which is given to you for conversion. Place God in the first place, then the risen Jesus will become your friend. Thank you for having responded to my call."*
**April 25, 1999** *"Dear children! Also today I call you to prayer. Little children, be joyful carriers of peace and love in this peaceless world. By fasting and prayer, witness that you are mine and that you live my messages. Pray and seek! I am praying and interceding for you before God that you convert; that your life and behavior always be Christian. Thank you for having responded to my call."*
**May 25, 1999** *"Dear children! Also today I call you to convert and to more firmly believe in God. Children, you seek peace and pray in different ways, but you have not yet given your hearts to God for Him to fill them with His love. So, I am with you to teach you and to bring you closer to the love of God. If you love God above all else, it will be easy for you to pray and to open your hearts to Him. Thank you for having responded to my call."*
**June 25, 1999** *"Dear children! Today I thank you for living and witnessing my messages with your life. Little children, be strong and pray so that prayer may give you strength and joy. Only in this way will each of you be mine and I will lead you on the way of salvation. Little children, pray and with your life witness my presence here. May each day be a joyful witness for you of God's love. Thank you for having responded to my call."*
**July 25, 1999** *"Dear children! Also today I rejoice with you and I call you all to prayer with the heart. I call all of you, little children, to give thanks to God here with me for the graces which He gives to you through me. I desire for you to comprehend that I want to realize here, not only a place of prayer but also a meeting of hearts. I desire for my, Jesus' and your heart to become one heart of love and peace. That is why, little children, pray and rejoice over everything that God does here, despite that satan provokes quarrels and unrest. I am with you and I lead you all on the way of love. Thank you for having responded to my call."*

**August 25, 1999** *"Dear children! Also today I call you to give glory to God the Creator in the colors of nature. He speaks to you also through the smallest flower about His beauty and the depth of love with which He has created you. Little children, may prayer flow from your hearts like fresh water from a spring. May the wheat fields speak to you about the mercy of God towards every creature. That is why, renew prayer of thanksgiving for everything He gives you. Thank you for having responded to my call."*
**September 25, 1999** *"Dear children! Today again I call you to become carriers of my peace. In a special way, now when it is being said that God is far away, He has truly never been nearer to you. I call you to renew prayer in your families by reading the Sacred Scripture and to experience joy in meeting with God who infinitely loves His creatures. Thank you for having responded to my call."*
**October 25, 1999** *"Dear children! Do not forget: this is a time of grace; that is why, pray, pray, pray! Thank you for having responded to my call."*
**November 25, 1999** *"Dear children! Also today I call you to prayer. In this time of grace, may the cross be a sign-post of love and unity for you through which true peace comes. That is why, little children, pray especially at this time that little Jesus, the Creator of peace, may be born in your hearts. Only through prayer will you become my apostles of peace in this world without peace. That is why, pray until prayer becomes a joy for you. Thank you for having responded to my call."*
**December 25, 1999** *"Dear children! This is the time of grace. Little children, today in a special way with little Jesus, whom I hold in my embrace, I am giving you the possibility to decide for peace. Through your 'yes' for peace and your decision for God, a new possibility for peace is opened. Only in this way, little children, this century will be for you a time of peace and well-being. Therefore, put little newborn Jesus in the first place in your life and He will lead you on the way of salvation. Thank you for having responded to my call."*
**January 25, 2000** *"Dear children! I call you, little children, to pray without ceasing. If you pray, you are closer to God and He will lead you on the way of peace and salvation. That is why I call you today to give peace to others. Only in God is there true peace. Open your hearts and become those who give a gift of peace and others will discover peace in you and through you and in this way you will witness God's peace and love which He gives you. Thank you for having responded to my call."*
**February 25, 2000** *"Dear children! Wake up from the sleep of unbelief and sin, because this is a time of grace which God gives you. Use this time and seek the grace of healing of your heart from God, so that you may see God and man with the heart. Pray in a special way for those who have not come to know God's love, and witness with your life so that they also can come to know God and His immeasurable love. Thank you for having responded to my call."*
**March 25, 2000** *"Dear children! Pray and make good use of this time, because this is a time of grace. I am with you and I intercede for each one of you before God, for your heart to open to God and to God's love. Little children, pray without ceasing, until prayer becomes a joy for you. Thank you for having responded to my call."*
**April 25, 2000** *"Dear children! Also today I call you to conversion. You are concerned too much about material things and little about spiritual ones. Open your hearts and start again to work more on your personal conversion. Decide every day to dedicate time to God and to prayer until prayer becomes a joyful meeting with God for you. Only in this way will your life have meaning and with joy you will contemplate eternal life. Thank you for having responded to my call."*
**May 25, 2000** *"Dear children! I rejoice with you and in this time of grace I call you to spiritual renewal. Pray, little children, that the Holy Spirit may come to dwell in you in fullness, so that you may be able to witness in joy to all those who are far from faith. Especially, little children, pray for the gifts of the Holy Spirit so that in the spirit of love, every day and in each situation, you may be closer to your fellow-man; and that in wisdom and love you may overcome every difficulty. I am with you and I intercede for each of you before Jesus. Thank you for having responded to my call."*
**June 25, 2000** *"Dear children! Today I call you to prayer. The one who prays is not afraid of the future. Little children do not forget, I am with you and I love you all. Thank you for having responded to my call."*
**July 25, 2000** *"Dear children! Do not forget that you are here on earth on the way to eternity and that your home is in Heaven. That is why, little children, be open to God's love and leave egoism and sin. May your joy be only in discovering God in daily prayer. That is why, make good use of this time and pray, pray, pray; and God is near to you in prayer and through prayer. Thank you for having responded to my call."*
**August 25, 2000** *"Dear children! I desire to share my joy with you. In my Immaculate Heart I feel that there are many of those who have drawn closer to me and are, in a special way, carrying the victory of my Immaculate Heart in their hearts by praying and converting. I desire to thank you and to inspire you to work even more for God and His kingdom with love and the power of the Holy Spirit. I am with you and I bless you with my motherly blessing. Thank you for having responded to my call."*
**September 25, 2000** *"Dear children! Today I call you to open yourselves to prayer. May prayer become joy for you. Renew prayer in your families and form prayer groups. In this way, you will experience joy in prayer and togetherness. All those who pray and are members of prayer groups are open to God's will in their hearts and joyfully witness God's love. I am with you, I carry all of you in my heart and I bless you with my motherly blessing. Thank you for having responded to my call."*

**October 25, 2000** *"Dear children! Today I desire to open my motherly heart to you and to call you all to pray for my intentions. I desire to renew prayer with you and to call you to fast which I desire to offer to my Son Jesus for the coming of a new time - a time of spring. In this Jubilee year many hearts have opened to me and the Church is being renewed in the Spirit. I rejoice with you and I thank God for this gift; and you, little children, I call to pray, pray, pray - until prayer becomes a joy for you. Thank you for having responded to my call."*

**November 25, 2000** *"Dear children! Today when Heaven is near to you in a special way, I call you to prayer so that through prayer you place God in the first place. Little children, today I am near you and I bless each of you with my motherly blessing so that you have the strength and love for all the people you meet in your earthly life and that you can give God's love. I rejoice with you and I desire to tell you that your brother Slavko has been born into Heaven and intercedes for you. Thank you for having responded to my call."*

**December 25, 2000** *"Dear children! Today when God granted to me that I can be with you, with little Jesus in my arms, I rejoice with you and I give thanks to God for everything He has done in this Jubilee year. I thank God especially for all the vocations of those who said 'yes' to God completely. I bless you all with my blessing and the blessing of the newborn Jesus. I pray for all of you for joy to be born in your hearts so that in joy you too carry the joy I have today. In this Child I bring to you the Savior of your hearts and the One who calls you to the holiness of life. Thank you for having responded to my call."*

**January 25, 2001** *"Dear children! Today I call you to renew prayer and fasting with even greater enthusiasm until prayer becomes a joy for you. Little children, the one who prays is not afraid of the future and the one who fasts is not afraid of evil. Once again, I repeat to you: only through prayer and fasting also wars can be stopped - wars of your unbelief and fear for the future. I am with you and am teaching you little children: your peace and hope are in God. That is why draw closer to God and put Him in the first place in your life. Thank you for having responded to my call."*

**February 25, 2001** *"Dear children! This is a time of grace. That is why pray, pray, pray until you comprehend God's love for each of you. Thank you for having responded to my call."*

**March 25, 2001** *"Dear children! Also today I call you to open yourselves to prayer. Little children, you live in a time in which God gives great graces but you do not know how to make good use of them. You are concerned about everything else, but the least for the soul and spiritual life. Awaken from the tired sleep of your soul and say yes to God with all your strength. Decide for conversion and holiness. I am with you, little children, and I call you to perfection of your soul and of everything you do. Thank you for having responded to my call."*

**April 25, 2001** *"Dear children! Also today, I call you to prayer. Little children, prayer works miracles. When you are tired and sick and you do not know the meaning of your life, take the Rosary and pray; pray until prayer becomes for you a joyful meeting with your Savior. I am with you, little children, and I intercede and pray for you. Thank you for having responded to my call."*

**May 25, 2001** *"Dear children! At this time of grace, I call you to prayer. Little children, you work much but without God's blessing. Bless and seek the wisdom of the Holy Spirit to lead you at this time so that you may comprehend and live in the grace of this time. Convert, little children, and kneel in the silence of your hearts. Put God in the center of your being so that, in that way, you can witness in joy the beauty that God continually gives in your life. Thank you for having responded to my call."*

**June 25, 2001** *"Dear children! I am with you and I bless you all with my motherly blessing. Especially today when God gives you abundant graces, pray and seek God through me. God gives you great graces, that is why, little children make good use of this time of grace and come closer to my heart so that I can lead you to my Son Jesus. Thank you for having responded to my call."*

**July 25, 2001** *"Dear children! In this time of grace, I call you to come even closer to God through your personal prayer. Make good use of the time of rest and give your soul and your eyes rest in God. Find peace in nature and you will discover God the Creator Whom you will be able to give thanks to for all creatures; then you will find joy in your heart. Thank you for having responded to my call."*

**August 25, 2001** *"Dear children! Today I call all of you to decide for holiness. May for you, little children, always in your thoughts and in each situation holiness be in the first place, in work and in speech. In this way, you will also put it into practice; little by little, step by step, prayer and a decision for holiness will enter into your family. Be real with yourselves and do not bind yourselves to material things but to God. And do not forget, little children, that your life is as passing as a flower. Thank you for having responded to my call."*

**September 25, 2001** *"Dear children! Also today I call you to prayer, especially today when satan wants war and hatred. I call you anew, little children: pray and fast that God may give you peace. Witness peace to every heart and be carriers of peace in this world without peace. I am with you and intercede before God for each of you. And you do not be afraid because the one who prays is not afraid of evil and has no hatred in the heart. Thank you for having responded to my call."*

**October 25, 2001** *"Dear children! Also today I call you to pray from your whole heart and to love each other. Little children, you are chosen to witness peace and joy. If there is no peace, pray and you will receive it. Through you and your prayer, little children, peace will begin to flow through the world. That is why, little children, pray, pray, pray, because prayer works miracles in human hearts and in the world. I am with you and I thank God for each of you who has accepted and lives prayer with seriousness. Thank you for having responded to my call."*

**November 25, 2001** *"Dear children! In this time of grace, I call you anew to prayer. Little children, pray and prepare your hearts for the coming of the King of Peace, that with His blessing He may give peace to the whole world. Peacelessness has begun to reign in hearts and hatred reigns in the world. That is why, you who live my messages be the light and extended hands to this faithless world that all may come to know the God of Love. Do not forget, little children, I am with you and bless you all. Thank you for having responded to my call."*
**December 25, 2001** *"Dear children! I call you today and encourage you to prayer for peace. Especially today I call you, carrying the newborn Jesus in my arms for you, to unite with Him through prayer and to become a sign to this peaceless world. Encourage each other, little children, to prayer and love. May your faith be an encouragement to others to believe and to love more. I bless you all and call you to be closer to my heart and to the heart of little Jesus. Thank you for having responded to my call."*
**January 25, 2002** *"Dear children! At this time while you are still looking back to the past year I call you, little children, to look deeply into your heart and to decide to be closer to God and to prayer. Little children, you are still attached to earthly things and little to spiritual life. May my call today also be an encouragement to you to decide for God and for daily conversion. You cannot be converted, little children, if you do not abandon sins and do not decide for love towards God and neighbor. Thank you for having responded to my call."*
**February 25, 2002** *"Dear children! In this time of grace, I call you to become friends of Jesus. Pray for peace in your hearts and work for your personal conversion. Little children, only in this way will you be able to become witnesses of peace and of the love of Jesus in the world. Open yourselves to prayer so that prayer becomes a need for you. Be converted, little children, and work so that as many souls as possible may come to know Jesus and His love. I am close to you and I bless you all. Thank you for having responded to my call."*
**March 25, 2002** *"Dear children! Today I call you to unite with Jesus in prayer. Open your heart to Him and give Him everything that is in it: joys, sorrows and illnesses. May this be a time of grace for you. Pray, little children, and may every moment belong to Jesus. I am with you and I intercede for you. Thank you for having responded to my call."*
**April 25, 2002** *"Dear children! Rejoice with me in this time of spring when all nature is awakening and your hearts long for change. Open yourselves, little children, and pray. Do not forget that I am with you and I desire to take you all to my Son that He may give you the gift of sincere love towards God and everything that is from Him. Open yourselves to prayer and seek a conversion of your hearts from God; everything else He sees and provides. Thank you for having responded to my call."*
**May 25, 2002** *"Dear children! Today I call you to put prayer in the first place in your life. Pray and may prayer, little children, be a joy for you. I am with you and intercede for all of you, and you, little children, be joyful carriers of my messages. May your life with me be joy. Thank you for having responded to my call."*
**June 25, 2002** *"Dear children! Today I pray for you and with you that the Holy Spirit may help you and increase your faith, so that you may accept even more the messages that I am giving you here in this holy place. Little children, comprehend that this is a time of grace for each of you; and with me, little children, you are secure. I desire to lead you all on the way of holiness. Live my messages and put into life every word that I am giving you. May they be precious to you because they come from Heaven. Thank you for having responded to my call."*
**July 25, 2002** *"Dear children! Today I rejoice with your patron saint and call you to be open to God's will, so that in you and through you, faith may grow in the people you meet in your everyday life. Little children, pray until prayer becomes joy for you. Ask your holy protectors to help you grow in love towards God. Thank you for having responded to my call."*
**August 25, 2002** *"Dear children! Also today I am with you in prayer so that God gives you an even stronger faith. Little children, your faith is small and you are not even aware how much, despite this, you are not ready to seek the gift of faith from God. That is why I am with you, little children, to help you comprehend my messages and put them into life. Pray, pray, pray and only in faith and through prayer your soul will find peace and the world will find joy to be with God. Thank you for having responded to my call."*
**September 25, 2002** *"Dear children! Also in this peaceless time, I call you to prayer. Little children, pray for peace so that in the world every person would feel love towards peace. Only when the soul finds peace in God, it feels content and love will begin to flow in the world. And in a special way, little children, you are called to live and witness peace - peace in your hearts and families - and, through you, peace will also begin to flow in the world. Thank you for having responded to my call."*
**October 25, 2002** *"Dear children! Also today I call you to prayer. Little children, believe that by simple prayer miracles can be worked. Through your prayer you open your heart to God and He works miracles in your life. By looking at the fruits, your heart fills with joy and gratitude to God for everything He does in your life and, through you, also to others. Pray and believe little children, God gives you graces and you do not see them. Pray and you will see them. May your day be filled with prayer and thanksgiving for everything that God gives you. Thank you for having responded to my call."*
**November 25, 2002** *"Dear children! I call you also today to conversion. Open your heart to God, little children, through Holy Confession and prepare your soul so that little Jesus can be born anew in your heart. Permit Him to transform you and lead you on the way of peace and joy. Little children, decide for prayer. Especially now, in this time of grace, may your heart yearn for prayer. I am close to you and intercede before God for all of you. Thank you for having responded to my call."*

**December 25, 2002** *"Dear children! This is a time of great graces, but also a time of great trials for all those who desire to follow the way of peace. Because of that, little children, again I call you to pray, pray, pray, not with words but with the heart. Live my messages and be converted. Be conscious of this gift that God has permitted me to be with you, especially today when in my arms I have little Jesus - the King of Peace. I desire to give you peace, and that you carry it in your hearts and give it to others until God's peace begins to rule the world. Thank you for having responded to my call."*
**January 25, 2003** *"Dear children! With this message I call you anew to pray for peace. Particularly now when peace is in crisis, you be those who pray and bear witness to peace. Little children, be peace in this peaceless world. Thank you for having responded to my call."*
**February 25, 2003** *"Dear children! Also today I call you to pray and fast for peace. As I have already said and now repeat to you, little children, only with prayer and fasting can wars also be stopped. Peace is a precious gift from God. Seek, pray and you will receive it. Speak about peace and carry peace in your hearts. Nurture it like a flower which is in need of water, tenderness and light. Be those who carry peace to others. I am with you and intercede for all of you. Thank you for having responded to my call."*
**March 25, 2003** *"Dear children! Also today I call you to pray for peace. Pray with the heart, little children, and do not lose hope because God loves His creatures. He desires to save you, one by one, through my coming here. I call you to the way of holiness. Pray, and in prayer you are open to God's will; in this way, in everything you do, you realize God's plan in you and through you. Thank you for having responded to my call."*
**April 25, 2003** *"Dear children! I call you also today to open yourselves to prayer. In the foregone time of Lent you have realized how small you are and how small your faith is. Little children, decide also today for God, that in you and through you He may change the hearts of people, and also your hearts. Be joyful carriers of the risen Jesus in this peaceless world, which yearns for God and for everything that is from God. I am with you, little children, and I love you with a special love. Thank you for having responded to my call."*
**May 25, 2003** *"Dear children! Also today I call you to prayer. Renew your personal prayer, and in a special way pray to the Holy Spirit to help you pray with the heart. I intercede for all of you, little children, and call all of you to conversion. If you convert, all those around you will also be renewed and prayer will be a joy for them. Thank you for having responded to my call."*
**June 25, 2003** *"Dear children! Also today, I call you with great joy to live my messages. I am with you and I thank you for putting into life what I am saying to you. I call you to renew my messages even more, with new enthusiasm and joy. May prayer be your daily practice. Thank you for having responded to my call."*
**July 25, 2003** *"Dear children! Also today I call you to prayer. Little children, pray until prayer becomes a joy for you. Only in this way each of you will discover peace in the heart and your soul will be content. You will feel the need to witness to others the love that you feel in your heart and life. I am with you and intercede before God for all of you. Thank you for having responded to my call."*
**August 25, 2003** *"Dear children! Also today I call you to give thanks to God in your heart for all the graces which He gives you, also through the signs and colors that are in nature. God wants to draw you closer to Himself and moves you to give Him glory and thanks. Therefore, little children, I call you anew to pray, pray, pray and do not forget that I am with you. I intercede before God for each of you until your joy in Him is complete. Thank you for having responded to my call."*
**September 25, 2003** *"Dear children! Also today I call you to come closer to my heart. Only in this way, will you comprehend the gift of my presence here among you. I desire, little children, to lead you to the heart of my Son Jesus; but you resist and do not desire to open your hearts to prayer. Again, little children, I call you not to be deaf but to comprehend my call, which is salvation for you. Thank you for having responded to my call."*
**October 25, 2003** *"Dear children! I call you anew to consecrate yourselves to my heart and the heart of my Son Jesus. I desire, little children, to lead you all on the way of conversion and holiness. Only in this way, through you, we can lead all the more souls on the way of salvation. Do not delay, little children, but say with all your heart: "I want to help Jesus and Mary that all the more brothers and sisters may come to know the way of holiness." In this way, you will feel the contentment of being friends of Jesus. Thank you for having responded to my call."*
**November 25, 2003** *"Dear children! I call you that this time be for you an even greater incentive to prayer. In this time, little children, pray that Jesus be born in all hearts, especially in those who do not know Him. Be love, joy and peace in this peaceless world. I am with you and intercede before God for each of you. Thank you for having responded to my call."*
**December 25, 2003** *"Dear children! Also today, I bless you all with my Son Jesus in my arms and I carry Him, who is the King of Peace, to you, that He grant you His peace. I am with you and I love you all, little children. Thank you for having responded to my call."*
**January 25, 2004** *"Dear children! Also today I call you to pray. Pray, little children, in a special way for all those who have not come to know God's love. Pray that their hearts may open and draw closer to my heart and the Heart of my Son Jesus, so that we can transform them into people of peace and love. Thank you for having responded to my call."*
**February 25, 2004** *"Dear children! Also today, as never up to now, I call you to open your hearts to my messages. Little children, be those who draw souls to God and not those who distance them. I am with you and*

*love you all with a special love. This is a time of penance and conversion. From the bottom of my heart, I call you to be mine with all your heart and then you will see that your God is great, because He will give you an abundance of blessings and peace. Thank you for having responded to my call."*
**March 25, 2004** *"Dear children! Also today, I call you to open yourselves to prayer. Especially now, in this time of grace, open your hearts, little children, and express your love to the Crucified. Only in this way, will you discover peace, and prayer will begin to flow from your heart into the world. Be an example, little children, and an incentive for the good. I am close to you and I love you all. Thank you for having responded to my call."*
**April 25, 2004** *"Dear children! Also today, I call you to live my messages even more strongly in humility and love so that the Holy Spirit may fill you with His grace and strength. Only in this way will you be witnesses of peace and forgiveness. Thank you for having responded to my call."*
**May 25, 2004** *"Dear children! Also today, I urge you to consecrate yourselves to my Heart and to the Heart of my Son Jesus. Only in this way will you be mine more each day and you will inspire each other all the more to holiness. In this way joy will rule your hearts and you will be carriers of peace and love. Thank you for having responded to my call."*
**June 25, 2004** *"Dear children! Also today, joy is in my heart. I desire to thank you for making my plan realizable. Each of you is important, therefore, little children, pray and rejoice with me for every heart that has converted and become an instrument of peace in the world. Prayer groups are powerful, and through them I can see, little children, that the Holy Spirit is at work in the world. Thank you for having responded to my call."*
**July 25, 2004** *"Dear children! I call you anew: be open to my messages. I desire, little children, to draw you all closer to my Son Jesus; therefore, you pray and fast. Especially I call you to pray for my intentions, so that I can present you to my Son Jesus; for Him to transform and open your hearts to love. When you will have love in the heart, peace will rule in you. Thank you for having responded to my call."*
**August 25, 2004** *"Dear children! I call you all to conversion of heart. Decide, as in the first days of my coming here, for a complete change of your life. In this way, little children, you will have the strength to kneel and to open your hearts before God. God will hear your prayers and answer them. Before God, I intercede for each of you. Thank you for having responded to my call."*
**September 25, 2004** *"Dear children! Also today, I call you to be love where there is hatred and food where there is hunger. Open your hearts, little children, and let your hands be extended and generous so that, through you, every creature may thank God the Creator. Pray, little children, and open your heart to God's love, but you cannot if you do not pray. Therefore, pray, pray, pray. Thank you for having responded to my call."*
**October 25, 2004** *"Dear children! This is a time of grace for the family and, therefore, I call you to renew prayer. May Jesus be in the heart of your family. In prayer, learn to love everything that is holy. Imitate the lives of saints so that they may be an incentive and teachers on the way of holiness. May every family become a witness of love in this world without prayer and peace. Thank you for having responded to my call."*
**November 25, 2004** *"Dear children! At this time, I call you all to pray for my intentions. Especially, little children, pray for those who have not yet come to know the love of God and do not seek God the Savior. You, little children, be my extended hands and by your example draw them closer to my Heart and the Heart of my Son. God will reward you with graces and every blessing. Thank you for having responded to my call."*
**December 25, 2004** *"Dear children! With great joy, also today I carry my Son Jesus in my arms to you; He blesses you and calls you to peace. Pray, little children, and be courageous witnesses of Good News in every situation. Only in this way will God bless you and give you everything you ask of Him in faith. I am with you as long as the Almighty permits me. I intercede for each of you with great love. Thank you for having responded to my call."*
**January 25, 2005** *"Dear children! In this time of grace again I call you to prayer. Pray, little children, for unity of Christians, that all may be one heart. Unity will really be among you inasmuch as you will pray and forgive. Do not forget: love will conquer only if you pray, and your heart will open. Thank you for having responded to my call."*
**February 25, 2005** *"Dear children! Today I call you to be my extended hands in this world that puts God in the last place. You, little children, put God in the first place in your life. God will bless you and give you strength to bear witness to Him, the God of love and peace. I am with you and intercede for all of you. Little children, do not forget that I love you with a tender love. Thank you for having responded to my call."*
**March 25, 2005** *"Dear children! Today I call you to love. Little children, love each other with God's love. At every moment, in joy and in sorrow, may love prevail and, in this way, love will begin to reign in your hearts. The risen Jesus will be with you and you will be his witnesses. I will rejoice with you and protect you with my motherly mantle. Especially, little children, I will watch your daily conversion with love. Thank you for having responded to my call."*
**April 25, 2005** *"Dear children! Also today, I call you to renew prayer in your families. By prayer and the reading of Sacred Scripture, may the Holy Spirit, who will renew you, enter into your families. In this way, you will become teachers of the faith in your family. By prayer and your love, the world will set out on a better way and love will begin to rule in the world. Thank you for having responded to my call."*
**May 25, 2005** *"Dear children! Anew I call you to live my messages in humility. Especially witness them now when we are approaching the anniversary of my apparitions. Little children, be a sign to those who are far from*

*God and His love. I am with you and bless you all with my motherly blessing. Thank you for having responded to my call."*

**June 25, 2005** *"Dear children! Today I thank you for every sacrifice that you have offered for my intentions. I call you, little children, to be my apostles of peace and love in your families and in the world. Pray that the Holy Spirit may enlighten and lead you on the way of holiness. I am with you and bless you all with my motherly blessing. Thank you for having responded to my call."*

**July 25, 2005** *"Dear children! Also today, I call you to fill your day with short and ardent prayers. When you pray, your heart is open and God loves you with a special love and gives you special graces. Therefore, make good use of this time of grace and devote it to God more than ever up to now. Do novenas of fasting and renunciation so that satan be far from you and grace be around you. I am near you and intercede before God for each of you. Thank you for having responded to my call."*

**August 25, 2005** *"Dear children! Also today I call you to live my messages. God gave you a gift of this time as a time of grace. Therefore, little children, make good use of every moment and pray, pray, pray. I bless you all and intercede before the Most High for each of you. Thank you for having responded to my call."*

**September 25, 2005** *"Dear children! In love I call you: convert, even though you are far from my heart. Do not forget, I am your mother and I feel pain for each one who is far from my heart; but I do not leave you alone. I believe you can leave the way of sin and decide for holiness. Thank you for having responded to my call."*

**October 25, 2005** *"Little children, believe, pray and love, and God will be near you. He will give you the gift of all the graces you seek from Him. I am a gift to you, because, from day to day, God permits me to be with you and to love each of you with immeasurable love. Therefore, little children, in prayer and humility, open your hearts and be witnesses of my presence. Thank you for having responded to my call."*

**November 25, 2005** *"Dear children! Also today I call you to pray, pray, pray until prayer becomes life for you. Little children, at this time, in a special way, I pray before God to give you the gift of faith. Only in faith will you discover the joy of the gift of life that God has given you. Your heart will be joyful thinking of eternity. I am with you and love you with a tender love. Thank you for having responded to my call."*

**December 25, 2005** *"Dear children! Also today, in my arms I bring you little Jesus, the King of Peace, to bless you with His peace. Little children, in a special way today I call you to be my carriers of peace in this peaceless world. God will bless you. Little children, do not forget that I am your mother. I bless you all with a special blessing, with little Jesus in my arms. Thank you for having responded to my call."*

**January 25, 2006** *"Dear children! Also today I call you to be carriers of the Gospel in your families. Do not forget, little children, to read Sacred Scripture. Put it in a visible place and witness with your life that you believe and live the Word of God. I am close to you with my love and intercede before my Son for each of you. Thank you for having responded to my call."*

**February 25, 2006** *"Dear children! In this Lenten time of grace, I call you to open your hearts to the gifts that God desires to give you. Do not be closed, but with prayer and renunciation say 'yes' to God and He will give to you in abundance. As in springtime the earth opens to the seed and yields a hundredfold, so also your heavenly Father will give to you in abundance. I am with you and love you, little children, with a tender love. Thank you for having responded to my call."*

**March 25, 2006** *"Courage, little children! I decided to lead you on the way of holiness. Renounce sin and set out on the way of salvation, the way which my Son has chosen. Through each of your tribulations and sufferings God will find the way of joy for you. Therefore, little children, pray. We are close to you with our love. Thank you for having responded to my call."*

**April 25, 2006** *"Dear children! Also today I call you to have more trust in me and my Son. He has conquered by His death and resurrection and, through me, calls you to be a part of His joy. You do not see God, little children, but if you pray you will feel His nearness. I am with you and intercede before God for each of you. Thank you for having responded to my call."*

**May 25, 2006** *"Dear children! Also today I call you to put into practice and to live my messages that I am giving you. Decide for holiness, little children, and think of heaven. Only in this way, will you have peace in your heart that no one will be able to destroy. Peace is a gift, which God gives you in prayer. Little children, seek and work with all your strength for peace to win in your hearts and in the world. Thank you for having responded to my call."*

**June 25, 2006** *"Dear children! With great joy in my heart I thank you for all the prayers that, in these days, you offered for my intentions. Know, little children, that you will not regret it, neither you nor your children. God will reward you with great graces and you will merit eternal life. I am near you and thank all those who, through these years, have accepted my messages, have poured them into their life and decided for holiness and peace. Thank you for having responded to my call."*

**July 25, 2006** *"Dear children! At this time, do not only think of rest for your body but, little children, seek time also for the soul. In silence may the Holy Spirit speak to you and permit Him to convert and change you. I am with you and before God I intercede for each of you. Thank you for having responded to my call."*

**August 25, 2006** *"Dear children! Also today I call you to pray, pray, pray. Only in prayer will you be near to me and my Son and you will see how short this life is. In your heart a desire for Heaven will be born. Joy will begin to rule in your heart and prayer will begin to flow like a river. In your words there will only be thanksgiving to God*

*for having created you and the desire for holiness will become a reality for you. Thank you for having responded to my call."*
**September 25, 2006** *"Dear children! Also today I am with you and call all of you to complete conversion. Decide for God, little children, and you will find in God the peace your heart seeks. Imitate the lives of saints and may they be an example for you; and I will inspire you as long as the Almighty permits me to be with you. Thank you for having responded to my call."*
**October 25, 2006** *"Dear children! Today the Lord permitted me to tell you again that you live in a time of grace. You are not conscious, little children, that God is giving you a great opportunity to convert and to live in peace and love. You are so blind and attached to earthly things and think of earthly life. God sent me to lead you toward eternal life. I, little children, am not tired, although I see that your hearts are heavy and tired for everything that is a grace and a gift. Thank you for having responded to my call."*
**November 25, 2006** *"Dear children! Also today I call you to pray, pray, pray. Little children, when you pray you are close to God and He gives you the desire for eternity. This is a time when you can speak more about God and do more for God. Therefore, little children, do not resist but permit Him to lead you, to change you and to enter into your life. Do not forget that you are travelers on the way toward eternity. Therefore, little children, permit God to lead you as a shepherd leads his flock. Thank you for having responded to my call."*
**December 25, 2006** *"Dear children! Also today I bring you the newborn Jesus in my arms. He who is the King of Heaven and earth, He is your peace. Little children, no one can give you peace as He who is the King of Peace. Therefore, adore Him in your hearts, choose Him and you will have joy in Him. He will bless you with His blessing of peace. Thank you for having responded to my call."*
**January 25, 2007** *"Dear children! Put Sacred Scripture in a visible place in your family and read it. In this way, you will come to know prayer with the heart and your thoughts will be on God. Do not forget that you are passing like a flower in a field, which is visible from afar but disappears in a moment. Little children, leave a sign of goodness and love wherever you pass and God will bless you with an abundance of His blessing. Thank you for having responded to my call."*
**February 25, 2007** *"Dear children! Open your heart to God's mercy in this Lenten time. The heavenly Father desires to deliver each of you from the slavery of sin. Therefore, little children, make good use of this time and through meeting with God in confession, leave sin and decide for holiness. Do this out of love for Jesus, who redeemed you all with his blood, that you may be happy and in peace. Do not forget, little children: your freedom is your weakness, therefore follow my messages with seriousness. Thank you for having responded to my call."*
**March 25, 2007** *"Dear children! I desire to thank you from my heart for your Lenten renunciations. I desire to inspire you to continue to live fasting with an open heart. By fasting and renunciation, little children, you will be stronger in faith. In God you will find true peace through daily prayer. I am with you and I am not tired. I desire to take you all with me to Heaven, therefore, decide daily for holiness. Thank you for having responded to my call."*
**April 25, 2007** *"Dear children! Also today I again call you to conversion. Open your hearts. This is a time of grace while I am with you, make good use of it. Say: 'This is the time for my soul'. I am with you and love you with immeasurable love. Thank you for having responded to my call."*
**May 25, 2007** *"Dear children! Pray with me to the Holy Spirit for Him to lead you in the search of God's will on the way of your holiness. And you, who are far from prayer, convert and, in the silence of your heart, seek salvation for your soul and nurture it with prayer. I bless you all individually with my motherly blessing. Thank you for having responded to my call."*
**June 25, 2007** *"Dear children! Also today, with great joy in my heart, I call you to conversion. Little children, do not forget that you are all important in this great plan, which God leads through Medjugorje. God desires to convert the entire world and to call it to salvation and to the way towards Himself, who is the beginning and the end of every being. In a special way, little children, from the depth of my heart, I call you all to open yourselves to this great grace that God gives you through my presence here. I desire to thank each of you for the sacrifices and prayers. I am with you and I bless you all. Thank you for having responded to my call."*
**July 25, 2007** *"Dear children! Today, on the day of the Patron of your Parish, I call you to imitate the lives of the Saints. May they be, for you, an example and encouragement to a life of holiness. May prayer for you be like the air you breathe in and not a burden. Little children, God will reveal His love to you and you will experience the joy that you are my beloved. God will bless you and give you an abundance of grace. Thank you for having responded to my call."*
**August 25, 2007** *"Dear children! Also today I call you to conversion. May your life, little children, be a reflection of god's goodness and not of hatred and unfaithfulness. Pray, little children, that prayer may become life for you. In this way, in your life you will discover the peace and joy which god gives to those who have an open heart to his love. And you who are far from god's mercy, convert so that god may not become deaf to your prayers and that it may not be too late for you. Therefore, in this time of grace, convert and put god in the first place in your life. Thank you for having responded to my call."*
**September 25, 2007** *"Dear children! Also today I call all of you for your hearts to blaze with more ardent love for the Crucified, and do not forget that, out of love for you, He gave His life so that you may be saved. Little children, meditate and pray that your heart may be open to God's love. Thank you for having responded to my call."*

**October 25, 2007** *"Dear children! God sent me among you out of love that I may lead you towards the way of salvation. Many of you opened your hearts and accepted my messages, but many have become lost on this way and have never come to know the God of love with the fullness of heart. Therefore, I call you to be love and light where there is darkness and sin. I am with you and bless you all. Thank you for having responded to my call."*
**November 25, 2007** *"Dear children! Today, when you celebrate Christ, the King of all that is created, I desire for Him to be the King of your lives. Only through giving, little children, can you comprehend the gift of Jesus´ sacrifice on the Cross for each of you. Little children, give time to God that He may transform you and fill you with His grace, so that you may be a grace for others. For you, little children, I am a gift of grace and love, which comes from God for this peaceless world. Thank you for having responded to my call."*
**December 25, 2007** *"Dear children! With great joy I bring you the King of Peace for Him to bless you with His blessing. Adore Him and give time to the Creator for whom your heart yearns. Do not forget that you are passers-by on this earth and that things can give you small joys, while through my Son, eternal life is given to you. That is why I am with you, to lead you towards what your heart yearns for. Thank you for having responded to my call."*
**January 25, 2008** *"Dear children! With the time of Lent, you are approaching a time of grace. Your heart is like ploughed soil and it is ready to receive the fruit which will grow into what is good. You, little children, are free to choose good or evil. Therefore, I call you to pray and fast. Plant joy and the fruit of joy will grow in your hearts for your good, and others will see it and receive it through your life. Renounce sin and choose eternal life. I am with you and intercede for you before my Son. Thank you for having responded to my call."*
**February 25, 2008** *"Dear children! In this time of grace, I call you anew to prayer and renunciation. May your day be interwoven with little ardent prayers for all those who have not come to know God's love. Thank you for having responded to my call."*
**March 25, 2008** *"Dear children! I call you to work on your personal conversion. You are still far from meeting with God in your heart. Therefore, spend all the more time in prayer and Adoration of Jesus in the Most Blessed Sacrament of the Altar, for Him to change you and to put into your hearts a living faith and a desire for eternal life. Everything is passing, little children, only God is not passing. I am with you and I encourage you with love. Thank you for having responded to my call."*
**April 25, 2008** *"Dear children! Also today, I call all of you to grow in God's love as a flower which feels the warm rays of spring. In this way, also you, little children, grow in God's love and carry it to all those who are far from God. Seek God's will and do good to those whom God has put on your way, and be light and joy. Thank you for having responded to my call."*
**May 25, 2008** *"Dear children! In this time of grace, when God has permitted me to be with you, little children, I call you anew to conversion. Work on the salvation of the world in a special way while I am with you. God is merciful and gives special graces, therefore, seek them through prayer. I am with you and do not leave you alone. Thank you for having responded to my call."*
**June 25, 2008** *"Dear children! Also today, with great joy in my heart, I call you to follow me and to listen to my messages. Be joyful carriers of peace and love in this peaceless world. I am with you and I bless you all with my Son Jesus, the King of Peace. Thank you for having responded to my call."*
**July 25, 2008** *"Dear children! At this time when you are thinking of physical rest, I call you to conversion. Pray and work so that your heart yearns for God the Creator who is the true rest of your soul and your body. May He reveal His face to you and may He give you His peace. I am with you and intercede before God for each of you. Thank you for having responded to my call."*
**August 25, 2008** *"Dear children! Also today I call you to personal conversion. You be those who will convert and, with your life, will witness, love, forgive and bring the joy of the Risen One into this world, where my Son died and where people do not feel a need to seek Him and to discover Him in their lives. You adore Him, and may your hope be hope to those hearts who do not have Jesus. Thank you for having responded to my call."*
**September 25, 2008** *"Dear children! May your life, anew, be a decision for peace. Be joyful carriers of peace and do not forget that you live in a time of grace, in which God gives you great graces through my presence. Do not close yourselves, little children, but make good use of this time and seek the gift of peace and love for your life so that you may become witnesses to others. I bless you with my motherly blessing. Thank you for having responded to my call."*
**October 25, 2008** *"Dear children! In a special way I call you all to pray for my intentions so that, through your prayers, you may stop satan's plan over this world, which is further from God every day, and which puts itself in the place of God and is destroying everything that is beautiful and good in the souls of each of you. Therefore, little children, arm yourselves with prayer and fasting so that you may be conscious of how much God loves you and may carry out God's will. Thank you for having responded to my call."*
**November 25, 2008** *"Dear children! Also today I call you, in this time of grace, to pray for little Jesus to be born in your heart. May He, who is peace itself, give peace to the entire world through you. Therefore, little children, pray without ceasing for this turbulent world without hope, so that you may become witnesses of peace for all. May hope begin to flow through your hearts as a river of grace. Thank you for having responded to my call."*
**December 25, 2008** *"Dear children! You are running, working, gathering - but without blessing. You are not praying! Today I call you to stop in front of the manger and to meditate on Jesus, Whom I give to you today also,*

*to bless you and to help you to comprehend that, without Him, you have no future. Therefore, little children, surrender your lives into the hands of Jesus, for Him to lead you and protect you from every evil. Thank you for having responded to my call."*

**January 25, 2009** *"Dear children! Also today I call you to prayer. May prayer be for you like the seed that you will put in my heart, which I will give over to my Son Jesus for you, for the salvation of your souls. I desire, little children, for each of you to fall in love with eternal life which is your future, and for all worldly things to be a help for you to draw you closer to God the Creator. I am with you for this long because you are on the wrong path. Only with my help, little children, you will open your eyes. There are many of those who, by living my messages, comprehend that they are on the way of holiness towards eternity. Thank you for having responded to my call."*

**February 25, 2009** *"Dear children! In this time of renunciation, prayer and penance, I call you anew: go and confess your sins so that grace may open your hearts, and permit it to change you. Convert little children, open yourselves to God and to His plan for each of you. Thank you for having responded to my call."*

**March 25, 2009** *"Dear children! In this time of spring, when everything is awakening from the winter sleep, you also awaken your souls with prayer so that they may be ready to receive the light of the risen Jesus. Little children, may He draw you closer to His Heart so that you may become open to eternal life. I pray for you and intercede before the Most High for your sincere conversion. Thank you for having responded to my call."*

**April 25, 2009** *"Dear children! Today I call you all to pray for peace and to witness it in your families so that peace may become the highest treasure on this peaceless earth. I am your Queen of Peace and your mother. I desire to lead you on the way of peace, which comes only from God. Therefore, pray, pray, pray. Thank you for having responded to my call."*

**May 25, 2009** *"Dear children! In this time, I call you all to pray for the coming of the Holy Spirit upon every baptized creature, so that the Holy Spirit may renew you all and lead you on the way of witnessing your faith - you and all those who are far from God and His love. I am with you and intercede for you before the Most High. Thank you for having responded to my call."*

**June 25, 2009** *"Dear children! Rejoice with me, convert in joy and give thanks to God for the gift of my presence among you. Pray that, in your hearts, God may be in the center of your life and with your life witness, little children, so that every creature may feel God's love. Be my extended hands for every creature, so that it may draw closer to the God of love. I bless you with my motherly blessing. Thank you for having responded to my call."*

**July 25, 2009** *"Dear children! May this time be a time of prayer for you. Thank you for having responded to my call."*

**August 25, 2009** *"Dear children! Today I call you anew to conversion. Little children, you are not holy enough and you do not radiate holiness to others, therefore pray, pray, pray and work on your personal conversion, so that you may be a sign of God's love to others. I am with you and am leading you towards eternity, for which every heart must yearn. Thank you for having responded to my call."*

**September 25, 2009** *"Dear children, with joy, persistently work on your conversion. Offer all your joys and sorrows to my Immaculate Heart that I may lead you all to my most beloved Son, so that you may find joy in His Heart. I am with you to instruct you and to lead you towards eternity. Thank you for having responded to my call."*

**October 25, 2009** *"Dear children! Also today I bring you my blessing, I bless you all and I call you to grow on this way, which God has begun through me for your salvation. Pray, fast and joyfully witness your faith, little children, and may your heart always be filled with prayer. Thank you for having responded to my call."*

**November 25, 2009** *"Dear children! In this time of grace I call you all to renew prayer in your families. Prepare yourselves with joy for the coming of Jesus. Little children, may your hearts be pure and pleasing, so that love and warmth may flow through you into every heart that is far from His love. Little children, be my extended hands, hands of love for all those who have become lost, who have no more faith and hope. Thank you for having responded to my call."*

**December 25, 2009** *"Dear children! On this joyful day, I bring all of you before my Son, the King of Peace, that He may give you His peace and blessing. Little children, in love share that peace and blessing with others. Thank you for having responded to my call."*

**January 25, 2010** *"Dear children! May this time be a time of personal prayer for you, so that the seed of faith may grow in your hearts; and may it grow into a joyful witness to others. I am with you and I desire to inspire you all: grow and rejoice in the Lord who has created you. Thank you for having responded to my call."*

**February 25, 2010** *"Dear children! In this time of grace, when nature also prepares to give the most beautiful colors of the year, I call you, little children, to open your hearts to God the Creator for Him to transform and mold you in His image, so that all the good which has fallen asleep in your hearts may awaken to a new life and a longing towards eternity. Thank you for having responded to my call."*

**March 25 2010** *"Dear children! Also today I desire to call you all to be strong in prayer and in the moments when trials attack you. Live your Christian vocation in joy and humility and witness to everyone. I am with you and I carry you all before my Son Jesus, and He will be your strength and support. Thank you for having responded to my call."*

**April 25, 2010** *"Dear children! At this time, when in a special way you are praying and seeking my intercession, I call you, little children, to pray so that through your prayers I can help you to have all the more hearts be opened to my messages. Pray for my intentions. I am with you and I intercede before my Son for each of you. Thank you for having responded to my call."*
**May 25, 2010** *"Dear children! God gave you the grace to live and to defend all the good that is in you and around you, and to inspire others to be better and holier; but satan, too, does not sleep and through modernism diverts you and leads you to his way. Therefore, little children, in the love for my Immaculate Heart, love God above everything and live His commandments. In this way, your life will have meaning and peace will rule on earth. Thank you for having responded to my call."*
**June 25, 2010** *"Dear children! With joy, I call you all to live my messages with joy; only in this way, little children, will you be able to be closer to my Son. I desire to lead you all only to Him, and in Him you will find true peace and the joy of your heart. I bless you all and love you with immeasurable love. Thank you for having responded to my call."*
**July 25, 2010** *"Dear children! Anew I call you to follow me with joy. I desire to lead all of you to my Son, your Savior. You are not aware that without Him you do not have joy and peace, nor a future or eternal life. Therefore, little children, make good use of this time of joyful prayer and surrender. Thank you for having responded to my call."*
**August 25, 2010** *"Dear children! With great joy, also today, I desire to call you anew: pray, pray, pray. May this time be a time of personal prayer for you. During the day, find a place where you will pray joyfully in a recollected way. I love you and bless you all. Thank you for having responded to my call."*
**September 25, 2010** *"Dear children! Today I am with you and bless you all with my motherly blessing of peace, and I urge you to live your life of faith even more, because you are still weak and are not humble. I urge you, little children, to speak less and to work more on your personal conversion so that your witness may be fruitful. And may your life be unceasing prayer. Thank you for having responded to my call."*
**October 25, 2010** *"Dear children! May this time be a time of prayer for you. My call, little children, desires to be for you a call to decide to follow the way of conversion; therefore, pray and seek the intercession of all the saints. May they be for you an example, an incentive and a joy towards eternal life. Thank you for having responded to my call."*
**November 25, 2010** *"Dear children! I look at you and I see in your heart death without hope, restlessness and hunger. There is no prayer or trust in God, that is why the Most High permits me to bring you hope and joy. Open yourselves. Open your hearts to God's mercy and He will give you everything you need and will fill your hearts with peace, because He is peace and your hope. Thank you for having responded to my call."*
**December 25, 2010** *"Dear children! Today, I and my Son desire to give you an abundance of joy and peace so that each of you may be a joyful carrier and witness of peace and joy in the places where you live. Little children, be a blessing and be peace. Thank you for having responded to my call."*
**January 25, 2011** *"Dear children! Also today I am with you and I am looking at you and blessing you, and I am not losing hope that this world will change for the good and that peace will reign in the hearts of men. Joy will begin to reign in the world because you have opened yourselves to my call and to God's love. The Holy Spirit is changing a multitude of those who have said 'yes'. Therefore I desire to say to you: thank you for having responded to my call."*
**February 25, 2011** *"Dear children! Nature is awakening and on the trees the first buds are seen which will bring most beautiful flowers and fruit. I desire that you also, little children, work on your conversion and that you be those who witness with their life, so that your example may be a sign and an incentive for conversion to others. I am with you and before my Son Jesus I intercede for your conversion. Thank you for having responded to my call."*
**March 25, 2011** *"Dear children! In a special way today I desire to call you to conversion. As of today, may new life begin in your heart. Children, I desire to see your 'yes', and may your life be a joyful living of God's will at every moment of your life. In a special way today, I bless you with my motherly blessing of peace, love and unity in my heart and in the heart of my Son Jesus. Thank you for having responded to my call."*
**April 25, 2011** *"Dear children! As nature gives the most beautiful colors of the year, I also call you to witness with your life and to help others to draw closer to my Immaculate Heart, so that the flame of love for the Most High may sprout in their hearts. I am with you and I unceasingly pray for you that your life may be a reflection of Heaven here on earth. Thank you for having responded to my call."*
**May 25, 2011** *"Dear children! My prayer today is for all of you who seek the grace of conversion. You knock on the door of my heart, but without hope and prayer, in sin, and without the Sacrament of Reconciliation with God. Leave sin and decide, little children, for holiness. Only in this way can I help you, hear your prayers and seek intercession before the Most High. Thank you for having responded to my call."*
**June 25, 2011** *"Dear children! Give thanks with me to the Most High for my presence with you. My heart is joyful watching the love and joy in the living of my messages. Many of you have responded, but I wait for, and seek, all the hearts that have fallen asleep to awaken from the sleep of unbelief. Little children, draw even closer to my Immaculate Heart so that I can lead all of you toward eternity. Thank you for having responded to my call."*

**July 25, 2011** *"Dear children! May this time be for you a time of prayer and silence. Rest your body and spirit, may they be in God's love. Permit me, little children, to lead you, open your hearts to the Holy Spirit so that all the good that is in you may blossom and bear fruit one hundred fold. Begin and end the day with prayer with the heart. Thank you for having responded to my call."*

**August 25, 2011** *"Dear children! Today I call you to pray and fast for my intentions, because satan wants to destroy my plan. Here I began with this parish and invited the entire world. Many have responded, but there is an enormous number of those who do not want to hear or accept my call. Therefore, you who have said 'yes', be strong and resolute. Thank you for having responded to my call."*

**September 25, 2010** *"Dear children! Today I am with you and bless you all with my motherly blessing of peace, and I urge you to live your life of faith even more, because you are still weak and are not humble. I urge you, little children, to speak less and to work more on your personal conversion so that your witness may be fruitful. And may your life be unceasing prayer. Thank you for having responded to my call."*

**October 25, 2011** *"Dear children! I am looking at you and in your hearts I do not see joy. Today I desire to give you the joy of the Risen One, that He may lead you and embrace you with His love and tenderness. I love you and I am praying for your conversion without ceasing before my Son Jesus. Thank you for having responded to my call."*

**November 25, 2011** *"Dear children! Today I desire to give you hope and joy. Everything that is around you, little children, leads you towards worldly things but I desire to lead you towards a time of grace, so that through this time you may be all the closer to my Son, that He can lead you towards His love and eternal life, for which every heart yearns. You, little children, pray and may this time for you be one of grace for your soul. Thank you for having responded to my call."*

**December 25, 2011** *"Dear children! Also today, in my arms I am carrying my Son Jesus to you, for Him to give you His peace. Pray, little children, and witness so that in every heart, not human but God's peace may prevail, which no one can destroy. It is that peace in the heart which God gives to those whom He loves. By your baptism you are all, in a special way called and loved, therefore witness and pray that you may be my extended hands to this world which yearns for God and peace. Thank you for having responded to my call."*

**January 25, 2012** *"Dear children! With joy, also today I call you to open your hearts and to listen to my call. Anew, I desire to draw you closer to my Immaculate Heart, where you will find refuge and peace. Open yourselves to prayer, until it becomes a joy for you. Through prayer, the Most High will give you an abundance of grace and you will become my extended hands in this restless world which longs for peace. Little children, with your lives witness faith and pray that faith may grow day by day in your hearts. I am with you. Thank you for having responded to my call."*

**February 25, 2012** *"Dear children! At this time, in a special way I call you: 'pray with the heart'. Little children, you speak much and pray little. Read and meditate on Sacred Scripture, and may the words written in it be life for you. I encourage and love you, so that in God you may find your peace and the joy of living. Thank you for having responded to my call."*

**March 25, 2012** *"Dear children! Also today, with joy, I desire to give you my motherly blessing and to call you to prayer. May prayer become a need for you to grow more in holiness every day. Work more on your conversion because you are far away, little children. Thank you for having responded to my call."*

**April 25, 2012** *"Dear children! Also today I am calling you to prayer, and may your heart, little children, open towards God as a flower opens towards the warmth of the sun. I am with you and I intercede for all of you. Thank you for having responded to my call."*

**May 25, 2012** *"Dear children! Also today I call you to conversion and to holiness. God desires to give you joy and peace through prayer but you, little children, are still far away - attached to the earth and to earthly things. Therefore, I call you anew: open your heart and your sight towards God and the things of God - and joy and peace will come to reign in your hearts. Thank you for having responded to my call."*

**June 25, 2012** "Dear children! With great hope in the heart, also today I call you to prayer. If you pray, little children, you are with me and you are seeking the will of my Son and are living it. Be open and live prayer and, at every moment, may it be for you the savor and joy of your soul. I am with you and I intercede for all of you before my Son Jesus. Thank you for having responded to my call."

**July 25, 2012** "Dear children! Today I call you to the 'good'. Be carriers of peace and goodness in this world. Pray that God may give you the strength so that hope and pride may always reign in your heart and life because you are God's children and carriers of His hope to this world that is without joy in the heart, and is without a future, because it does not have its heart open to God who is your salvation. Thank you for having responded to my call."

**August 25, 2012** "Dear children! Also today, with hope in the heart, I am praying for you and am thanking the Most High for every one of you who lives my messages with the heart. Give thanks to God's love that I can love and lead each of you through my Immaculate Heart also toward conversion. Open your hearts and decide for holiness, and hope will give birth to joy in your hearts. Thank you for having responded to my call."

**September 25, 2012** "Dear children! When in nature you look at the richness of the colors which the Most High gives to you, open your heart and pray with gratitude for all the good that you have and say: 'I am here created for eternity' – and yearn for heavenly things because God loves you with immeasurable love. This is why He also gave me to you to tell you: 'Only in God is your peace and hope, dear children'. Thank you for having responded to my call."

**October 25, 2012** "Dear children! Today I call you to pray for my intentions. Renew fasting and prayer because Satan is cunning and attracts many hearts to sin and perdition. I call you, little children, to holiness and to live in grace. Adore my Son so that He may fill you with His peace and love for which you yearn. Thank you for having responded to my call."

**November 25, 2012** "Dear children! In this time of grace, I call all of you to renew prayer. Open yourselves to Holy Confession so that each of you may accept my call with the whole heart. I am with you and I protect you from the ruin of sin, but you must open yourselves to the way of conversion and holiness, that your heart may burn out of love for God. Give Him time and He will give Himself to you and thus, in the will of God you will discover the love and the joy of living. Thank you for having responded to my call."

**December 25, 2012** Our Lady came with little Jesus in her arms and she did not give a message, but little Jesus began to speak and said: "I am your peace, live my commandments." With a sign of the cross, Our Lady and little Jesus blessed us together.

**January 25, 2013** "Dear children! Also today I call you to prayer. May your prayer be as strong as a living stone, until with your lives you become witnesses. Witness the beauty of your faith. I am with you and intercede before my Son for each of you. Thank you for having responded to my call."

**February 25, 2013** "Dear children! Also today I call you to prayer. Sin is pulling you towards worldly things and I have come to lead you towards holiness and the things of God, but you are struggling and spending your energies in the battle with the good and the evil that are in you. Therefore, little children, pray, pray, pray until prayer becomes a joy for you and your life will become a simple walk towards God. Thank you for having responded to my call."

**March 25, 2013** "Dear children! In this time of grace I call you to take the cross of my beloved Son Jesus in your hands and to meditate on His passion and death. May your suffering be united in His suffering and love will win, because He who is love gave Himself out of love to save each of you. Pray, pray, pray until love and peace begin to reign in your hearts. Thank you for having responded to my call."

**April 25, 2013** "Dear children! Pray, pray, keep praying until your heart opens in faith as a flower opens to the warm rays of the sun. This is a time of grace which God gives you through my presence but you are far from my heart, therefore, I call you to personal conversion and to family prayer. May Sacred Scripture always be an incentive for you. I bless you all with my motherly blessing. Thank you for having responded to my call."

**May 25, 2013** "Dear children! Today I call you to be strong and resolute in faith and prayer, until your prayers are so strong so as to open the Heart of my beloved Son Jesus. Pray little children, pray without ceasing until your heart opens to God's love. I am with you and I intercede for all of you and I pray for your conversion. Thank you for having responded to my call."

**June 25, 2013** "Dear children! With joy in the heart I love you all and call you to draw closer to my Immaculate Heart so I can draw you still closer to my Son Jesus, and that He can give you His peace and love, which are nourishment for each one of you. Open yourselves, little children, to prayer – open yourselves to my love. I am your mother and cannot leave you alone in wandering and sin. You are called, little children, to be my children, my beloved children, so I can present you all to my Son. Thank you for having responded to my call."

**July 25, 2013** "Dear children! With joy in my heart I call all of you to live your faith and to witness it with your heart and by your example in every way. Decide, little children, to be far from sin and temptation and may there be joy and love for holiness in your hearts. I love you, little children, and accompany you with my intercession before the Most High. Thank you for having responded to my call."

**August 25, 2013** "Dear children! Also today, the Most High is giving me the grace to be with you and to lead you towards conversion. Every day I am sowing and am calling you to conversion, that you may be prayer, peace, love - the grain that by dying will give birth a hundredfold. I do not desire for you, dear children, to have to repent for everything that you could have done but did not want to. Therefore, little children, again, with enthusiasm say: 'I want to be a sign to others.' Thank you for having responded to my call."

**September 25, 2013** "Dear children! Also today I call you to prayer. May your relationship with prayer be a daily one. Prayer works miracles in you and through you, therefore, little children, may prayer be a joy for you. Then your relationship with life will be deeper and more open and you will comprehend that life is a gift for each of you. Thank you for having responded to my call."

**October 25, 2013** "Dear children! Today I call you to open yourselves to prayer. Prayer works miracles in you and through you. Therefore, little children, in the simplicity of heart seek of the Most High to give you the strength to be God's children and for Satan not to shake you like the wind shakes the branches. Little children, decide for God anew and seek only His will, and then you will find joy and peace in Him. Thank you for having responded to my call."

**November 25, 2013** "Dear children! Today I call all of you to prayer. Open the doors of your heart profoundly to prayer, little children, to prayer with the heart; and then the Most High will be able to act upon your freedom and conversion will begin. Your faith will become firm so that you will be able to say with all your heart: 'My God, my all.' You will comprehend, little children, that here on earth everything is passing. Thank you for having responded to my call."

**December 25, 2013** "Dear children! I am carrying to you the King of Peace that He may give you His peace. You, little children, pray, pray, pray. The fruit of prayer will be seen on the faces of the people who have decided for God and His Kingdom. I, with my Son Jesus, bless you all with a blessing of peace. Thank you for having responded to my call."
**January 25, 2014** "Dear children! Pray, pray, pray for the radiance of your prayer to have an influence on those whom you meet. Put the Sacred Scripture in a visible place in your families and read it, so that the words of peace may begin to flow in your hearts. I am praying with you and for you, little children, that from day to day you may become still more open to God's will. Thank you for having responded to my call."

# Part II.
## Monthly Messages to Mirjana
## (2004-2013)

Beginning on August 2, 1987 Our Lady began appearing to Mirjana on the 2nd of every month to pray with her for unbelievers. Our Lady defines unbelievers as: Those who have not yet experienced God's love. These 2nd of the month apparitions were private for about 10 years. Then, in 1997, Our Lady asked that the apparitions be made public. In fall 2004 Our Lady began to give public messages during most of the apparitions, and at present, messages are being given on every 2nd of the month. When Mirjana was asked if these messages are only meant for unbelievers, she responded that they were for everyone. The 2nd of the month messages from 2004-2009 were translated from Croatian to English by my wife Ana Shawl, and from 2009-2012, by Miki Musa, who is one of the senior guides in Medjugorje.

**October 2, 2004** *"Dear children, today, watching you with a heart full of love, I want to tell you that, what you persistently seek, what you long for, my little children, is before you. It is sufficient with a clean heart to put my Son in the first place, and then you will see. Listen to me and let me lead you on this motherly way.*
**November 2, 2004** *"Dear children, I need you. I call you and ask for your help. Make peace with yourselves, with God and with your neighbors. Then help me. Convert unbelievers. Wipe the tears from my face."*
**December 2, 2004** *"Dear children, I come to you as a mother, who, above all, loves her children. My children, I want to teach you to love! I pray for this! I pray that in each of your neighbors you recognize my Son, because the path to my Son, who is true peace and love, leads you through love towards your neighbors. My children, pray and fast that your hearts be open for this my intention."*
**January 2, 2005** *"Dear children, my motherly heart begs you to accept prayer, because it is your salvation! Pray, pray, pray, my children."*
**March 2, 2005** *"Dear children, do as I do! Come, give your love and give everyone an example of my son!"*
**April 2, 2005** Mirjana: I would not call this a message. Our Lady blessed everyone and all the things that were to be blessed, with her motherly blessing, but she again stressed that the most important blessing is from the priest.- Our Lady said: *"At this point I'm asking you to renew the Church!"*- Mirjana asked: Is this possible can we do it?- Our Lady replied: *"My children, but I will be with you. My Apostles, I'll be with you and help you. Renew first yourself and your family and then everything will be easier."*- Then, Mirjana said: Then Mother, just be with us.
**May 2, 2005** *"Dear children, I am with you that I can take you all to my Son. I wish to lead you all to salvation. Follow me, because in just this way you will find true peace and happiness. My little children come with me!"*
**July 2, 2005** *"Dear Children, as your mother, I rejoice with you, for as a mother I invited you. I am bringing my Son to you. My Son, Your God. Cleanse your hearts and bow your head before your only God. Let my motherly heart leap with joy. Thank you."*
**August 2, 2005** *"Dear children, I came to you with open arms, so that I could take you all into my arms, under my mantle. I cannot do this while your hearts are filled with false light and false idols. Clean them and let my*

*angels sing in them. Then, I will take you under my mantle and give you my Son, true peace, and happiness. Do not wait my children. Thank you!"*
**September 2, 2005** *"Dear children, I, as a mother come to and am showing you how much your God, your Father loves you. And you? Where are you, my children? What takes the first place in your hearts? Why do you not put my Son in the first place? My Children, allow God's blessings to fall upon you. Let God's peace overcome you. Peace, that my Son gives, only He."*
**October 2, 2005** *"Dear children, I come to you as a mother. I bring to you my Son, peace, and love. Cleanse your hearts, and take my Son with you. Give others this true peace and happiness."*
**December 2, 2005** *"Dear children, let it be at this holy time, that love and the grace of my Son descends upon you. Only a pure heart, filled with prayer and compassion can feel the love of my Son. Pray for those who do not have the grace to feel the love of my Son. My children, help me! Thank you."*
**January 2, 2006** *"Dear children, My son was born! Your savior is here with you! What prevents your hearts from accepting Him? What is it that is false within your hearts? Cleanse them with fasting and prayer. Recognize and accept my Son. True peace and true love, that only He can give you. The path to eternal life is He, my Son. Thank you."*
***March 2, 2006*** *She greeted us sadly with: "Praised be Jesus." She blessed all articles that we brought to be blessed and all those present. She talked to me about the situation in the world, with emphasis on those who did not know the love of God. Three times she repeated: "God is love!" I asked her some questions about the sick and the like, and Our Lady responded.*
**June 2, 2006** Our Lady appeared to Mirjana this 2nd of the month and here is what Mirjana shared with us: Our Lady blessed all present and all religious articles that we brought for blessing. With a serious expression on her face, she emphasized once again the priestly blessing. With pain and love she said: *"Remember my children, that is my Son blessing you. Do not accept this so lightly."* After that Our Lady talked about some things that are supposed to happen and she said: *"There is no path without my Son. Do not think that you will have peace and joy if He is not in the first place."* Our Lady was not sad or Joyful, I would say that she was more concerned, with a look of care on her face.
**April 2, 2007** *"Dear children, Do not be hard hearted towards the mercy of God, which has been pouring out upon you for so long a time. In this special time of prayer, permit me to transform your hearts so that you may help me to have my Son resurrect in all hearts, and that my heart may triumph. Thank you!"Mirjana said, Our Lady added: "Your shepherds need your prayers." Our Lady blessed all of us, and all religious articles, and once again emphasized that she gives her motherly blessing. But the greatest blessing is the blessing from the priests.*
**May 2, 2007** *"Dear children, today I come to you with a motherly desire that you give me your hearts. My children, do so with complete confidence and without fear. I will put in your hearts my Son and His mercy. Then you, my children, with different eyes, see the world around you. You will see your neighbor. You will feel his pain and suffering. You will not turn your head from those who suffer, because my son is turning their heads. Children, do not hesitate."*
**June 2, 2007** *"Dear children! Also in this difficult time God's love sends me to you. My children, do not be afraid, I am with you. With complete trust give me your hearts, that I may help you to recognize the signs of the time in which you live. I will help you to come to know the love of my Son. I will triumph through you. Thank you."*
Our Lady blessed all of us, and all religious articles brought for blessing. Once again She reminded us to pray for priests, and that a priest's blessing is a blessing from Her Son Jesus.
**July 2, 2007** *"Dear children! In the great love of God, I come to you today to lead you on the way of humility and meekness. The first station on that way, my children, is confession. Reject your arrogance and kneel down before my Son. Comprehend, my children, that you have nothing and you can do nothing. The only thing that you have and that you possess is sin. Be cleansed and accept meekness and humility. My Son could have won with strength, but He chose meekness, humility and love. Follow my Son and give me your hands so that, together, we may climb the mountain* and win. Thank you."*

Again Our Lady spoke about the importance of priests, and their blessing. *Our Lady referred to this as a spiritual climb.

**August 2, 2007** *"Dear children, Today I look in your hearts and looking at them my heart seizes with pain. My children! I desire from you unconditional, pure love for God. You will know that you are on the right path when with your body you are on the earth, and with your soul you are always with God. Through this unconditional and pure love you will see my Son in every person. You will feel in union with God. As a Mother I will be happy because I will have your holy and unified hearts. My children, I will have your salvation. Thank you."*
At the beginning of the apparition Our Lady showed Mirjana what is waiting for us if there is not the holiness in our hearts, and our brotherly union in Christ. It was not nice. She asked us to pray for our shepherds because she said that without them there is no unity.

**September 2, 2007** *"Dear children, In this time of God's signs, do not be afraid because I am with you. The great love of God sends me to lead you to salvation. Give me your simple hearts, purified by fasting and prayer. Only in the simplicity of your hearts is your salvation. I will be with you and lead you. Thank you."*
**October 2, 2007** *"Dear children, I call you to accompany me in my mission of God with an open heart and complete trust. The path on which I lead you towards God is difficult, but persistent and in the end we will all rejoice in God. Therefore, my children, do not stop praying for the gift of faith. Only faith in God's Word will be the light in this darkness which desires to envelop us. Do not be afraid, I am with you. Thank you."*
Mirjana described that at the end of the apparition, she saw an intense strong light as Heaven was opening, and Our Lady was entering into Heaven through that light.

**November 2, 2007** *"Dear children, Today I call you to open your hearts to the Holy Spirit and permit Him to transform you. My children, God is the immeasurable good and therefore, as a mother, I implore you: Pray, pray, pray, fast and hope that it is possible to achieve good, because from that good love is born. The Holy Spirit will strengthen that love in you and you will be able to call God your Father. Through this exalted love, you will truly come to love all people and, through God, you will regard them as brothers and sisters. Thank you."*
*While Our Lady was blessing, She said: "On the way on which I lead you to my Son, those who represent Him walk beside me."*
***December 2, 2007*** *She blessed all of us, and all religious articles. Our Lady was very sad. All the time her eyes were filled with tears."Dear children! Today, while I am looking at your hearts, my heart is filled with pain and trepidation. My children, stop for a moment and look into your hearts. Is my Son, your God truly in the first place? Are His commandments truly the measure of your life? I am warning you again: without faith there is neither closeness of God nor the word of God which is the light of salvation and the light of common sense."*
Mirjana added: I painfully asked Our Lady not to leave us, and not to take her hands away from us. She painfully smiled at my request and left. This time Our Lady did not say: Thank you.

**January 2, 2008** *"Dear children! With all the strength of my heart, I love you and give myself to you. As a mother fights for her children, I pray and fight for you. I ask you not to be afraid to open yourselves, so as to be able to love with the heart and give yourselves to others. The more that you do this with the heart, the more you will receive and the better you will understand my Son and His gift to you. Through the love of my Son and me, may you all be recognized. Thank you."Our Lady blessed all those present and religious articles brought for blessing. She asked for prayer and fasting for our shepherds.*
**February 2, 2008** *"Dear Children, I am with you. As a mother I am gathering you, because I was to erase from your hearts, that which I see now. Accept the love of my Son and erase from your hearts fear, pain, suffering and disappointment. I have chosen you in a special way to be a light of the love of my Son. Thank you."*
**March 2, 2008** *"Dear Children, Please especially during this Lenten season, respond to God's goodness, because He has chosen you and me He has sent to be among you. Cleanse yourselves of sin and in Jesus, my Son, recognize the peaceful sacrifice for the sins of the whole world. Let Him be the purpose in your lives. May your lives be in service of the Divine love of my Son. Thank you my children."*
Our Lady Blessed us all and all our religious articles and again, she asked us to pray for our Shepherds.

**April 2, 2008** *"Dear children, Also today as I am with you in the great love of God I desire to ask you: Are you also with me? Are your hearts open for me? Do you permit me with my love to purify and prepare them for my Son? My children, you have been chosen because, in your time, the great grace of God has descended on earth. Do not hesitate to accept it. Thank you."*
Our Lady blessed everyone present and all the religious articles. As she was leaving, behind her in the blueness was a most beautiful warm light.

**May 2, 2008** *"Dear children, By God's will I am here with you in this place. I desire that you open your hearts to me and to accept me as a mother. With my love I will teach you simplicity of life and richness of mercy and I will lead you to my Son. The way to Him can be difficult and painful but do not be afraid, I will be with you. My hands will hold you to the very end, to eternal happiness; therefore do not be afraid to open yourselves to me. Thank you. Pray for priests. My Son gave them to you as a gift."*
**June 2, 2008** *"Dear children, I am with you by the grace of God, to make you great. Great in faith and love, all of you. You whose hearts have been made hard as a stone by sin and guilt*, and you devout souls, I desire to illuminate with a new light. Pray that my prayer may meet open hearts. That I may be able to illuminate them with the strength of faith and open the ways of love and hope. Be persevering. I will be with you."*
Our Lady blessed all those present, and all religious articles brought for blessing.*As Our Lady said this, she was looking at those present to whom this referred to, with a painful expression and tears in her eyes.

**July 2, 2008** *"Dear children! With motherly love I desire to encourage you to love your neighbor. Let my Son be the source of that love. He, who could have done everything by force, chose love and gave an example to you. Also today, through me, God expresses to you immeasurable goodness, and you my children are obliged to respond to it. Behave with the same goodness and generosity towards the souls whom you meet. May your love convert them. In that way my Son and His love will arise in you. Thank you."*
Our Lady added: "Your shepherds should be in your hearts and your prayers."

**August 2, 2008** *"Dear children; In my coming to you, here among you, the greatness of God is reflected and the way with God to eternal happiness is opened. Do not feel weak, alone or abandoned. With faith, prayer and love climb to the hill of salvation. May the Mass, the most exalted and most powerful act of your prayer, be the center of your spiritual life. Trust and love, my children. Those whom my Son chose and called will help you in this as well. To you and to them especially, I give my motherly blessing. Thank you."*
Our Lady blessed all people present, and all religious articles brought for blessing.

**September 2, 2008** *"Dear children, Today, with my motherly heart, I call you gathered around me to love your neighbor. My children, stop. Look in the eyes of your brother and see Jesus, my Son. If you see joy, rejoice with him. If there is pain in the eyes of your brother, with your tenderness and goodness, cast it away, because without love you are lost. Only love is effective; it works miracles. Love will give you unity in my Son and victory of my heart. Therefore, my children, love."*
Our Lady blessed all those who were present, and all of the religious articles. Once again she called us to pray for our shepherds.

**October 2, 2008** *"Dear children; Again I call you to faith. My motherly heart desires for your heart to be open, so that it could say to your heart: believe. My children, only faith will give you strength in life's trials. It will renew your soul and open the way of hope. I am with you. I gather you around me because I desire to help you, so that you can help your neighbors to discover faith, which is the only joy and happiness of life. Thank you."Our Lady blessed all those present, and all religious articles. Once again she called us to pray for priests, especially at this time.*
**November 2, 2008** *"Dear children, today I call you to a complete union with God. Your body is on earth, but I ask that your souls, as often as possible be in God's nearness. You will achieve this through prayer, prayer with an open heart. In that way you will thank God for the immeasurable goodness which He gives to you through me and, with a sincere heart, you will accept the obligation to treat the souls whom you meet with equal goodness. Thank you, my children."Our Lady added, "With the heart I pray to God to give strength and love to your shepherds to help you in this and to lead you."*
**December 2, 2008** *"Dear children; In this holy time of joyful expectation, God has chosen you little ones to realize His great intentions. My children, be humble. Through your humility, God, with His wisdom, will make of your souls a chosen home. You will illuminate it with good works and thus, with an open heart, you will welcome the birth of my Son in all of His generous love. Thank you dear children."*

---

**January 2, 2009** *"Dear children, While great heavenly grace is being lavished upon you, your hearts remain hard and without response. My children, why do you not give me your hearts completely? I only desire to put in them peace and salvation, my Son. With my Son your souls will be directed to noble goals and you will never get lost. Even in greatest darkness you will find the way. My children, decide for a new life with the name of my Son on your lips. Thank you."*
**February 2, 2009** *"Dear children, With a motherly heart, today I want to remind you, namely, of God's infinite love, and the patience which ensues from it. Your Father sends me and waits. He is waiting for your open hearts, ready for His works. He is waiting for your hearts united in Christian love and mercy in the spirit of my Son. Do not waste time children, because you are not the masters of time. Thank you."*
**March 2, 2009** *"Dear children! Here I am among you. I am looking into your wounded and restless hearts. You have become lost, my children. Your wounds from sin are becoming greater and greater and are distancing you all the more from the real truth. You are seeking hope and consolation in the wrong places, while I am offering you sincere devotion which is nurtured by love, sacrifice and truth. I am giving you my Son."*
Our Lady blessed everyone present, and all the religious articles that were brought to be blessed and she was sad!

**April 2, 2009** *"Dear children, God's love is in my words. My children, that is the love which desires to turn you to righteousness and truth. That is the love which desires to save you from delusion. And you, my children? Your* *hearts remain closed, they are hard and do not respond to my calls, they are insincere. With motherly love I am praying for you because I desire for all of you to resurrect in my Son. Thank you."*

**May 2, 2009** *Our Lady was very sad. She blessed us and gave this message: "Dear children! Already for a long time I am giving you my motherly heart and offering my Son to you. You are rejecting me. You are permitting sin to overcome you more and more. You are permitting it to master you and to take away your power of discernment. My poor children, look around you and look at the signs of the times. Do you think that you can do without God's blessing? Do not allow darkness to envelop you. From the depth of your hearts cry out for my Son. His Name disperses even the greatest darkness. I will be with you, just call on me: 'Here we are Mother, lead us.' Thank you."*

**June 2, 2009** *"Dear children! My love seeks your complete and unconditional love which will not leave you the same as you are, instead it will change you and teach you to trust in my Son. My children, with my love I am saving you and making you true witnesses of the goodness of my Son. Therefore, my children, do not be afraid to witness love in the name of my Son. Thank you."*

While Our Lady was leaving Mirjana saw a cross, and in the middle of the cross a heart, with a crown of thorns around the heart. Our Lady was not sad.

**July 2, 2009** *"Dear children! I am calling you because I need you. I need hearts ready for immeasurable love. Hearts that are not burdened by vanity. Hearts that are ready to love as my Son loved, that are ready to sacrifice themselves as my Son sacrificed Himself. I need you. In order to come with me, forgive yourselves, forgive others and adore my Son. Adore Him also for those who have not come to know Him, those who do not love Him. Therefore, I need you. Therefore, I call you. Thank you."*

**October 2, 2009** *"Dear Children, As I look at you, my heart seizes with pain. Where are you going my children? Have you sunk so deeply into sin that you do not know how to stop yourselves? You justify yourselves with sin and live according to it. Kneel down beneath the Cross and look at my Son. He conquered sin and died so that you, my children, may live. Permit me to help you not to die but to live with my Son forever. Thank you!"*

**December 2, 2009** *"Dear children, At this time of preparation and joyful expectation I, as a mother, desire to point you to what is the most important, to your soul. Can my Son be born in it? Is it cleansed by love from lies, arrogance, hatred and malice? Above all else does your soul love God as your Father and does it love your fellow brother in Christ? I am pointing you to the way which will raise your soul to a complete union with my Son. I desire for my Son to be born in you. What a joy that would be for me as mother. Thank you."*

---

**January 2, 2010** *"Dear children, Today I am calling you to, with complete trust and love, set out with me because I desire to acquaint you with my Son. Do not be afraid, my children, I am here with you; I am next to you. I am showing you the way to forgive yourselves, to forgive others, and, with sincere repentance of heart, to kneel before the Father. Make everything die in you that hinders you from loving and saving, that you may be with Him and in Him. Decide for a new beginning, a beginning of sincere love of God Himself. Thank you."*

**February 2, 2010** *"Dear children; with motherly love, today I call you to be a lighthouse to all souls who wander in the darkness of ignorance of God's love. That you may shine all the brighter and draw all the more souls, do not permit the untruths which come out of your mouth to silence your conscience. Be perfect. I am leading you with my motherly hand, a hand of love. Thank you."*

**April 2, 2010** *"Dear children; Today I bless you in a special way and I pray for you to return to the right way, to my Son, your Savior, your Redeemer, to Him who gave you eternal life. Reflect on everything human, on everything that does not permit you to set out after my Son, on transience, imperfection and limitation, and then think of my Son, of His Divine infiniteness. By your surrender and prayer ennoble your body and perfect your soul. Be ready, my children. Thank you."*

**May 2, 2010** *"Dear children; Today, through me, the good Father calls you to, with your soul filled with love, to set out on a spiritual visitation. Dear children, be filled with grace, sincerely repent for your sins and yearn for the good. Yearn also in the name of those who have not come to know the perfection of the good. You will be more pleasing to God. Thank you."*

**June 2, 2010** *"Dear Children; Today I call you with prayer and fasting to clear the path in which my Son will enter into your hearts. Accept me as a mother and a messenger of God's love and His desire for your salvation. Free yourself of everything from the past which burdens you, that gives you a sense of guilt, that which previously led you astray in error and darkness. Accept the light. Be born anew in the righteousness of my Son. Thank you."*

**July 2, 2010** *"Dear children; my motherly call, which I direct to you today, is a call of truth and life. My Son, who is life, loves you and knows you in truth. To come to know and to love yourself, you must come to know my Son; to come to know and to love others, you must see my Son in them. Therefore, my children, pray, pray, that you may comprehend and surrender with a spirit that is free, be completely transformed and, in this way, may have the Kingdom of Heaven in your heart on earth. Thank you!"*

**August 2, 2010** *"Dear children! Today I call you, together with me, to begin to build the Kingdom of Heaven in your hearts; that you may forget that what is personal and, led by the example of my Son, think of what is of God. What does He desire of you? Do not permit satan to open the paths of earthly happiness, the paths without my Son. My children, they are false and last a short while. My Son exists. I offer you eternal happiness and peace and unity with my Son, with God; I offer you the Kingdom of God. Thank you."*
**September 2, 2010** *"Dear children; I am beside you because I desire to help you to overcome trials, which this time of purification puts before you. My children, one of those is not to forgive, and not to ask for forgiveness. Every sin offends love and distances you from it and love is my Son. Therefore, my children, if you desire to walk with me towards the peace of God's love, you must learn to forgive and to ask for forgiveness. Thank you."*
**October 2, 2010** *"Dear children; Today I call you to a humble, my children, humble devotion. Your hearts need to be just. May your crosses be your means in the battle against the sins of the present time. May your weapon be patience and boundless love, a love that knows to wait and which will make you capable of recognizing God's signs, that your life, by humble love, may show the truth to all those who seek it in the darkness of lies. My children, my apostles, help me to open the paths to my Son. Once again I call you to pray for your shepherds. Alongside them, I will triumph. Thank you."*
**November 2, 2010** *"Dear children; With motherly perseverance and love I am bringing you the light of life to destroy the darkness of death in you. Do not reject me, my children. Stop and look within yourselves and see how sinful you are. Be aware of your sins and pray for forgiveness. My children, you do not desire to accept that you are weak and little, but you can be strong and great by doing God's will. Give me your cleansed hearts that I may illuminate them with the light of life, my Son. Thank you."*
**December 2, 2010** *"Dear children; Today I am praying here with you that you may gather the strength to open your hearts and thus to become aware of the mighty love of the suffering God. Through His love, goodness and meekness, I am also with you. I invite you for this special time of preparation to be a time of prayer, penance and conversion. My children, you need God. You cannot go forward without my Son. When you comprehend and accept this, what was promised to you will be realized. Through the Holy Spirit the Kingdom of Heaven will be born in your hearts. I am leading you to this. Thank you."*

---

**January 2, 2011** *"Dear children; Today I call you to unity in Jesus, my Son. My motherly heart prays that you may comprehend that you are God's family. Through the spiritual freedom of will, which the Heavenly Father has given you, you are called to become cognizant (to come to the knowledge) of the truth, the good or the evil. May prayer and fasting open your hearts and help you to discover the Heavenly Father through my Son. In discovering the Father, your life will be directed to carrying out of God's will and the realization of God's family, in the way that my Son desires. I will not leave you alone on this path. Thank you."*
**February 2, 2011** *"Dear children; You are gathering around me, you are seeking your way, you are seeking, you are seeking the truth but are forgetting what is the most important, you are forgetting to pray properly. Your lips pronounce countless words, but your spirit does not feel anything. Wandering in darkness, you even imagine God Himself according to yourselves, and not such as He really is in His love. Dear children, proper prayer comes from the depth of your heart, from your suffering, from your joy, from your seeking the forgiveness of sins. This is the way to come to know the right God and by that also yourselves, because you are created according to Him. Prayer will bring you to the fulfillment of my desire, of my mission here with you, to the unity in God's family. Thank you."*
Our Lady blessed everyone present, thanked them, and called us to pray for priests.

**March 2, 2011** *"Dear children; My motherly heart suffers tremendously as I look at my children who persistently put what is human before what is of God; at my children who, despite everything that surrounds them and despite all the signs that are sent to them, think that they can walk without my Son. They cannot! They are walking to eternal perdition. That is why I am gathering you, who are ready to open your heart to me, you who are ready to be apostles of my love, to help me; so that by living God's love you may be an example to those who do not know it. May fasting and prayer give you strength in that and I bless you with motherly blessing in the name of the Father and of the Son and of the Holy Spirit. Thank you."*
Our Lady was very sad.

**April 2, 2011** *"Dear children; With motherly love I desire to open the heart of each of you and to teach you personal unity with the Father. To accept this, you must comprehend that you are important to God and that He is calling you individually. You must comprehend that your prayer is a conversation of a child with the Father; that love is the way by which you must set out love for God and for your neighbor. That is, my children, the love that has no boundaries. That is the love that emanates from truth and goes to the end. Follow me, my children, so that also others, in recognizing the truth and love in you, may follow you. Thank you."* Once again Our Lady

*called us to pray for our shepherds (priests) and said: "They have a special place in my heart. They represent my Son."*
**May 2, 2011** *"Dear children; God the Father is sending me to show you the way of salvation, because He, my children, desires to save you and not to condemn you. That is why I, as a mother, am gathering you around me, because with my motherly love I desire to help you to be free of the dirtiness of the past and to begin to live anew and differently. I am calling you to resurrect in my Son. Along with confession of sins, renounce everything that has distanced you from my Son and that has made your life empty and unsuccessful. Say 'yes' to the Father with the heart and set out on the way of salvation to which He is calling you through the Holy Spirit. Thank you. I am especially praying for the shepherds (priests), for God to help them to be alongside you with a fullness of heart."*
***June 2, 2011*** *"Dear children! As I call you to prayer for those who have not come to know the love of God, if you were to look into your hearts you would comprehend that I am speaking about many of you. With an open heart, sincerely ask yourselves if you want the living God or do you want to eliminate Him and live as you want. Look around you, my children, and see where the world is going, the world that thinks of doing everything without the Father, and which wanders in the darkness of temptation. I am offering to you the light of the Truth and the Holy Spirit. According to God's plan I am with you to help you to have my Son, His Cross and Resurrection, triumph in your hearts. As a mother, I desire and pray for your unity with my Son and His works. I am with you; you decide. Thank you."*
**July 2, 2011** *"Dear children; today I call you to a difficult and painful step for your unity with my Son. I call you to complete admission and confession of sins, to purification. An impure heart cannot be in my Son and with my Son. An impure heart cannot give the fruit of love and unity. An impure heart cannot do correct and just things; it is not an example of the beauty of God's love to those who surround it and to those who have not come to know that love. You, my children, are gathering around me full of enthusiasm, desires and expectations, and I implore the Good Father to, through the Holy Spirit, put my Son faith, into your purified hearts. My children, obey me, set out with me."*
*As Our Lady was leaving, to her left she showed darkness and to her right a Cross in golden light."*
**August 2, 2011** *"Dear children; Today I call you to be born anew in prayer and through the Holy Spirit, to become a new people with my Son; a people who knows that if they have lost God, they have lost themselves; a people who knows that, with God, despite all sufferings and trials, they are secure and saved. I call you to gather into God's family and to be strengthened with the Father's strength. As individuals, my children, you cannot stop the evil that wants to begin to rule in this world and to destroy it. But, according to God's will, all together, with my Son, you can change everything and heal the world. I call you to pray with all your heart for your shepherds, because my Son chose them. Thank you."*
***September 2, 2011*** *"Dear children; With all my heart and soul full of faith and love in the Heavenly Father, I gave my Son to you and am giving Him to you anew. My Son has brought you, the people of the entire world, to know the only true God and His love. He has led you on the way of truth and made you brothers and sisters. Therefore, my children, do not wander, do not close your heart before that truth, hope and love. Everything around you is passing and everything is falling apart, only the glory of God remains. Therefore, renounce everything that distances you from the Lord. Adore Him alone, because He is the only true God. I am with you and I will remain with you. I am especially praying for the shepherds that they may be worthy representatives of my Son and may lead you with love on the way of truth. Thank you."*
**October 2, 2011** *"Dear children; Also today my motherly heart calls you to prayer, to your personal relationship with God the Father, to the joy of prayer in Him. God the Father is not far away from you and He is not unknown to you. He revealed Himself to you through my Son and gave you Life that is my Son. Therefore, my children, do not give in to temptations that want to separate you from God the Father. Pray! Do not attempt to have families and societies without Him. Pray! Pray that your hearts may be flooded with the goodness which comes only from my Son, Who is sincere goodness. Only hearts filled with goodness can comprehend and accept God the Father. I will continue to lead you. In a special way I implore you not to judge your shepherds. My children, are you forgetting that God the Father called them? Pray! Thank you."*
**November 2, 2011** *"Dear children, the Father has not left you to yourselves. Immeasurable is His love, the love that is bringing me to you, to help you to come to know Him, so that, through my Son, all of you can call Him 'Father' with the fullness of heart; that you can be one people in God's family. However, my children, do not forget that you are not in this world only for yourselves, and that I am not calling you here only for your sake. Those who follow my Son think of the brother in Christ as of their very selves and they do not know selfishness. That is why I desire that you be the light of my Son, that to all those who have not come to know the Father, to all those who wander in the darkness of sin, despair, pain and loneliness, you may illuminate the way, and that with your life, you may show them the love of God. I am with you. If you open your hearts, I will lead you. Again I am calling you: pray for your shepherds. Thank you."*
***December 2, 2011*** *"Dear children; As a mother I am with you so that with my love, prayer and example I may help you to become a seed of the future, a seed that will grow into a firm tree and spread its branches throughout the world. For you to become a seed of the future, a seed of love, implore the Father to forgive you your omissions up to now. My children, only a pure heart, unburdened by sin, can open itself and only honest*

*eyes can see the way by which I desire to lead you. When you become aware of this, you will become aware of the love of God, it will be given (as a gift) to you. Then you will give it (as a gift) to others as a seed of love. Thank you."*

---

**January 2, 2012** *"Dear children; As with motherly concern I look in your hearts, in them I see pain and suffering; I see a wounded past and an incessant search; I see my children who desire to be happy but do not know how. Open yourselves to the Father. That is the way to happiness, the way by which I desire to lead you. God the Father never leaves His children alone, especially not in pain and despair. When you comprehend and accept this, you will be happy. Your search will end. You will love and you will not be afraid. Your life will be hope and truth which is my Son. Thank you. I implore you, pray for those whom my Son has chosen. Do not judge because you will all be judged."*
**February 2, 2012** *"Dear children; I am with you for so much time and already for so long I have been pointing you to God's presence and His infinite love, which I desire for all of you to come to know. And you, my children? You continue to be deaf and blind as you look at the world around you and do not want to see where it is going without my Son. You are renouncing Him - and He is the source of all graces. You listen to me while I am speaking to you, but your hearts are closed and you are not hearing me. You are not praying to the Holy Spirit to illuminate you. My children, pride has come to rule. I am pointing out humility to you. My children, remember that only a humble soul shines with purity and beauty because it has come to know the love of God. Only a humble soul becomes heaven, because my Son is in it. Thank you. Again I implore you to pray for those whom my Son has chosen - those are your shepherds."*
***March 2, 2012*** *"Dear children; Through the immeasurable love of God I am coming among you and I am persistently calling you into the arms of my Son. With a motherly heart I am imploring you, my children, but I am also repeatedly warning you, that concern for those who have not come to know my Son be in the first place for you. Do not permit that by looking at you and your life, they are not overcome by a desire to come to know Him. Pray to the Holy Spirit for my Son to be impressed within you. Pray that you can be apostles of the divine light in this time of darkness and hopelessness. This is a time of your trial. With a rosary in hand and love in the heart set out with me. I am leading you towards Easter in my Son. Pray for those whom my Son has chosen that they can always live through Him and in Him, the High Priest. Thank you."*
**April 2, 2012** *"Dear children, As the Queen of Peace, I desire to give peace to you, my children, true peace which comes through the heart of my Divine Son. As a mother I pray that wisdom, humility and goodness may come to reign in your hearts; that peace may reign; that my Son may reign. When my Son will be the ruler in your hearts, you will be able to help others to come to know Him. When heavenly peace comes to rule over you, those who are seeking it in the wrong places, thus causing pain to my motherly heart, will recognize it. My children, great will be my joy when I see that you are accepting my words and that you desire to follow me. Do not be afraid, you are not alone. Give me your hands and I will lead you. Do not forget your shepherds. Pray that in their thoughts they may always be with my Son who called them to witness Him. Thank you."*
**May 02, 2012** "Dear children! With motherly love I implore you to give me your hands, permit me to lead you. I, as a mother, desire to save you from restlessness, despair and eternal exile. My Son, by His death on the Cross, showed how much He loves you; He sacrificed Himself for your sake and the sake of your sins. Do not keep rejecting His sacrifice and do not keep renewing His sufferings with your sins. Do not keep shutting the doors of Heaven to yourselves. My children, do not waste time. Nothing is more important than unity in my Son. I will help you because the Heavenly Father is sending me so that, together, we can show the way of grace and salvation to all those who do not know Him. Do not be hard hearted. Have confidence in me and adore my Son. My children, you cannot be without the shepherds. May they be in your prayers every day. Thank you."
**June 02, 2012** "Dear children, I am continuously among you because, with my endless love, I desire to show you the door of Heaven. I desire to tell you how it is opened: through goodness, mercy, love and peace - through my Son. Therefore, my children, do not waste time on vanities. Only knowledge of the love of my Son can save you. Through that salvific love and the Holy Spirit He chose me and I, together with Him, am choosing you to be apostles of His love and will. My children, great is the responsibility upon you. I desire that by your example you help sinners regain their sight, enrich their poor souls and bring them back into my embrace. Therefore, pray, pray, fast and confess regularly. If receiving my Son in the Eucharist is the center of your life then do not be afraid, you can do everything. I am with you. Every day I pray for the shepherds and I expect the same of you. Because, my children, without their guidance and strengthening through their blessing, you cannot do it. Thank you."
**July 02, 2012** "My children; Again, in a motherly way, I implore you to stop for a moment and to reflect on yourselves and on the transience of this your earthly life. Then reflect on eternity and the eternal beatitude. What do you want? Which way do you want to set out on? The Father`s love sends me to be a mediatrix for you, to show you with motherly love the way which leads to the purity of soul; a soul unburdened by sin; a soul that will come to know eternity. I am praying that the light of the love of my Son may illuminate you, so that you may triumph over weaknesses and come out of misery. You are my children and I desire for all of you to be on the way of salvation. Therefore, my children, gather around me that I may have you come to know the love of

my Son and thus open the door of eternal beatitude. Pray as I do for your shepherds. Again I caution you: do not judge them, because my Son chose them. Thank you."
**August 02, 2012** "Dear children, I am with you and I am not giving up. I desire to have you come to know my Son. I desire for my children to be with me in eternal life. I desire for you to feel the joy of peace and to have eternal salvation. I am praying that you may overcome human weaknesses. I am imploring my Son to give you pure hearts. My dear children, only pure hearts know how to carry a cross and know how to sacrifice for all those sinners who have offended the Heavenly Father and who, even today, offend Him, although they have not come to know Him. I am praying that you may come to know the light of true faith which comes only from prayer of pure hearts. It is then that all those who are near you will feel the love of my Son. Pray for those whom my Son has chosen to lead you on the way to salvation. May your mouth refrain from every judgment. Thank you."
**September 02, 2012** "Dear children, as my eyes are looking at you, my soul is seeking those souls with whom it desires to be one – the souls who have understood the importance of prayer for those of my children who have not come to know the love of the Heavenly Father. I am calling you because I need you. Accept the mission and do not be afraid, I will strengthen you. I will fill you with my graces. With my love I will protect you from the evil spirit. I will be with you. With my presence I will console you in difficult moments. Thank you for your open hearts. Pray for priests. Pray that the unity between my Son and them may be all the stronger, that they may be one. Thank you."
**October 02, 2012** "Dear children; I am calling you and am coming among you because I need you. I need apostles with a pure heart. I am praying, and you should also pray, that the Holy Spirit may enable and lead you, that He may illuminate you and fill you with love and humility. Pray that He may fill you with grace and mercy. Only then will you understand me, my children. Only then will you understand my pain because of those who have not come to know the love of God. Then you will be able to help me. You will be my light-bearers of God's love. You will illuminate the way for those who have been given eyes but do not want to see. I desire for all of my children to see my Son. I desire for all of my children to experience His Kingdom. Again I call you and implore you to pray for those whom my Son has called. Thank you."
**December 02, 2012** "Dear children, with motherly love and motherly patience anew I call you to live according to my Son, to spread His peace and His love, so that, as my apostles, you may accept God's truth with all your heart and pray for the Holy Spirit to guide you. Then you will be able to faithfully serve my Son, and show His love to others with your life. According to the love of my Son and my love, as a mother, I strive to bring all of my strayed children into my motherly embrace and to show them the way of faith. My children, help me in my motherly battle and pray with me that sinners may become aware of their sins and repent sincerely. Pray also for those whom my Son has chosen and consecrated in His name. Thank you."

---

**January 02, 2013** "Dear children, with much love and patience I strive to make your hearts like unto mine. I strive, by my example, to teach you humility, wisdom and love because I need you; I cannot do without you my children. According to God's will I am choosing you, by His strength I am strengthening you. Therefore, my children, do not be afraid to open your hearts to me. I will give them to my Son and in return, He will give you the gift of Divine peace. You will carry it to all those whom you meet, you will witness God's love with your life and you will give the gift of my Son through yourselves. Through reconciliation, fasting and prayer, I will lead you. Immeasurable is my love. Do not be afraid. My children, pray for the shepherds. May your lips be shut to every judgment, because do not forget that my Son has chosen them and only He has the right to judge. Thank you."
**February 02, 2013** "Dear children, love is bringing me to you - the love which I desire to teach you also - real love; the love which my Son showed you when He died on the Cross out of love for you; the love which is always ready to forgive and to ask for forgiveness. How great is your love? My motherly heart is sorrowful as it searches for love in your hearts. You are not ready to submit your will to God's will out of love. You cannot help me to have those who have not come to know God's love to come to know it, because you do not have real love. Consecrate your hearts to me and I will lead you. I will teach you to forgive, to love your enemies and to live according to my Son. Do not be afraid for yourselves. In afflictions my Son does not forget those who love. I will be beside you. I will implore the Heavenly Father for the light of eternal truth and love to illuminate you. Pray for your shepherds so that through your fasting and prayer they can lead you in love. Thank you."
**March 02, 2013** "Dear children! Anew, in a motherly way, I am calling you not to be of a hard heart. Do not shut your eyes to the warnings which the Heavenly Father sends to you out of love. Do you love Him above all else? Do you repent for having often forgotten that the Heavenly Father, out of His great love, sent his Son to redeem us by the Cross? Do you repent for not yet having accepted the message? My children, do not resist the love of my Son. Do not resist hope and peace. Along with your prayer and fasting, by His cross, my Son will cast away the darkness that wants to surround you and come to rule over you. He will give you the strength for a new life. Living it according to my Son, you will be a blessing and a hope to all those sinners who wander in the darkness of sin. My children, keep vigil. I, as a mother, am keeping vigil with you. I am especially praying and watching over those whom my Son called to be light-bearers and carriers of hope for you - for your shepherds. Thank you."

**April 02, 2013** "Dear children, I am calling you to be one with my Son in spirit. I am calling you, through prayer, and the Holy Mass when my Son unites Himself with you in a special way, to try to be like Him; that, like Him, you may always be ready to carry out God's will and not seek the fulfillment of your own. Because, my children, it is according to God's will that you are and that you exist, and without God's will you are nothing. As a mother I am asking you to speak about the glory of God with your life because, in that way, you will also glorify yourself in accordance to His will. Show humility and love for your neighbour to everyone. Through such humility and love, my Son saved you and opened the way for you to the Heavenly Father. I implore you to keep opening the way to the Heavenly Father for all those who have not come to know Him and have not opened their hearts to His love. By your life, open the way to all those who still wander in search of the truth. My children, be my apostles who have not lived in vain. Do not forget that you will come before the Heavenly Father and tell Him about yourself. Be ready! Again I am warning you, pray for those whom my Son called, whose hands He blessed and whom He gave as a gift to you. Pray, pray, pray for your shepherds. Thank you."
**May 02, 2013** "Dear children; Anew, I am calling you to love and not to judge. My Son, according to the will of the Heavenly Father, was among you to show you the way of salvation, to save you and not to judge you. If you desire to follow my Son, you will not judge but love like your Heavenly Father loves you. And when it is the most difficult for you, when you are falling under the weight of the cross do not despair, do not judge, instead remember that you are loved and praise the Heavenly Father because of His love. My children, do not deviate from the way on which I am leading you. Do not recklessly walk into perdition. May prayer and fasting strengthen you so that you can live as the Heavenly Father would desire; that you may be my apostles of faith and love; that your life may bless those whom you meet; that you may be one with the Heavenly Father and my Son. My children, that is the only truth, the truth that leads to your conversion, and then to the conversion of all those whom you meet - those who have not come to know my Son - all those who do not know what it means to love. My children, my Son gave you a gift of the shepherds. Take good care of them. Pray for them. Thank you."
**June 02, 2013** "Dear children, In this restless time, anew I am calling you to set out after my Son - to follow Him. I know of the pain, suffering and difficulties, but in my Son you will find rest; in Him you will find peace and salvation. My children, do not forget that my Son redeemed you by His Cross and enabled you, anew, to be children of God; to be able to, anew, call the Heavenly Father: "Father". To be worthy of the Father, love and forgive, because your Father is love and forgiveness. Pray and fast, because that is the way to your purification, it is the way of coming to know and becoming cognizant of the Heavenly Father. When you become cognizant of the Father, you will comprehend that He is all you need. I, as a mother, desire my children to be in a community of one single people where the Word of God is listened to and carried out.* Therefore, my children, set out after my Son. Be one with Him. Be God's children. Love your shepherds as my Son loved them when He called them to serve you. Thank you."*Our Lady said this resolutely and with emphasis.
**July 02, 2013** "Dear children, with a motherly love I am imploring you to give me the gift of your hearts, so I can present them to my Son and free you – free you from all the evil enslaving and distancing you all the more from the only Good – my Son – from everything which is leading you on the wrong way and is taking peace away from you. I desire to lead you to the freedom of the promise of my Son, because I desire for God's will to be fulfilled completely here; and that through reconciliation with the Heavenly Father, through fasting and prayer, apostles of God's love may be born – apostles who will freely, and with love, spread the love of God to all my children – apostles who will spread the love of the trust in the Heavenly Father and who will keep opening the gates of Heaven. Dear children, extend the joy of love and support to your shepherds, just as my Son has asked them to extend it to you. Thank you."
**August 02, 2013** "Dear children, If only you would open your hearts to me with complete trust, you would comprehend everything. You would comprehend with how much love I am calling you; with how much love I desire to change you, to make you happy; with how much love I desire to make you followers of my Son and give you peace in the fullness of my Son. You would comprehend the immeasurable greatness of my motherly love. That is why, my children, pray because through prayer your faith grows and love is born, the love along which even the cross is not unendurable because you do not carry it alone. In union with my Son you glorify the name of the Heavenly Father. Pray, pray for the gift of love, because love is the only truth: it forgives everything, it serves everyone and it sees a brother in everyone. My children, my apostles, great is the trust that the Heavenly Father has given you through me, His handmaid, to help those who do not know Him, that they may reconcile with Him and follow Him. That is why I am teaching you love, because only if you have love will you be able to respond to Him. Again I am calling you to love your shepherds and to pray that, at this difficult time, the name of my Son may be glorified under their guidance. Thank you."
**September 02, 2013** "Dear children, I love you all. All of you, all of my children, all of you are in my heart. All of you have my motherly love, and I desire to lead all of you to come to know God's joy. This is why I am calling you. I need humble apostles who, with an open heart, will accept the Word of God and help others to comprehend the meaning of their life along side God's word. To be able to do this my children, through prayer and fasting, you must learn to listen with the heart and to learn to keep submitting yourselves. You must learn to keep rejecting everything that distances you from God's word and to yearn only for that which draws you closer to it. Do not be afraid. I am here. You are not alone. I am imploring the Holy Spirit to renew and strengthen you. I

am imploring the Holy Spirit that, as you help others, you too may be healed. I am imploring Him that, through Him, you may be God's children and my apostles."
Then with great concern Our Lady said: "For the sake of Jesus, for the sake of my Son, love those whom He has called and long for the blessing only from the hands which He has consecrated. Do not permit evil to come to reign. Anew I repeat – only along side your shepherds will my heart triumph. Do not permit evil to separate you from your shepherds. Thank you."

**October 02, 2013** "Dear children, I love you with a motherly love and with a motherly patience I wait for your love and unity. I pray that you may be a community of God's children, of my children. I pray that as a community you may joyfully come back to life in the faith and in the love of my Son. My children, I am gathering you as my apostles and am teaching you how to bring others to come to know the love of my Son; how to bring to them the Good News, which is my Son. Give me your open, purified hearts and I will fill them with the love for my Son. His love will give meaning to your life and I will walk with you. I will be with you until the meeting with the Heavenly Father. My children, it is those who walk towards the Heavenly Father with love and faith who will be saved. Do not be afraid. I am with you. Put your trust in your shepherds as my Son trusted when He chose them, and pray that they may have the strength and the love to lead you. Thank you."
**November 02, 2013** "Dear children, anew, in a motherly way, I am calling you to love, to continually pray for the gift of love, to love the Heavenly Father above everything. When you love Him you will love yourself and your neighbor. This cannot be separated. The Heavenly Father is in each person. He loves each person and calls each person by name. Therefore, my children, through prayer hearken to the will of the Heavenly Father. Converse with Him. Have a personal relationship with the Father, which will deepen even more your relationship as a community of my children - my apostles. As a mother I desire that, through the love for the Heavenly Father, you may be raised above earthly vanities and may help others to gradually come to know and come closer to the Heavenly Father. My children, pray, pray, pray for the gift of love because 'love' is my Son. Pray for your shepherds that they may always have love for you as my Son had, and showed by giving His life for your salvation. Thank you."
**December 02, 2013** "Dear children, with a motherly love and a motherly patience I am looking at your ceaseless wandering and how lost you are. That is why I am with you. I desire to help you to first find and come to know yourself, so that, then, you would be able to recognize and to admit everything that does not permit you to get to know the love of the Heavenly Father, honestly and wholeheartedly. My children, the Father comes to be known through the cross. Therefore, do not reject the cross. Strive to comprehend and accept it with my help. When you will be able to accept the cross you will also understand the love of the Heavenly Father; you will walk with my Son and with me; you will differ from those who have not come to know the love of the Heavenly Father, those who listen to Him but do not understand Him, those who do not walk with Him - who have not come to know Him. I desire for you to come to know the truth of my Son and to be my apostles; that, as children of God, you may rise above the human way of thinking and always, and in everything, seek God's way of thinking, anew. My children, pray and fast that you may be able to recognize all of this which I am seeking of you. Pray for your shepherds and long to come to know the love of your Heavenly Father, in union with them. Thank you.

# Part III.
# Annual Messages to Mirjana (1995-2013)

The visionaries Mirjana Dragicevic-Soldo, Ivanka Ivankovic-Elez, and Jakov Colo have received all ten secrets, and Our Lady appears to them once per year, and will do so for the rest of their lives. For Ivanka, who received her 10th secret on May 7, 1985, it is on the anniversary date of the apparitions, June 25. For Jakov, who received his 10th secret on September 12, 1998, it is on Christmas day. For Mirjana, who received her 10th secret on Christmas 1982, it is on March 18. In addition, Our Lady told Mirjana that she would experience extraordinary apparitions as well.

These messages were obtained from the parish in Medjugorje (Information Center MIR Medjugorje, http://www.medjugorje.hr).

**Mirjana Dragicevic-Soldo**
Mirjana Dragicevic-Soldo had daily apparitions from June 24, 1981 to December 25, 1982. On that day, Our Lady told her:

*"Mirjana, I chose you, and I told you everything that is necessary. I entrusted you with the knowledge of many abominations, which you must carry with dignity. Think of me, and how much I too shed tears because of this. You must always be brave. You quickly understood my messages, and so you must understand that now I must leave. Be brave!"*
Entrusting to her the tenth secret, Our Lady told her that for the rest of her life she would have one yearly apparition, on March 18th.

**March 18, 1995**The apparition lasted ten minutes. After it, Mirjana, in tears, withdrew to her room. Here is what she said about her meeting with Our Lady.
I prayed the Our Father and the Glory Be with our Lady three times. The first one was for unbelievers, especially for those who have not experienced God's love. The second was for the souls in purgatory and the third for the intentions of those who were present at the apparition. Our Lady blessed all those present, and also all the religious articles. Our Lady was not happy during the apparition as she has been known to be during past apparitions for my birthday. She talked to me about the secrets but I cannot say anything about that.

In answer to questions why Mirjana cried and if Our Lady gave any message, the visionary answered:

It is hard for me when Our Lady goes away. The meeting with Our Lady is a fulfillment of everything. I feel completed. But when she leaves, I realize that I'm here, on earth, and that I'm going on without her as if I were forsaken, even though I know I am not. It is really hard, so hard.

In the message, Our Lady spoke about the love that we need. Her wish is that people love one another because God is love, and if we love God, we will love one another. I understand this message as one of consolation, and that we don't have to fear anything if we have love. And this was Our Lady's message:

*"Dear children! Already for many years as a Mother, I have been teaching you faith and God's love. You have not shown gratitude to the dear Father nor have you given him glory. You have become empty and your heart has become hard and without love toward your neighbors' sufferings. I am teaching you love and showing you that the dear Father loved you but you have not loved Him. He sacrificed his Son for your salvation, my children. As long as you do not love, you will not know your Father's love. You won't get to know him because God is love. Love and don't be afraid, my children, because there is no fear in love. If your hearts are open to the Father and if they are full of love toward him, then why any fear of what is to come? Those who are afraid are the ones who do not love because they are waiting for punishments and because they know how empty and hard they are. Children, I am leading you to love, to the dear Father. I am leading you to eternal life. Eternal life is my Son. Receive him and you have received love."*
**March 18, 1996**After the apparition, Mirjana transmitted Our Lady's message:
*"Dear children! On this message, which I give you today through my servant, I desire for you to reflect a long time. My children, great is the love of God. Do not close your eyes, do not close your ears, while I repeat to you: Great is his love! Hear my call and my supplication, which I direct to you. Consecrate your heart and make in it the home of the Lord. May he dwell in it forever. My eyes and my heart will be here, even when I will no longer appear. Act in everything as I ask you and lead you to the Lord. Do not reject from yourself the name of God, that you may not be rejected. Accept my messages that you may be accepted. Decide, my children, it is the time of decision. Be of just and innocent heart that I may lead you to your Father, for this that I am here, is his great love. Thank you for being here!"*
**March 18, 1997**The apparition was at 1:50pm and lasted six minutes. Our Lady did not speak about the secrets, but gave the following message:
*"Dear children! As a mother I beseech you, do not go on the way you have been going. That is a way without love toward neighbor and toward my Son. On that way, you will find only hardness and emptiness of heart, and*

*not the peace that everyone is crying out for. Genuine peace will be had only by the one who sees and loves my Son in his neighbor. In whose heart my Son reigns, that one knows what peace is and tranquility. Thank you having responded to my call."*

**March 18, 1998**The apparition lasted between four and five minutes. Our Lady spoke to her about the secrets, blessed all those present, and gave the following message:

*"Dear children! I call you to be my light, in order to enlighten all those who still live in darkness, to fill their hearts with Peace, my Son. Thank you for having responded to my call!"*

**March 18, 1999**The apparition lasted for six minutes from 10:14am to 10:20am. Our Lady spoke about the secrets. She blessed everyone.

*"Dear children! I want you to surrender your hearts to me so that I may take you on the way, which leads to the light and to eternal life. I do not want your hearts to wander in today's darkness. I will help you. I will be with you on this way of discovery of the love and the mercy of God. As a mother, I ask you to permit me to do this. Thank you for having responded to my call."*

**March 18, 2000**The apparition started at 9:55am, and lasted about 5 minutes. Our Lady prayed over everyone, and blessed everyone. Mirjana especially recommended the sick. This time Our Lady did not say anything about the secrets.

*"Dear children! Do not seek peace and happiness in vain, in the wrong places and in wrong things. Do not permit your hearts to become hard by loving vanity. Invoke the name of my Son. Receive Him in your heart. Only in the name of my Son will you experience true happiness and true peace in your heart. Only in this way will you come to know the love of God and spread it further. I am calling you to be my apostles."*

**March 18, 2001**The apparition lasted 5 minutes from 9:45am to 9:50am. Our Lady blessed everyone and gave a message. She was resolute and clear in Her words.

*"Dear children! Today I call you to love and mercy. Give love to each other as your Father gives it to you. Be merciful (pause) - with the heart. Do good works, not permitting them to wait for you too long. Every mercy that comes from the heart brings you closer to my Son."*

**March 18, 2002**The apparition lasted from 9:27am to 9:34am, and Our Lady gave the following message.

*"Dear Children! As a mother, I implore you, open your heart and offer it to me, and fear nothing. I will be with you and will teach you how to put Jesus in the first place. I will teach you to love Him and to belong to Him completely. Comprehend, dear children that without my Son there is no salvation. You should become aware that He is your beginning and your end. Only with this awareness can you be happy and merit eternal life. As your mother, I desire this for you. Thank you for having responded to my call."*

**March 18, 2003**The apparition lasted from 8:55am to 9:02am, and Our Lady gave the following message:

*"Dear children! Particularly at this holy time of penance and prayer, I call you to make a choice. God gave you free will to choose life or death. Listen to my messages with the heart that you may become cognizant of what you are to do and how you will find the way to life. My children, without God you can do nothing; do not forget this even for a single moment. For, what are you and what will you be on earth, when you will return to it again. Do not anger God, but follow me to life. Thank you for being here."*

**March 18, 2004**This year several thousand pilgrims gathered to pray the Rosary at the Cenacolo Community in Medjugorje. The apparition lasted from 1:58pm to 2:03pm and Our Lady gave the following message:

*"Dear children! Also today, watching you with a heart full of love, I desire to tell you that what you persistently seek, what you long for, my little children, is before you. It is sufficient that, in a cleaned heart, you place my Son in the first place, and then you will be able to see. Listen to me and permit me to lead you to this in a motherly way."*

**March 18, 2005**This year several thousand pilgrims gathered to pray the Rosary at the Cenacolo Community in Medjugorje. The apparition lasted from 2:09pm to 2:14pm, and Our Lady gave the following message:

*"Dear children! I come to you as the mother who, above all, loves her children. My children, I desire to teach you to love also. I pray for this. I pray that you will recognize my Son in each of your neighbors. The way to my Son, who is true peace and love, passes through the love for all neighbors. My children, pray and fast for your heart to be open for this my intention."*

**March 18, 2006**This year several thousand pilgrims gathered to pray the Rosary at the Cenacolo Community in Medjugorje. The apparition lasted from 1:59pm to 2:04pm, and Our Lady gave the following message:

*"Dear children! In this Lenten time, I call you to interior renunciation. The way to this leads you through love, fasting, prayer and good works. Only with total interior renunciation will you recognize God's love and the signs of the time in which you live. You will be witnesses of these signs and will begin to speak about them. I desire to bring you to this. Thank you for having responded to me."*

**March 18, 2007**This year several thousand pilgrims gathered to pray the Rosary at the Cenacolo Community in Medjugorje. The apparition lasted from 2:07pm to 2:12pm, and Our Lady gave the following message:

*"Dear children! I come to you as a Mother with gifts. I come with love and mercy. Dear children, mine is a big heart. In it, I desire all of your hearts, purified by fasting and prayer. I desire that, through love, our hearts may triumph together. I desire that through that triumph you may see the real Truth, the real Way and the real Life. I desire that you may see my Son. Thank you."*

Our Lady blessed all of us, and all religious articles. Again she emphasized that it is only Her Motherly blessing, and she asked for daily prayers for those whom she said my Son has chosen and blessed. Mirjana clarified that she believed Our Lady was referring to priests.

**March 18, 2008**This year several thousand pilgrims gathered to pray the Rosary at the Cenacolo Community in Medjugorje. The apparition lasted from 2:01pm to 2:08pm.
Mirjana transmitted the following: I have never seen Our Lady address us in this manner. She extended her hands towards us and with her hands extended in this way, she said:

*"Dear children, today I extend my hands towards you. Do not be afraid to accept them. They desire to give you love and peace and to help you in salvation. Therefore, my children, receive them. Fill my heart with joy and I will lead you towards holiness. The way on which I lead you is difficult and full of temptations and falls. I will be with you and my hands will hold you. Be persevering so that, at the end of the way, we can all together, in joy and love, hold the hands of my Son. Come with me; fear not. Thank you."*
**March 18, 2009**Several thousand pilgrims gathered in prayer of the Rosary at the Blue Cross. The apparition lasted from 1:52pm to 1:58pm.
*"Dear children! Today I call you to look into your hearts sincerely and for a long time. What will you see in them? Where is my Son in them and where is the desire to follow me to Him? My children, may this time of renunciation be a time when you will ask yourself: 'What does my God desire of me personally? What am I to do?' Pray, fast and have a heart full of mercy. Do not forget your shepherds. Pray that they may not get lost, that they may remain in my Son so as to be good shepherds to their flock."*
Our Lady looked at all those present and added: *"Again I say to you, if you knew how much I love you, you would cry with happiness. Thank you."*
**March 18, 2010**Several thousand pilgrims gathered in prayer of the Rosary at the Blue Cross. The apparition lasted from 1:50pm to 1:54pm.
*"Dear children! Today I call you to love with all your heart and with all your soul. Pray for the gift of love, because when the soul loves it calls my Son to itself. My Son does not refuse those who call Him and who desire to live according to Him. Pray for those who do not comprehend love, who do not understand what it means to love. Pray that God may be their Father and not their Judge. My children, you be my apostles, be my river of love. I need you. Thank you."*
**March 18, 2011**Several thousand pilgrims gathered in prayer of the Rosary at the Blue Cross. The apparition lasted from 1:46pm to 1:50pm.
*"Dear children! I am with you in the name of the greatest Love, in the name of dear God, who has come close to you through my Son and has shown you real love. I desire to lead you on the way of God. I desire to teach you real love so that others may see it in you, that you may see it in others, that you may be a brother to them and that others may see a merciful brother in you. My children do not be afraid to open your hearts to me. With motherly love, I will show you what I expect of each of you, what I expect of my apostles. Set out with me. Thank you."*
**March 18, 2012**Several thousand pilgrims gathered in prayer of the Rosary at the Blue Cross. The apparition lasted from 2:00pm to 2:05pm.
*"Dear children! I am coming among you because I desire to be your mother - your intercessor. I desire to be the bond between you and the Heavenly Father - your mediatrix. I desire to take you by the hand and to walk with you in the battle against the impure spirit. My children, consecrate yourselves to me completely. I will take your lives into my motherly hands and I will teach them peace and love, and then I will give them over to my Son. I am asking of you to pray and fast because only in this way will you know how to witness my Son in the right way through my motherly heart. Pray for your shepherds that, united in my Son, they can always joyfully proclaim the Word of God. Thank you."*
**March 18, 2013:** *"Dear children! I call you to, with complete trust and joy, bless the name of the Lord and, day by day, to give Him thanks from the heart for His great love. My Son, through that love which He showed by the Cross, gave you the possibility to be forgiven for everything; so that you do not have to be ashamed or to hide, and out of fear not to open the door of your heart to my Son. To the contrary, my children, reconcile with the Heavenly Father so that you may be able to come to love yourselves as my Son loves you. When you come to love yourselves, you will also love others; in them you will see my Son and recognize the greatness of His love. Live in faith! Through me, my Son is preparing you for the works which He desires to do through you – works through which He desires to be glorified. Give Him thanks. Especially thank Him for the shepherds - for your intercessors in the reconciliation with the Heavenly Father. I am thanking you, my children. Thank you."*

# Part IV.
# Annual Messages to Ivanka
# (1995-2013)

Ivanka Ivankovic-Elez had daily apparitions from June 24, 1981 to May 7, 1985. On that day, Our Lady told her:

*"My dear child, today is our last meeting, but do not be sad because I will come to you on every anniversary except this one. My child, do not think that you have done something wrong, and that's why I no longer come. No, this isn't true. The plan which my Son and I have, you accepted with all your heart and completed your part. Be happy because I am your mother and I love you with all my heart. Ivanka, thank you for having responded to the invitation of my Son and for persevering and for always being close to Him and staying until He had completed that for which He asked of you. My child, tell your friends that both I and my Son will always be there for you when you seek or call us. That which I told you during these years about the secrets, it is still not time to tell anyone. Ivanka, the grace which you and the others received, nobody on this earth has received up until now!"*
Confiding to her the tenth secret, Our Lady told her that for the rest of her life, she would have one yearly apparition on June 25th, the anniversary of the apparitions.

**June 25, 1995**Ivanka had the six minute apparition at her family home at the end of which she brought this message of Our Lady to those present: Our Lady blessed every one present at the apparition. She spoke to me about the secrets. She called us to pray for families because satan desires to destroy them. In addition, Our Lady called on all people to be messengers of peace.
At the end Ivanka added: Now I will have to wait a whole year again for another meeting.

**June 25, 1996**The apparition took place in her family home, and lasted seven minutes. After the apparition, Ivanka said that this had been one of the most beautiful apparitions that she had had up to the present. Our Lady thanks us for our prayer, and for our love and desires that prayer and love become interwoven into every day. In conclusion, she invited us to pray for those who were under diabolic possession.
**June 25, 1997**Ivanka had the six minute apparition in her own family home. After the apparition Ivanka said: Our Lady talked to me about the fifth secret, and spoke the following message:
*"Dear children, pray with the heart to know how to forgive and how to be forgiven. I thank you for your prayers and the love you give to me."*
**June 25, 1998**Ivanka had the apparition in her home and it lasted six minutes. After the apparition Ivanka said: Our Lady was joyful. I asked her to bless everyone, which she did. Our Lady talked to me about all the secrets. She invited us to pray for families at this time, and especially to pray for the sick. She called us to open our hearts and to thank her Son for the grace He has given us. At the end, Our Lady thanked us for our prayers and love.
**June 25, 1999**Ivanka had the apparition, which lasted eight minutes, in her own family home. Present for the apparition were only Ivanka's family, husband and three children. After the apparition, Ivanka said that during the apparition, she prayed for the parish and families, and she recommended all in her prayer. Our Lady gave the following message:
*"Dear children, thank my Son for all the graces that he has given you. Pray for peace, pray for peace, pray for peace!"*
**June 25, 2000**The apparition lasted seven minutes, and Ivanka had it in her family home. Present for the apparition were only Ivanka's family, husband and three children. Our Lady gave the following message:
*"I introduced myself as 'Queen of Peace'. Again, I call you to peace, fasting, prayer. Renew family prayer and receive my blessing."*
Ivanka told us that Our Lady was happy, and that she spoke to her about the sixth secret.

**June 25, 2001**Ivanka had the apparition in the presence of her family. She says that Our Lady was joyful, and that she spoke to her about the future of the Church. Our Lady gave the following message:
*"Dear angels! Thank you for your prayers, because through them my plan is being realized. This is why, angels, pray, pray, pray, so that my plan may be realized. Receive my motherly blessing!"*
**June 25, 2002**The apparition lasted six minutes. Ivanka had the apparition at home in the presence of her family, her husband and three children. Our Lady gave the following message:
*"Dear Children, do not tire of prayer. Pray for peace, peace, peace."*
Our Lady related to Ivanka some new details about her life. She gave us her motherly blessing. Our Lady was joyful.

**June 25, 2003**The apparition lasted ten minutes. Ivanka had the apparition at home in the presence of her family, her husband and her three children. Our Lady gave the following message:
*"Dear children! Do not be afraid, I am always with you. Open your heart for love and peace to enter into it. Pray for peace, peace, peace."*
Our Lady came joyful and spoke to Ivanka more extensively about her life.

**June 25, 2004**The apparition lasted nine minutes. Ivanka had the apparition at home in the presence of her family, her husband and her three children. Our Lady gave the following message:
*"Dear children! Pray for those families who have not come to know the love of my Son. Receive my motherly blessing."*
Our Lady came joyful and spoke to Ivanka more extensively about her life.

**June 25, 2005**The apparition lasted ten minutes. Ivanka had the apparition at home in the presence of her family, her husband and her three children. Our Lady gave the following message:
*"Dear children, love each other with the love of my Son. Peace, peace, peace."*
Our Lady was joyful and spoke to Ivanka about the 6th secret.

**June 25, 2006**The apparition lasted seven minutes. Ivanka had the apparition at home in the presence of her family, her husband and her three children. Our Lady gave the following message:
*"Dear children, thank you for having responded to my call. Pray, pray, pray."*
Our Lady was joyful, and spoke about the seventh secret.

**June 25, 2007**The apparition lasted seventeen minutes. Ivanka had the apparition at home in the presence of her family, her husband and her three children.
After the apparition, the visionary Ivanka said: Our Lady remained with me for seventeen minutes. She was joyful and spoke to me about Her life. Our Lady said: *"Dear children, receive my motherly blessing."*
**June 25, 2008**The apparition lasted six minutes. Ivanka had the apparition at home in the presence of her family, her husband and her three children. After the apparition, the visionary Ivanka said: Our Lady spoke to me about the ninth secret. She gave us her motherly blessing.
**June 25, 2009**The apparition lasted ten minutes. Ivanka had the apparition at home in the presence of her family, her husband and her three children. After the apparition, the visionary Ivanka said: Our Lady remained with me for 10 minutes and spoke to me of the tenth secret. Our Lady said:
*"Dear children, I call you to be apostles of peace. Peace, peace, peace."*
**June 25, 2010**The apparition, which lasted six minutes, took place at Ivanka's family home. Only Ivanka's family was present at the apparition. After the apparition Ivanka said: Our Lady spoke to me about the fifth secret and, at the end, said: *"Dear children, receive my motherly blessing."*
**June 25, 2011**The apparition, which lasted eight minutes, took place at Ivanka's family home. Only Ivanka's family was present at the apparition. After the apparition Ivanka said: Our Lady spoke to me about the first secret and, at the end, said: *"Dear children, receive my motherly blessing."*
**June 25, 2012**The apparition, which lasted 7 minutes, took place at Ivanka's family home. Only Ivanka's family was present at the apparition. After the apparition, Ivanka said: Our Lady spoke to me about the 5th secret and at the end said: "I am giving you my motherly blessing. Pray for peace, peace, peace."
**June 25, 2013**The apparition, which lasted 2 minutes, took place at Ivanka's family home. Only Ivanka's family was present at the apparition. After the apparition, Ivanka said: "Our Lady did not give a message. She blessed us with her motherly blessing."

# Part V.
# Annual Messages to Jakov
# (1995-2013)

Jakov Colo had daily apparitions from June 25, 1981 to September 12, 1998. On that day, Our Lady told him:

*"Dear child! I am your mother and I love you unconditionally. From today, I will not be appearing to you every day, but only on Christmas, the birthday of my Son. Do not be sad, because as a mother, I will always be with you and like every true mother, I will never leave you. And you continue further to follow the way of my Son, the way of peace and love and try to persevere in the mission that I have confided to you. Be an example of that man who has known God and God's love. Let people always see in you an example of how God acts on people and how God acts through them. I bless you with my motherly blessing and I thank you for having responded to my call."*
Entrusting to him the tenth secret, Our Lady told him that for the rest of his life he would have one yearly apparition, on Christmas Day.

**December 25, 1998**After the apparition, which began at 11.50am, and lasted twelve minutes, Jakov wrote: Our Lady came joyful. She greeted me, as always, with *"Praised be Jesus!"* She spoke to me about the secrets and afterwards gave me this message:
*"Dear children! Today, on the birthday of my Son, my heart is filled with immeasurable joy, love and peace. As your mother, I desire for each of you to feel that same joy, peace and love in the heart. That is why do not be afraid to open your heart and to completely surrender yourself to Jesus, because only in this way can He enter into your heart and fill it with love, peace and joy. I bless you with my motherly blessing."*
Jakov prayed with his family. He prepared himself for the apparition with Confession and Holy Mass. After the apparition, he cried for a while.

**December 25, 1999**The apparition began at 3:00pm and lasted for ten minutes. Our Lady came joyfully in a golden dress with the child Jesus in her arms. She talked about the secrets. She blessed everyone. Our Lady gave the following message:
*"Dear children! Today on the birthday of my Son, when my heart is filled with immeasurable joy and love, I invite you to open fully and surrender fully to God. Throw out all the darkness from your heart and let God's light and God's love enter your heart and dwell there forever. Be carriers of God's light and love to all people, so everyone, in you and through you, can feel and experience the authentic light and love that only God is able to give you. I am blessing you with my motherly blessing!"*
**December 25, 2000**The apparition began at 3:20 pm and lasted ten minutes. Our Lady came joyful with baby Jesus in her arms. She blessed everyone and gave a message:
*"Dear children! Today when Jesus is born and by His birth brings immeasurable joy, love and peace, I call you, in a special way to say your 'yes' to Jesus. Open your hearts so that Jesus enters into them, comes to dwell in them and starts to work through you. Only in this way will you be able to comprehend the true beauty of God's love, joy and peace. Dear children, rejoice in the birth of Jesus and pray for all those hearts that have not opened to Jesus so that Jesus may enter into each of their hearts and may start working through them, so that every person would be an example of a true person through whom God works."*
**December 25, 2001**The apparition began at 3:30pm and lasted five minutes. Our Lady gave the following message:
*"Dear Children, today when Jesus is born anew for you, in a special way, I want to call you to conversion. Pray, pray, pray for the conversion of your heart, so that Jesus may be born in you all and may dwell in you and come to reign over your entire being. Thank you for having responded to the call."*

**December 25, 2002**Our Lady came with the Child Jesus in her arms. The apparition began at 5:20pm and lasted seven minutes. Our Lady gave the following message:
*"Dear children! Today, on the day of love and peace, with Jesus in my arms, I call you to prayer for peace. Little children, without God and prayer you cannot have peace. Therefore, little children, open your heart so that the King of Peace may be born in your heart. Only in this way, you can witness and carry God's peace to this peaceless world. I am with you and bless you with my motherly blessing."*
**December 25, 2003**The apparition began at 3:15pm and lasted eight minutes. Our Lady gave the following message:
*"Dear children! Today, when in a special way, Jesus desires to give you His peace, I call you to pray for peace in your hearts. Children, without peace in your hearts you cannot feel the love and joy of the birth of Jesus. Therefore, little children, today in a special way, open your hearts and begin to pray. Only through prayer and complete surrender, will your heart be filled with the love and peace of Jesus. I bless you with my motherly blessing."*
**December 25, 2004**The apparition began at 2:30pm and lasted seven minutes. Our Lady gave the following message:
*"Dear children! Today, on a day of grace, with little Jesus in my arms, in a special way I call you to open your hearts and to start to pray. Little children, ask Jesus to be born in each of your hearts and to begin to rule in your lives. Pray to Him for the grace to be able to recognize Him always and in every person. Little children, ask Jesus for love, because only with God's love can you love God and all people. I carry you all in my heart and give you my Motherly blessing."*
**December 25, 2005**The apparition began at 2:45pm and lasted seven minutes. Our Lady gave the following message:
*"Dear children! Today, with Jesus in my arms, in a special way I call you to conversion. Children, through all this time which God permitted me to be with you, I continuously called you to conversion. Many of your hearts remained closed. Little children, Jesus is peace, love and joy; therefore now decide for Jesus. Start to pray. Pray to Him for the gift of conversion. Little children, only with Jesus can you have peace, joy and a heart filled with love. Little children, I love you. I am your mother and give you my motherly blessing."*
**December 25, 2006**The apparition began at 3:23pm and lasted six minutes. Our Lady gave the following message:
*"Today is a great day of joy and peace. Rejoice with me. Little children, in a special way, I call you to holiness in your families. I desire, little children, that each of your families be holy and that God's joy and peace, which God sends you today in a special way, may come to rule and dwell in your families. Little children, open your hearts today on this day of grace, decide for God and put Him in the first place in your family. I am your Mother. I love you and give you my Motherly Blessing."*
**December 25, 2007**The apparition began at 2:29pm and lasted six minutes. Our Lady gave the following message:
*"Dear children! Today, in a special way I call you to become open to God and for each of your hearts today to become a place of Jesus' birth. Little children, through all this time that God permits me to be with you, I desire to lead you to the joy of your life. Little children, the only true joy of your life is God. Therefore, dear children, do not seek joy in things of this earth but open your hearts and accept God. Little children, everything passes, only God remains in your heart. Thank you for having responded to my call."*
**December 25, 2008**The apparition began at 9:49am and lasted six minutes. Our Lady gave the following message:
*"Dear children! Today, in a special way, I call you to pray for peace. Without God you cannot have peace or live in peace. Therefore, little children, today on this day of grace open your hearts to the King of peace, for Him to be born in you and to grant you His peace - and you be carriers of peace in this peaceless world. Thank you for having responded to my call."*
**December 25, 2009**The apparition began at 2:35pm and lasted twelve minutes. Our Lady gave the following message:
*"Dear children! All of this time in which God in a special way permits me to be with you, I desire to lead you on the way that leads to Jesus and to your salvation. My little children, you can find salvation only in God and therefore, especially on this day of grace with little Jesus in my arms, I call you to permit Jesus to be born in your hearts. Only with Jesus in your heart can you set out on the way of salvation and eternal life. Thank you for having responded to my call."*
**December 25, 2010**The apparition began at 2:25pm and lasted seven minutes. Jakov said: Our Lady spoke to me about the secrets and at the end said: *"Pray, pray, pray."*
**December 25, 2011**The apparition began at 3:30pm and lasted eleven minutes. Our Lady gave the following message:
*"Dear children! Today, in a special way, I desire to take you to and give you over to my Son. Little children, open your hearts and permit Jesus to be born in you, because only in this way, little children, you yourselves will be able to experience your new birth and set out with Jesus in your hearts towards the way of salvation. Thank you for having responded to my call."*

**December 25, 2012**The apparition began at 2:15pm and lasted 10 minutes. Afterwards Jakov transmitted this message:
*"Dear children, give the gift of your life to me and completely surrender to me so that I may help you to comprehend my motherly love and the love of my Son for you. My children, I love you immeasurably and today, in a special way, on the day of the birth of my Son, I desire to receive each of you into my heart and to give a gift of your lives to my Son. My children, Jesus loves you and gives you the grace to live in His mercy, but sin has overtaken many of your hearts and you live in darkness. Therefore, my children, do not wait, say 'no' to sin and surrender your hearts to my Son, because only in this way will you be able to live God's mercy and, with Jesus in your hearts, set out on the way of salvation."*
**December 25th 2013**The apparition began at 3:07 pm and lasted 8 minutes. Afterwards Jakov transmitted the message:
*"Little children, today in a special way, Jesus desires to come to dwell in each of your hearts and to share with you your every joy and pain. Therefore, little children, today in a special way, peer into your hearts and ask yourselves if the peace and joy of the birth of Jesus have truly taken hold of your hearts. Little children, do not live in darkness, aspire towards the light and towards God's salvation. Children, decide for Jesus and give Him your life and your hearts, because only in this way will the Most High be able to work in you and through you."*

CPSIA information can be obtained
at www.ICGtesting.com
Printed in the USA
BVHW091356221221
624599BV00015B/1449